F. W. MAITLAND: STATE, TRUST AND CORPORATION

The essays collected in *State, Trust and Corporation* contain the reflections of England's greatest legal historian on the legal, historical and philosophical origins of the idea of the state. All written in the first years of the twentieth century, Maitland's essays are classics both of historical writing and of political theory. They contain a series of profound insights into the way the character of the state has been shaped by the non-political associations that exist alongside it, and their themes are of continuing relevance today.

This is the first new edition of these essays for sixty years, and the first of any kind to contain full translations, glossary and expository introduction. It has been designed to make Maitland's writings fully accessible to the non-specialist, and to make available to anyone interested in the idea of the state some of the most important modern writings in English on that subject.

DAVID RUNCIMAN is University Lecturer in Political Theory at the University of Cambridge.

MAGNUS RYAN is Lecturer in Late Medieval Studies at the Warburg Institute, and a Fellow of All Souls College, Oxford.

D0840950

CAMBRIDGE TEXTS IN THE
HISTORY OF POLITICAL THOUGHT

Series editors

RAYMOND GUESS, *Reader in Philosophy, University of Cambridge*
QUENTIN SKINNER, *Regius Professor of Modern History in the
University of Cambridge*

Cambridge Texts in the History of Political Thought is now firmly established as the major student textbook series in political theory. It aims to make available to students all the most important texts in the history of Western political thought, from ancient Greece to the early twentieth century. All the familiar classic texts will be included, but the series seeks at the same time to enlarge the conventional canon by incorporating an extensive range of less well-known works, many of them never before available in a modern English edition. Wherever possible, texts are published in complete and unabridged form, and translations are specially commissioned for the series. Each volume contains a critical introduction together with chronologies, biographical sketches, a guide to further reading and any necessary glossaries and textual apparatus. When completed, the series will aim to offer an outline of the entire evolution of Western political thought.

For a list of titles published in the series, please see end of book

F. W. MAITLAND

State, Trust and Corporation

EDITED BY

DAVID RUNCIMAN

Faculty of Social and Political Sciences, University of Cambridge

AND

MAGNUS RYAN

The Warburg Institute, University of London and All Souls College, University of Oxford

CAMBRIDGE
UNIVERSITY PRESS

PUBLISHED BY THE PRESS SYNDICATE OF THE UNIVERSITY OF CAMBRIDGE
The Pitt Building, Trumpington Street, Cambridge, United Kingdom

CAMBRIDGE UNIVERSITY PRESS
The Edinburgh Building, Cambridge, CB2 2RU, UK
40 West 20th Street, New York, NY 10011–4211, USA
477 Williamstown Road, Port Melbourne, VIC 3207, Australia
Ruiz de Alarcón 13, 28014 Madrid, Spain
Dock House, The Waterfront, Cape Town 8001, South Africa

http://www.cambridge.org

First published 2003

Printed in the United Kingdom at the University Press, Cambridge

Typeface Ehrhardt 9.5/12 pt.   *System* LaTeX 2$_\varepsilon$ [TB]

A catalogue record for this book is available from the British Library

ISBN 0 521 82010 3 hardback
ISBN 0 521 52630 2 paperback

Contents

Contents

Acknowledgements

For their help on a variety of specific matters the editors wish to thank Paul Brand, George Garnett, Birke Häcker, John Hudson, Kent Lerch, Scott Mandelbrote, Richard Nolan, Benjamin Thompson, Anne Thomson and John Watts. They also wish to thank Raymond Guess and Quentin Skinner for their support and editorial advice. At Cambridge University Press they wish to thank Susan Beer for her help in correcting the text, and Richard Fisher for overseeing this project from beginning to end.

Editors' introduction

Life and work

F. W. Maitland (1850–1906) was a legal historian who began and ended his intellectual career writing about some of the enduring problems of modern political thought – What is freedom? What is equality? What is the state? His first publication, printed privately in 1875, was an extended essay entitled 'A historical sketch of liberty and equality as ideals of English political philosophy from the time of Hobbes to the time of Coleridge'. This sketch takes as its starting point the basic question, 'What is it that governments ought to do?', only to conclude that such questions are 'not one[s] which can be decided by a bare appeal to first principles, but require much economic and historical discussion'.[1] Among his final publications, written nearly thirty years later, are the series of shorter essays collected in this book, each of which addresses itself less directly but with equal force to the question of what it is that states, and by extension the governments of states, actually are. In between these excursions into political theory, Maitland produced the work on which his fame has come to rest, the historical investigations into the foundations and workings of English law and of English life which have gained him the reputation as perhaps the greatest of all modern historians of England. This work and that reputation have tended to overshadow what preceded it and what followed it. In the case of the early historical sketch this is perhaps fair. But the later essays are different, not least for the fact that they flow out of the historical interests that drove Maitland for most of his life, above all his

---

[1] F. W. Maitland, *Collected papers*, ed. H. A. L. Fisher (Cambridge: Cambridge University Press, 1911), vol. 1, p. 161.

interest in what made English law and English legal institutions work. As a result, the essays contain some detailed and fairly technical discussions of a legal or historical kind, and it is one of the purposes of this edition to make those discussions accessible to the non-specialist whose primary interest is in political thought. But they also contain a series of reflections on the historical and legal origins of the concept of the state, and its historical and legal relation to other kinds of human association, which, as Maitland himself recognised, take legal history right to the heart of political thought, just as they remind us that the origins of much political thought lie in legal history. These five essays, written between 1900 and 1904, not only address the question of what the state actually is. They also make it abundantly clear why that question is not merely a question about the state, and why it cannot simply be answered in accordance with the ideals of English political philosophy.

Maitland's 'Historical sketch' was originally written as a dissertation to be submitted for a Fellowship in Moral and Mental Science at Trinity College, Cambridge. It was printed privately after the Fellows rejected it, awarding the Fellowship instead to James Ward, a psychologist. Following this rebuff, Maitland gave up his early undergraduate ambitions to pursue an academic career and moved from Cambridge to London, where he was called to the bar in 1876. There he worked as a barrister with limited success for nearly a decade, specialising in conveyancing cases, until, in 1884, the chance came to return to Cambridge as a Reader in English Law. By this time Maitland's interests had turned from the history of ideas to the history of legal actions, and he had started to make use of the vast and largely untapped resources of the Public Record Office, publishing in 1884 the *Pleas of the Crown for the County of Gloucester, 1221* ('a slim and outwardly insignificant volume', as his friend and biographer H. A. L. Fisher describes it; 'but it marks an epoch in the history of history').[2] So began perhaps the most remarkable burst of sustained productivity ever seen from an English historian, as Maitland published articles on and editions of anything and everything he found to interest him in the early documents of English legal history, as anything and everything did, ranging from the monumental one-offs of Bracton and Domesday book to the constant and evolving record of medieval England to be found in its Year Books and Parliament Rolls. In 1888 Maitland was appointed Downing

[2] H. A. L. Fisher, *Frederick William Maitland: a biographical sketch* (Cambridge: Cambridge University Press, 1910), p. 25.

x

Professor of English Law at Cambridge and in 1895 he published, with Sir Frederick Pollock, his best-known work, *The history of English law up to the time of Edward I*. Ill health, which plagued him throughout his life, was the reason he gave for refusing the Regius Professorship of Modern History, which was offered to him following the death of Lord Acton in 1902. But it did not prevent him writing, publishing, teaching and administering the early history of English law up until his death, in 1906, at the age of fifty-six.

Gierke

Two factors combined towards the end of his life to draw some of Maitland's attention from the history of law to the history of certain philosophical and political concepts with which the law is entwined. The first was his growing interest in one particular anomaly of English law, the idea of the corporation sole,[3] which he believed was responsible for some of the anomalies in the English conception of the state. The second was his encounter with the work of the German jurist and legal historian Otto von Gierke, whose English editor and translator Maitland became. Gierke's massive *Das deutsche Genossenschafisrecht*, which appeared in four volumes between 1868 and 1913, was an attempt to describe and comprehend the whole history of group life in Germany, as that in turn related to legal, political and philosophical understandings of the forms of human association. The size and subject matter of the enterprise made it effectively untranslatable as a whole (not least because it was unfinished at the time of Maitland's death), and Maitland chose to publish in English simply a short extract from the third of Gierke's volumes, which dealt with medieval conceptions of representation, group personality and the state. For this edition, which appeared in 1900, Maitland then wrote a relatively brief introduction,[4] in which he sought to explain why Gierke's endeavour – to make sense of the ways in which lawyers, politicians

---

[3] The idea of the 'corporation sole' is anomalous because it allows for the attribution of corporate personality to legal entities which would otherwise be identified as single (or 'sole') individuals (for example, in the classic case, a parish parson). This is in contrast to the more familiar 'corporation aggregate', which allows for the ascription of corporate personality to groups (or 'aggregations') of individuals. Maitland's interest in this distinction originally stemmed from his work on Bracton, where 'his keen eye had detected, as early as 1891, "the nascent law about corporations aggregate and corporations sole" ' (see Fisher, *Frederick William Maitland*, p. 75).

[4] Part of which is included here as a Preface to this collection of essays.

and philosophers have sought to make sense of the identity of groups – though quintessentially German, was of real interest for English audiences too.

The first step he took in making this case came in his translation of the title. What was in German *Die publicistischen Lehren des Mittelalters* becomes in English *The political theories of the Middle Age.*[5] An English audience needed to understand that questions of public law are also questions of political theory. But in calling public law political theory Maitland was also indicating to his readers that political speculation makes no sense apart from the juristic speculation that underpins it. In England that connection had been broken – there were simply not enough 'juristic speculators, of whom there are none or next to none in this country'.[6] Thus there was no 'publicistic' doctrine in England, and nothing to bridge the gap between the practical concerns of the private lawyers and the grand ideals of the moral philosophers, in whom England continued to abound. Maitland's introduction to Gierke served as an initial attempt to bridge that gap, and the tool he chose was the theory of the corporation ('*Korporationslehre*'). His argument was, in outline at least, a simple one. Corporations are, like states, organised and durable groups of human beings, and though we may try to organise them in different ways, the way we organise the one has a lasting impact on how we choose to organise the other. This had been lost sight of in England, because in England there lacked the conceptual framework to see the connection between the legal activities of groups and the philosophical doctrines of politics. But Gierke makes that connection clear, and in doing so he helps to make clear what we are missing.

Thus Maitland's first, and perhaps most difficult task, as he saw it, was simply to translate for an English audience words, concepts and arguments for which there was no English equivalent.[7] But in trying to make clear for his readers how things stood in Germany he also saw the value of helping them to understand how things looked in England from a German

---

[5] 'Now turning to translate Gierke's chapt. on "Publicistic Doctrine of M. A." – O. G. has given consent – will make lectures (if I return) and possibly book – but what to do with "Publicistic"?' (Letter to Frederick Pollock, 4 Dec. 1899, *Letters of F. W. Maitland*, ed. C. H. S. Fifoot (London: Selden Society, 1965), p. 253).

[6] O. von Gierke, *Political theories of the Middle Age*, ed. F. W. Maitland (Cambridge: Cambridge University Press, 1900), p. ix.

[7] This including the overarching concept of Gierke's whole enterprise – *Die Genossenschaft* – which translates into English variously as 'fellowship' or 'co-operative', but is only comprehensible in the light of the German forms of 'folk-law' from which it evolves and the Roman forms of both public and private law against which it is a reaction.

perspective. 'We Englishmen', who, as he puts it elsewhere, 'never clean our slates',[8] were rarely afforded the vantage point from which to judge whether the law by which they lived made sense as a set of ideas, not least because they were too busily and successfully living by it. But a German, who believed that it was not possible to live by law unless it cohered intellectually, could not fail to be both puzzled and intrigued by some of the governing concepts of English law, particularly those that related to the life of groups, up to and including the continuous life of that group we call the state. England, like Germany and other European countries, had received the Roman doctrine of *persona ficta*[9] as the technical mechanism by which groups might be afforded a continuous life – that is, a life independent of the mortal lives of those individuals who are its members or officers or representatives at any given moment. But England, unlike Germany and other European countries, had sought to bypass some of the more restrictive aspects of that doctrine – most notably, the presupposition that continuing group life depends on the approval of the state, on whom all legal fictions must depend – by running it alongside a series of competing legal techniques for promoting corporate identity. Some of these were, to continental eyes, not simply puzzling but straightforwardly paradoxical. How could there be, as there undoubtedly was under the English law of trusts, such a thing as an 'unincorporate body' – a contradiction in terms when one thinks that a body is inherently 'corporate' even if it is not necessarily 'corporeal'?[10] How could there be, as there undoubtedly was in both ecclesiastical and what passed for English public law, such a thing as a 'corporation sole', that is, something that called itself a corporation but was identified solely with one, named individual?[11] Here we have enduring groups that are not corporations and corporations that are not groups at all. Alongside the puzzlement, as Maitland gratefully conceded, went some envy, for who would not envy a legal system that seemed unembarrassed by questions of consistency when more pressing questions, both of civil freedom and of practical convenience, were at stake? But still it remained to be asked whether freedom or convenience were in the end

---

[8] See below, 'Moral personality and legal personality', p. 67.

[9] Otherwise known, by Maitland among others, as the 'Fiction theory'.

[10] 'Suppose that a Frenchman saw it, what would he say? "Unincorporate body: inanimate soul!"' [body: *corpus* (Lat.); soul: *anima* (Lat.)]. (See below, 'Moral personality and legal personality', p. 62.)

[11] This entity is to be distinguished from the so-called 'one-man corporation', a much later, business invention designed to screen individuals from personal liability, which Maitland also discusses (see endnote viii to the Preface, below).

best served by laws that it was difficult, if not impossible, to understand. So Maitland, when he had completed his translation of Gierke, set out to see whether they could be understood, which meant first of all trying to understand where they came from.

Corporation sole

Making sense of the idea of the corporation sole meant dealing with two distinct though related questions. First, it was necessary to discover what application the concept had, which involved understanding why it had come into being in the first place; but second, it was necessary to ask what forms of law the use of this concept had excluded. Law, in ruling some things in, is always ruling some things out (though it was by implication the English genius to stretch the terms of this proposition as far as they would go). Even English law could not conjure up terms of art that were infinitely adaptable. That the corporation sole was a term of art, contrived to meet a particular practical problem rather than deduced from a set of general juristic precepts, could not be doubted. Nor could it be doubted that the application of this contrivance was rather limited. But what was surprising was how much, nonetheless, was ruled in, and how much ruled out.

The origins of the corporation sole Maitland traced to a particular era and a particular problem. The era was the sixteenth century, and coincides with what Maitland calls 'a disintegrating process . . . within the ecclesiastical groups',[12] when enduring corporate entities (corporations 'aggregate', which were, notwithstanding the misleading terminology, more than the sum of their parts) were fracturing under political, social and legal pressure. However, the particular problem was not one of groups but of individuals; or rather, it was a problem of one individual, the parish parson, and of one thing, the parish church. Was this thing, a church, plausibly either the subject or the object of property rights? The second question – of objectivity – was the more pressing one, as it concerned something that was unavoidable as a cause of legal dispute, namely 'an exploitable and enjoyable mass of wealth'.[13] But it could not be addressed without considering the other question, and the possibility that the ownership of this wealth does not attach to any named individuals but to the

---

[12] See below, 'Corporation sole', p. 9.
[13] See below, 'Corporation sole', p. 9.

church itself. The law could probably have coped with this outcome, but the named individuals involved, including not only the parson but also the patron who nominates him and the bishop who appoints him, could not. It placed exploitation and enjoyment at too great a remove. Instead, an idea that had been creeping towards the light during the fifteenth century was finally pressed into service, and the parson was deemed the owner, not in his own right, but as a kind of corporation, called a 'corporation sole'.

What this meant, in practice, was that the parson could enjoy and exploit what wealth there was but could not alienate it. But what it meant in theory was that the church belonged to something that was both more than the parson but somewhat less than a true corporation. That it was more than the parson was shown by the fact that full ownership, to do with as he pleased, did not belong to any one parson at any given time; that it was less than a corporation was shown by the fact that when the parson died, ownership did not reside in anybody or anything else, but went into abeyance.[14] Essentially, the corporation sole was a negative idea. It placed ultimate ownership beyond anyone. It was a 'subjectless right, a fee simple in the clouds'.[15] It was, in short, an absurdity, which served the practical purpose of many absurdities by standing in for an answer to a question for which no satisfactory answer was forthcoming. The image Maitland chose to describe what this entailed was an organic one: the corporation sole, he wrote, was a 'juristic abortion',[16] something brought to life only to have all life snuffed out from it, because it was not convenient to allow it, as must be allowed all true corporations, a life of its own.

Why, though, should absurdity matter, if convenience was served? Parsons, though numerous, were not the most important persons in the realm, and parish churches, though valuable, were not priceless in legal or any other terms. Yet it mattered because, even in the man-made environment of law, life is precious, and energies are limited, and one life, even unlived, is not simply transformable into another. More prosaically,

---

[14] It is, as Maitland insisted, one of the characteristics of all 'true' corporations that they endure as legal entities even when their 'heads', or 'members', or both, cease to exist; it is also characteristic of such bodies that their heads or members can transact with them, that is, that there is something distinct from both head and members for them to transact with. Neither was true of the corporation sole, which dissolved when detached from its only member, and whose only member could not transact with it, being at any given moment identifiable with it, such that the parson would be transacting with himself.

[15] See below, 'Corporation sole', p. 9.

[16] See below, 'Corporation sole', p. 9.

the idea of the corporation sole is 'prejudicial', and prejudicial to the idea of corporations as fictions in particular. Maitland was careful not to implicate himself too deeply in the great German controversy that set up 'realism' in permanent opposition to the idea of the *persona ficta*, and argued for group personality in broadly ontological terms ('as to philosophy', Maitland wrote, 'that is no affair of mine'[17]).[18] But he was conscious that the idea of the corporation sole gave legal fictions a bad name. If corporations were fictitious persons they were at least fictions we should take seriously, or, as Maitland himself put it, 'fictions we needs must feign'.[19] But the corporation sole was a frivolous idea, which implied that the personification of things other than natural persons was somehow a less than serious matter. It was not so much that absurdity bred absurdity, but that it accustoms us to absurdity, and all that that entails. Finally, however, the idea of the corporation sole was serious because it encouraged something less than seriousness about another office than parson. Although the class of corporations sole was slow to spread ('[which] seems to me', Maitland wrote, 'some proof that the idea was sterile and unprofitable'),[20] it was found serviceable by lawyers in describing at least one other person, or type of person: the Crown.

To think of the Crown as a corporation sole, whose personality is neither equivalent to the actual person of the king nor detachable from it, is, Maitland says, 'clumsy'.[21] It is in some ways less clumsy than the use of the concept in application to a parson. The central difficulty, that of 'abeyance' when one holder of the office dies, is unlikely to arise in this case: when a parson dies there may be some delay before another is appointed, but when a king dies there is considerable incentive to allow no delay, whatever the legal niceties (hence: 'The King is dead; long live the King'). Nor is it necessarily more clumsy than other, more famous doctrines: it is no more ridiculous to make two persons of one body than it is to make two bodies of one person.[22] But where it is clumsy, it is, Maitland suggests, seriously inconvenient. It makes a 'mess' of the idea of the civil service (by allowing it to be confused with 'personal' service of the

---

[17] See below, 'Moral personality and legal personality', p. 62.
[18] This was the doctrine of which, as Maitland said, 'Dr Otto Gierke, of Berlin, has been . . . principal upholder' (see below, 'Corporation sole', p. 10, n. 4).
[19] See below, 'Moral personality and legal personality', p. 62.
[20] See below, 'Crown as corporation', p. 32.
[21] See below, 'Corporation sole', p. 9.
[22] See Ernst H. Kantorowicz, *The King's two bodies: a study in medieval political theology* (Princeton: Princeton University Press, 1957).

king); it cannot cope with the idea of a national debt (whose security is not aided by the suggestion that the money might be owed by the king); it even introduces confusion into the postal service (by encouraging the view that the Postmaster-General is somehow freeholder of countless post offices). It also gets things out of proportion, for just as it implies that a single man is owner of what rightly belongs to the state, so it also suggests that affairs of state encompass personal pastimes ('it is hard to defend the use of the word unless the Crown is to give garden parties').[23] The problem with absurd legal constructions is not simply that serious concerns may be trivialised, but also that trivial matters may be taken too seriously, which is just as time-consuming. 'So long as the State is not seen to be a person [in its own right], we must either make an unwarrantably free use of the King's name, or we must be forever stopping holes through which a criminal might glide.'[24]

There is nothing, to Maitland's eyes, particularly sinister about this, though the Crown first came to be identified as a corporation sole at a sinister time, during the reign of Henry VIII. In most important respects, as touching on the fundamental questions of politics, the British state had long been afforded its own identity as a corporation aggregate, distinct from the persons of any individuals who might make it up at any given moment. The British state had a secure national debt, which had been owed for some time by the British 'Publick', and the British public had been relatively secure since the end of the seventeenth century in the rights that it had taken from the Crown. The problems, such as they were, were problems of convenience and not of freedom. But precisely because the idea of the Crown as a corporation sole remained tied up in the domain of private law, it illustrated the gap that existed in England between legal and political conceptions of the state. For lawyers, the Crown was a kind of stopgap, and it served to block off any broader understanding of the relationship between legal questions of ownership and political questions of right. That there was such a relation was obvious, since the ability of the state to protect itself and its people's freedoms depended on their ability as a public to own what the state owed. But the fact that the Crown was still understood as a corporation sole implied that there was some distinction to be drawn between matters of basic political principle and mere questions of law. This was unsustainable. It was not simply that it was not clear on what

[23] See below, 'Crown as corporation', p. 41, n. 31.
[24] See below, 'Crown as corporation', p. 32.

basis this distinction could conceivably rest – it was impossible, after all, to argue that the corporation sole was useful in matters of law, since it had shown itself to be so singularly useless. It was also far from clear where to draw the line. Maitland devotes considerable attention to the problems that the British Crown was experiencing at the turn of the twentieth century in understanding its relationship with its own colonies. That they were its 'own', and had begun their life as pieces of property, meant that there was a legal argument for seeing them still as the property of the Crown, which was itself seen still as the corporate personality of Her Majesty the Queen. This was convoluted, unworkable and anachronistic. It was also ironic. It meant that in what was obviously a political relationship the supposedly dominant partner was still conceived as an essentially private entity, and therefore restricted by the conventions of private law; while the colony itself, which had begun life as a chartered corporation created by the Crown, was able to use that identity as a corporation aggregate to generate a distinct identity for itself as ' "one body corporate and politic in fact and name" '.[25] The thing that was owned was better placed than the thing that supposedly owned it to make the connection between corporate and political personality. This was embarrassing.

And all this, as Maitland puts it, because English law had allowed 'the foolish parson [to] lead it astray'.[26] But English law would not have been so easy to lead astray if so much of the domain of public law had not remained uncharted territory. In mapping some of it out, Maitland suggests the obvious solution to the incongruous position of the Crown as a kind of glorified parish priest, and that is to follow the example of the colonies and allow that in all matters, public and private, the British state is best understood as a corporate body in its own right. It might be painful, but it would not be dangerous. 'There is nothing in this idea that is incompatible with hereditary kingship. "The king and his subjects together compose the corporation, and he is incorporated with them and they with him, and he is the head and they are the members." '[27] It might also be liberating, at least with regard to time spent in the company of lawyers.[28] However, English law does not make it so simple. If it were just a straight choice between corporate bodiliness and a fragmentary individualism, the 'true'

---

[25] See below, 'Crown as corporation', p. 32.
[26] See below, 'Crown as corporation', p. 32.
[27] See below, 'Crown as corporation, p. 32.
[28] 'This is the language of statesmanship, of the statute book, of daily life. But then comes the lawyer with theories in his head . . .' (See below, 'Crown as corporation', p. 32.)

corporation aggregate has all the advantages over 'this mere ghost of a fiction',[29] the corporation sole. But English law offers another option, which has advantages of its own: bodiliness without incorporation, the 'unincorporate body'. To make sense of this option, and the possibility that it might be the appropriate vehicle for unifying the legal and political identity of the state, Maitland found it necessary to enter another part of the English legal terrain, the swampy regions of the law of trusts.

Unincorporate body

The story of the second great anomaly of English law as it relates to the life of groups is in some ways the opposite of the first. Whereas the corporation sole was a narrow and useless idea that somehow found its way to encompass the grandest political institution of all, the unincorporate body was a broad and extremely useful idea that could encompass everything (the Stock Exchange, the Catholic Church, the Jockey Club, charitable activities, family life, business ventures, trades unions, government agencies) except, finally, the state itself. Both ideas had their origins in highly contingent circumstances, and just as the corporation sole needed lawyers to kill it, so the unincorporate body needed lawyers, with their 'wonderful conjuring tricks',[30] to bring it to life.[31] But once alive, this new way of thinking about group identity soon 'found the line of least resistance'[32] and started to grow. And the more successfully it grew, the less pressing was the need to explain exactly how this new conception related to the existing thickets of law through which it was pushing. The idea of the 'unincorporate body' exemplified the English assumption that what works must make sense, rather than that something must make sense if it is to work.

In seeking to make sense of how this idea in fact works, Maitland was also in some ways attempting the opposite of what he sought to achieve in his introduction to Gierke. There he was trying to make German conceptions

---

[29] See below, 'Corporation sole', p. 28.

[30] Gierke, *Political theories of the Middle Age*, p. xxvii.

[31] Though the gift of life went both ways: 'If the Court of Chancery saved the Trust, the Trust saved the Court of Chancery.' (See below, 'Trust and corporation', p. 84.) Maitland was also very aware that one of the reasons lawyers were so eager to utilise this device was that the Inns of Court to which they belonged could, and did, organise themselves around the idea of 'unincorporate bodiliness', that is, trusts allowed them to have an identity which was enduring but which did not depend on incorporation by the Crown.

[32] See below, 'Trust and corporation', p. 75.

of the group intelligible to English readers; here he is trying to make English law intelligible to Germans.[33] ' "I do not understand your trust," ' writes a 'very learned German' of Maitland's acquaintance.[34] The problem is that the ownership conferred by the law of trusts does not seem to belong either to persons or to things, and German legal theory recognises ownership of no other kind. Yet this is precisely what allows non-persons such as 'unincorporate bodies' to be the beneficiaries of trusteeship. Ownership does not belong to persons because trusteeship allows ownership in 'strict law' to rest with one set of persons (the trustees) and ownership in 'equity' to rest with another group entirely (the beneficiaries);[35] it does not belong to things because trusteeship allows the things owned to vary and to be variously invested without the rights of ownership having to alter (hence the trust 'fund'). Instead, the law of trust rests on the idea of 'good conscience'. If men can be trusted to act as owners in law for those who have an equitable claim on the thing owned, and if those with whom they deal can be trusted to see the matter in the same light,[36] then it is possible to provide an enduring legal identity for all manner of people and things that do not otherwise fit into the typology of *ius in personam* and *ius in rem*. Indeed, as it turned out, almost anyone or anything could be the beneficiary of a trust, and it became the vehicle of what Maitland calls 'social experimentation' as lawyers sought to use this branch of law

[33] The essay translated here as 'Trust and corporation' was originally published in German in *Grünhut's Zeitschrift für das Privat- und öffentliche Recht* Bd. xxxii.

[34] See below, 'Unincorporate body', p. 53.

[35] These may be named persons or individuals – and originally would have been such – but the law of trusts was extended as it was applied to include 'purposes' as substitutes for such persons, which proved particularly useful in setting up charities under the protections of trusteeship.

[36] This, though, created a problem when trustees had dealings with corporations, who did not, as 'fictions', have consciences at all, whether good or bad (it was indeed precisely to avoid the imputation of 'consciencelessness' in this sense that many groups chose to organise themselves as around the law of trusts, so that they should not be seen to be dependent on the state for such moral life as they had). In the end, during the second half of the nineteenth century, as trustees had increasingly to deal with the rapidly growing number of corporations that had been created in the aftermath of the 1862 Companies Act, it was decided for the purposes of the trust law to allow 'consciences' to such corporations. Maitland discusses this curious and complicated process in 'The unincorporate body'. There he implies that the story is essentially a progressive one, and evidence of a gradual emancipation from that 'speculative theory of corporations to which we do lip-service' i.e. the theory of the *persona ficta*. (See below, 'Unincorporate body', p. xix.) But another way of seeing it is as an essentially circular story, as a body of law that originated to allow some escape from the restrictions of this 'speculative' theory of fictitious persons is required in the end to fall back on fictions of its own.

to protect and preserve all manner of social forms,[37] including all manner of groups that were unable or unwilling to be seen as corporations. 'The trust deed might be long; the lawyer's bill might be longer; new trustees would be wanted from time to time; and now and again an awkward obstacle would require ingenious evasion; but the organised group could live and prosper, and be all the more autonomous because it fell under no solemn legal rubric.'[38]

The advantages of this way of organising group life were plain enough. It meant that it was possible for groups to arrange their own internal affairs in any way that they chose, so long as what they chose could be agreed on and set down in a deed of trust, and suitable persons could be found to act as trustees. An examination of the organisational principles governing religious, political and other bodies that existed in unincorporate form in England did indeed reveal 'almost every conceivable type of organisation from centralised and absolute monarchy to decentralised democracy and the autonomy of the independent congregation'.[39] In contrast to the *persona ficta* of classic corporation theory, whose identity as given by the state is also decided upon by the state, the unincorporate body could choose its form without having to rely upon permission from above. Indeed, having come into being, it could also evolve, 'slowly and silently chang[ing] its shape many times before it is compelled to explain its constitution to a public tribunal'.[40] There was in this system of self-government born of self-fashioning an inbuilt reticence about taking the affairs of the group before the courts.[41] In a way, the English law of trusts bypassed the perennial dilemma of political pluralism – how to protect social entities against the state without encroaching on the state, and thereby making them more than social entities – by organising the life of groups around a principle which in each case made sense only in its own, and not in more broadly political, terms. The state had chartered corporations during its early life because it had recognised in corporations something of itself,

---

[37] Among them, as Maitland describes it, the ability of a woman to own property after marriage. 'Some trustees are to be owners. We are only going to speak of duties. What is to prevent us, if we use words enough, from binding them to pay the income of a fund into the very hands of the wife and to take her written receipt for it? But the wedge was in, and could be driven home.' (See below, 'Trust and corporation', p. 75.)

[38] Gierke, *Political theories of the Middle Age*, p. xxxi.

[39] See below, 'Trust and corporation', p. 75.

[40] See below, 'Trust and corporation', p. 75.

[41] 'Disputes there will be; but the disputants will be very unwilling to call in the policeman.' (See below, 'Trust and corporation', p. 75.)

and had been correspondingly fearful;[42] but it had allowed the trust to develop unhindered because each trust was *sui generis*, and in that sense no threat – 'though the usual trusts might fall under a few great headings, still all the details (which had to be punctually observed) were to be found in lengthy documents; and a large liberty of constructing unusual trusts was both conceded in law and exercised in fact'.[43] The plurality of political forms of unincorporate bodies that were themselves sometimes political, sometimes religious, and sometimes something else entirely, testified to the success of the experiment.

However, Maitland was aware that 'all this has its dark side'.[44] The unincorporate body was the product of privilege, though it stood in contrast to those chartered corporations whose *privilegia* of self-government were bestowed directly by the state. Trusts existed behind a wall 'that was erected in the interests of the richest and most powerful class of Englishmen',[45] and though those interests included a desire to bestow charity as well as to hold money and goods within the family, both charitable and family trusts were ways of retaining control over wealth just as they were means of redistributing it. It was also true that the law of trusts, in treating each unincorporate body on its own terms, thereby made no categorical distinctions between the purposes for which such bodies might be established. There was nothing to distinguish the Catholic Church in this sense from a football club, apart from whatever was distinct about their particular deeds of trust. The implications ran both ways. On the one hand, something grand and serious and historic, with compelling claims over its individual members, was seemingly being trivialised and 'privatised'; on the other, that same body was being made to feel comfortable, perhaps 'too comfortable' in Maitland's words,[46] about what took place behind the wall of the trust, away from the glare of the state. Nor did the contrast between unincorporate and corporate bodies run only one way. Part of

---

[42] In Hobbes's classic formulation: 'Another infirmity of a Common-wealth, is . . . the great number of Corporations, which are as it were many lesser Common-wealths in the bowels of a greater, like wormes in the entrayles of a naturall man' (T. Hobbes, *Leviathan*, ed. R. Tuck (Cambridge: Cambridge University Press, [1651] 1996), p. 230). In his introduction to Gierke, Maitland has an imaginary German commentator on English *Korporationslehre* remark: ' "That great 'trust' concept of yours stood you in good stead when the days were evil: when your Hobbes, for example, was instituting an unsavoury comparison between corporations and *ascarides* [worms]" ' (Gierke, *Political theories of the Middle Age*, p. xxxiii).

[43] See below, 'Trust and corporation', p. 75.

[44] See below, 'Trust and corporation', p. 75.

[45] See below, 'Trust and corporation', p. 75.

[46] See below, 'Trust and corporation', p. 75.

Maitland's purpose in writing his account of the English law of trusts was to explain the background to a notorious recent case relating to one prominent class of unincorporate bodies, the trade union.[47] Corporations were liable for the actions of their agents, but unincorporate bodies, because in law technically the property of the trustees, were not. In 1900 the Amalgamated Society of Railway Servants (ASRS) was sued by the Taff Vale railway company for damages following a strike. Because the ASRS was an unincorporate body, the courts, up to the Court of Appeal, held that the agents were personally liable and that the funds of the union were therefore not to be touched. But in 1901 the House of Lords overturned this verdict and ordered the ASRS to pay more than £42,000 in damages. This was highly inconvenient for the union, and not in itself much of an advertisement for the liberating effects of incorporation. But it involved a recognition that questions of identity cannot in the end be detached from questions of responsibility, and groups, if they are to have a life of their own, must be willing to be held responsible for what their agents do.

Finally, there was the matter of the state itself. The history of the English law of trusts represents an avoidance of and not an answer to the question of whether groups can be organised on principles wholly distinct from the organisation of the state. It remained to be asked why, if clubs and churches, unions and even organs of local government could live and prosper behind the wall of trusteeship, the state should not do likewise. Maitland does not really answer this question. He acknowledges that the Crown can be understood as both the beneficiary of trusts and also as a trustee acting on behalf of other beneficiaries, among them 'the Publick'. But though it does not much matter for these purposes whether the Crown is a corporation sole – it is the whole point of the law of trusts that neither trustee nor beneficiary needs be compromised by the law of corporations – the relationship of trusteeship cannot serve as a general guide to the political identity of the public or of anyone else. This is because it cannot serve as a general guide to anything – trusts are, by their nature, nothing more than the documents in which they are set down. In the absence of such documents, the trust that exists between political bodies is, as Maitland admits, nothing more than 'a metaphor'.[48] What he does not go on to say is that a metaphorical trust is, really, no trust at all.

---

[47] The essay 'The unincorporate body' was written 'to assign to this Taff Vale case its place in a long story' (see below, 'The unincorporate body', p. 52).

[48] See below, 'Trust and corporation', p. 75.

State, trust and corporation

Founding the state on a metaphorical trust is like founding the state on a hypothetical contract. Both are forms of relation that depend upon the terms of the specific relation established in each case. To ask whether the state makes sense as a trust is a purely speculative question, since trusts only make sense when they work in law, and always make sense when they work in law. The question is therefore whether the state is a trust in law, and the answer is that it was only haphazardly and infrequently one, and then only when the state was identified with the Crown. It was perhaps possible to find themes and strands which connect the various instances of the Crown's status as trustee or beneficiary in various cases, but, as Maitland says, 'to classify trusts is like classifying contracts'.[49] Seeking to abstract from actual trusts or contracts to an idea of trust or contract is a speculative enterprise of the kind that English political philosophers specialised in: speculation detached rather than drawn from the workings of the law itself, thereby ignoring 'certain peculiarities of the legal system in which they live'.[50] From his earliest work in the history of ideas Maitland had been deeply sceptical of the possibility of deriving a moral basis for the state from the legal idea of contract, not least because 'for centuries the law has abhorred a perpetuity'.[51] The point about contracts is that they are specific to time and place, and the same is true of trusts: the law of trusteeship proved almost limitlessly flexible except in one respect – trusts cannot be established by law in perpetuity. These are not, and cannot be, timeless ideals of political philosophy.

It is, however, a separate question to ask what difference it makes to think as though they were. 'We may remember', Maitland writes 'that the State did not fall to pieces when philosophers and jurists declared it was the outcome of a contract'.[52] To hypothesise or to poeticise legal relationships is not necessarily dangerous, if that is all you are doing. It is also revealing of what you wish you were doing, and Maitland suggests that 'to a student of *Staatswissenschaft* legal metaphors should be of great interest, especially when they have become the commonplaces of political debate'.[53] Nevertheless, the result is to close the state off in a speculative

---

[49] See below, 'Trust and corporation', p. 75.
[50] See below, 'Moral personality and legal personality', p. 62.
[51] Maitland, *Collected papers*, vol. 1, p. 65.
[52] See below, 'Trust and corporation', p. 75.
[53] See below, 'Trust and corporation', p. 75.

realm of its own, in which lip-service is paid to the language of law but the connection with the life of the law, or any other kind of life, is broken. There are attractions to this: it takes a lot of the heat out of political theory, and just as it spares political philosophers too much attention to the detailed consequences of their theories, so it spares groups within the state from the detailed attentions of the political philosophers.[54] But it is not a sustainable theory because it is not a working theory, and if the theory is required to do any real work there is the chance it will either break down or start to do some real damage.

In the only essay of those collected in this volume written for an avowedly non-specialist audience (the members of Newnham College, Cambridge), Maitland goes further than in any of the others in setting out what he thinks a sustainable theory might be. Still, he does not go very far. The national contrast he draws in 'Moral personality and legal personality' is not with Germany, but with France – 'a country where people take their legal theories seriously',[55] and where groups had suffered at the hands of an excessively rigid and technical theory of incorporation. In this respect, England had all the advantages. But because in France the theories had been so seriously applied, it was clearer there what was missing, whereas, as he puts it elsewhere in relation to England, 'the inadequacy of our theories was seldom brought to the light of day'.[56] What was missing was an acknowledgment that many groups were 'right-and-duty-bearing units' regardless of whether they were so recognised by the state, and therefore likely to suffer if the state failed to recognise them. Furthermore, if this was true of groups within the state, then it must be true of the state as well, which bore greater rights and duties than most. Maitland calls these 'moral' facts though he professes to be unconcerned as to their broader philosophical status, whether as truths or merely necessary fictions. That is a question for philosophers. But, Maitland suggests, if these groups have a life of their own then lawyers at least must recognise it, which means recognising that the life of the law cannot be divorced altogether from philosophical speculation, just as philosophical speculation is mere speculation when divorced from the life of the law. *Staatslehre* and

---

[54] Hobbes is an exception to this (see Hobbes, *Leviathan*, chapter XXII, '*Of* SYSTEMES *Subject, Political and Private*'). But it was one of the consistent themes of Maitland's writings that the theories of Thomas Hobbes had never been taken all that seriously in England.

[55] See below, 'Moral personality and legal personality', p. 62.

[56] See below, 'Trust and corporation', p. 75.

Korporationslehre cannot exist apart from each other, because they inhabit the same world.

Significance

Despite the reticence of some of Maitland's conclusions and the specialist nature of the historical accounts on which those conclusions were based, the writing that contained them proved enormously influential, albeit for a relatively short period of time. A group of English political theorists, who came collectively to be known as the political pluralists, found in Maitland, and via Maitland in Gierke, support for the case they wished to make against the excessive claims that were being made on behalf of the state in the early years of the last century. Both the excessive individualism of conventional juristic theory in England – exemplified by the theory of sovereignty associated with John Austin – and the excessive statism of more recent political philosophy – identified by the turn of the century with Bernard Bosanquet's *The philosophical theory of the State* (1899) – were challenged by Maitland's account of the complex interrelationship between states and other groups. Many of the pluralists were, like Maitland, historians (they included J. N. Figgis, Ernest Barker, G. D. H. Cole and Harold Laski) but they were not legal historians; nor did they for the most part share his scruples about straying from the world of history into the more speculative regions of political philosophy. As a result, many of the subtleties of Maitland's account were lost in the assault on the overmighty state, and political pluralism became, in its various forms, a somewhat wishful and excessively 'moralised' doctrine. It also became increasingly detached from the practical political world which it sought both to describe and reform, and in the aftermath of the First World War it was repudiated by many of its adherents, who found it unable to cope with the new realities of political life. Certainly political pluralism was a philosophy which shared little of Maitland's fascination with the interconnectedness of legal practicalities and political understanding, and in some ways exemplified what he called 'our specifically English addiction to ethics'.[57]

Of course, because Maitland's work is historical, it has also been subject to revision and updating by other historians working from other sources or reworking the sources that Maitland used, although in contrast to some

---

[57] See below, 'Moral personality and legal personality', p. 62.

of Maitland's other writing, there has been little sustained criticism of the historical substance of these particular essays.[58] It is true, however, that many of the legal problems Maitland writes about were soon to become things of the past. Already at the time he was writing, as the essays suggest, the pressures being placed upon some of the anomalies of English law could not be sustained, and practical solutions were being found which served to rationalise and harmonise the law as it related to corporate and unincorporate bodies. This process continued throughout the twentieth century, so that it would be hard to say now that any great political or philosophical principles hang on the distinction between the law of trusts and the law of corporations, though very many practical questions of course still depend on it. The idea of the 'corporation sole' no longer impedes our understanding of the legal responsibilities of the Crown, because those responsibilities have long since been parcelled out among various government agencies, each of which is subject to a vast and increasingly complex range of legal provisions. The law, in other words, has moved on and, in adapting itself to the massively complex requirements of modern corporate life, has become too complex to be easily reconciled with speculative theories at all.

Yet despite their apparent datedness in these two respects, Maitland's essays are still relevant to our understanding of the state and its relation to the groups that exist alongside it. Very many of the themes he discusses have a clear and continuing resonance. Almost everything Maitland alludes to in these highly allusive essays[59] has some connection with current political concerns. He writes about the growth of the giant American corporation under the protection of the law of trusts (in this respect, as in that of the political identity of the former colonies, America seems to point the way to the future in these essays); he writes about the inadequacy of abstract theories of sovereignty; he writes about the dilemmas of colonialism, and federalism, and empire; he describes the tensions between English

---

[58] Some of the reservations that legal historians have come to have about Maitland's other work are alluded to in the address given by S. F. C. Milsom to mark the unveiling of a memorial tablet for Maitland in Westminster Abbey in 2001 (see S. F. C. Milsom, 'Maitland', *Cambridge Law Journal* (60, 2001), 265–70). This ongoing critical engagement stands in contrast to the treatment of the essays Maitland wrote on early modern and modern history of state, trust and corporation. As George Garnett notes of the essays on the Crown republished here, historians have 'largely ignored [them] since they were written' (G. Garnett, 'The origins of the Crown', in *The history of English law: centenary essays on Pollock and Maitland*, ed. J. Hudson (Oxford, 1996) p. 172).

[59] 'Undoubtedly over-allusive, not from ostentation but from absorption', as H. A. L. Fisher puts it (Fisher, *Frederick William Maitland*, p. 106).

and European systems of law, and the possible coming together of these; he raises the problems of national government, and local government, and self-government; he describes some of the conditions of social diversity and religious toleration; he isolates many of the difficulties of what would now be called 'corporate governance'; he identifies the gap between legal and moral notions of trust; he maps the relation between the public and the private sphere. Almost none of this is explicit, but all of it is there.

However, the deepest resonance of Maitland's writings arises not from the issues he addresses but from the way he addresses them. This is partly, but not wholly, a question of style. There is, underlying everything that he writes, a historian's sense of irony, and the certainty that nothing plays itself out historically in exactly the fashion that was intended. Notwithstanding various attempts by the pluralists and others to claim Maitland as the exponent of a particular political philosophical creed,[60] he is a dismantler of creeds and a chronicler of the relationship between contingency and necessity. Rather than a doctrine of 'real group personality' or anything else, Maitland presents us with a series of choices, and not simple choices between truth and fiction, but choices between different kinds of truth or different kinds of fiction. There is nothing relativist about this, because behind it all lies a clear conception that what lasts legally and politically is what works, and what works is not just a question of opinion. But what works is not always straightforward, and things can work in different ways. There are convenient legal theories that do their work now but store up trouble for the future, just as there are inconvenient theories that point the way forward towards something better. It is a luxury to live under a legal system that does not need to cohere, but luxury is not the same as security. Likewise, to allow a gap to open up between political and legal conceptions of the state is not simply a mark of failure but also evidence of a kind of success. There is something to be said for what Maitland calls 'muddling along' with 'sound instincts . . . towards convenient conclusions'.[61] But with it comes a narrowing of horizons, and a corresponding uncertainty about what exists over the horizon, except for the sky. What he describes therefore is not a solution or a doctrine but a predicament – the predicament of group life, or of living under laws. The account he gives of that predicament is essentially historical, and it is highly contingent: the subjects of these essays are determined by historical circumstance,

[60] For example, 'Moral personality and legal personality' is included in R. Scruton (ed.), *Conservative texts* (Basingstoke: Macmillan, 1991).
[61] See below, 'Moral personality and legal personality', p. 62.

and have no universal application. But just because the predicament is historical, and just because these essays are essays in the history of legal and political thought, they show us what the history of legal and political thought contributes to the understanding of our predicament.[62]

---

[62] Cf. Quentin Skinner in 'A reply to my critics': 'Suppose we have the patience to go back to the start of our own history and find out in detail how it developed. This will not only enable us to illuminate the changing applications of some of our key concepts; it will also enable us to uncover the points at which they may have become confused or misunderstood in a way that marked their subsequent history. And if we can do this . . . we can hope not merely to illuminate but to dissolve some of our current philosophical perplexities' (J. Tully (ed.), *Meaning and context: Quentin Skinner and his critics* (Cambridge: Polity Press, 1988), p. 288). To dissolve philosophical perplexities is not the same as solving the problems that produced them.

Note on the text

The essays reproduced here are taken from the 1911 edition of Maitland's *Collected papers* published by Cambridge University Press. We have tried to remain as faithful as possible to this edition, and have included Maitland's footnotes as they appear in the original, with their idiosyncratic and not always consistent scheme of referencing. (Some suggestions for how to interpret these references are given in the bibliographical note that follows.) However, we have corrected a small number of typographical errors that appear in the 1911 edition, updated some of the spelling and punctuation, and removed footnotes that were added by the editor of the 1911 edition, H. A. L. Fisher.

We have reproduced the essays in the order of their appearance in the 1911 edition. They do not need to be read in this order, and readers wanting to start with the most accessible should begin with 'Moral personality and legal personality'. However, 'The corporation sole' and 'The Crown as corporation' are essentially two parts of a single essay and need to be read in sequence. With the exception of 'Moral personality and legal personality', these essays were written for a fairly specialist audience of lawyers and legal historians, and even 'Moral personality and legal personality' makes some fairly heavy demands for a talk originally given to a largely undergraduate audience. (The *Newnham College Letter* of 1904 contains the following report on the occasion: 'The Henry Sidgwick Memorial Lecture was delivered this year by Professor Maitland on October 22nd. The subject was *Moral and Legal Personality* and Professor Maitland gave a very brilliant and interesting lecture, though most of the very considerable audience found the task of following him in this difficult and intricate subject a severe intellectual exercise.') In the case of 'Trust and corporation' Maitland's audience was originally German, and the essay reflects this in its allusions and its extensive use of German terms. All the essays as they appeared in 1911 contain a number of words, phrases and longer passages of text in German, Latin, French and Anglo-Norman left untranslated by Maitland. Where possible, we have given English versions of these. In the case of longer passages, we have replaced the original with a direct translation. For shorter phrases and single words, where there is a reasonably straightforward English equivalent we have given this alongside the original. Words and phrases for which there is no direct translation (particularly terms of German and Roman law) are included as entries in their own right in the glossary of technical terms.

Much of the appeal (and some of the frustration) of Maitland's essays lies in their style, which is allusive, ironic and knowing. We have tried not to interrupt this too much, while offering as much help as we can to the reader who may not be familiar with the things Maitland is alluding to. In the case of the translation of foreign words and phrases, it has sometimes been necessary to use the English and original terms interchangeably. This is particularly true of 'Trust and corporation', in which Maitland often uses a German term in place of the English to make clear the particular areas and forms of law he is writing about. We have retained these German terms and provided translations at their first appearance in the text. But for stylistic reasons we have not always given a translation for every subsequent appearance of the term, particularly when it appears often in the same relatively brief passage of the text. We have also sought to do justice to one of Maitland's most important themes: the lexical translatability but conceptual and historical incommensurability of German and English legal terms. For example, *Zweckvermögen*, which we have translated as 'special purpose fund', is sometimes used by Maitland to refer to the formal character that a certain type of trust would have under German law, but which it cannot have precisely because it is not under German law. In other words, there are some terms in 'Trust and corporation' for which it is possible to provide an English equivalent but which Maitland wishes to imply are effectively untranslatable.

Our translations are included in the text in square brackets. The original text also includes a small number of translations by Maitland, which appear either within round brackets or in unbracketed quotation marks.

Bibliographical notes

Maitland's sources and abbreviations

Maitland's footnotes to these essays refer to a series of legal sources that he clearly anticipated would be familiar to his readers. We have left the footnotes in their original form, as integral parts of the essays. Very few of the references are full by modern standards, but many of them are nevertheless self-explanatory. However, Maitland also uses a series of abbreviations, not all of them consistent, to refer to some essential literature and sources. What follows is a glossary of these abbreviations.

1, 2, 3, etc. followed by name of monarch (e.g. 39 Hen. VI) This refers to the year of the reign of the monarch in question. When this entry is followed by an f., the reference is to a Year Book (f. or fo. standing for folio), with the subsequent abbreviations referring to the term of the year (Hilary [Hil.], Easter [Pasch.], Trinity [Trin.], Michaelmas [Mich.]) and then the number of the plea (pl. 1, 2 etc.) Very occasionally Maitland will preface these references with Y.B. When the year and monarch's name is followed by a c., the reference is to a statute (c. standing for the chapter of the statute, occasionally followed by s. or sec. for section, and pr. for *proemium*, or preamble). Very occasionally Maitland will preface these references with Stat. In the main text of 'The corporation sole' Maitland uses Arabic rather than Roman numerals to refer to the monarch in question, and an abbreviated name (e.g. E. 4, H. 6, etc.)

App. Cas. Appeal Case

J. de Athon Athon's *Constitutiones legitime seu legatine regionis anglicane* (first published in 1504)

B.G.B. *Bürgerliches Gesetzbuch* (1896)

Bracton Bracton's *De legibus et consuetudinibus angliae*. A recent edition is: Bracton, *De legibus et consuetudinibus angliae* ed. G. E. Woodbine, trans. with revisions and notes by S. E. Thorne, 4 vols. (London: Selden Society, 1968–77)

Ch.D. Chancery Division

Co. lit. *Coke upon Littleton* (in full *The first part of the institutes of the lawes of England: or a commentary upon Littleton*, first published in 1628)

C.P.D. Common Pleas Division

Comm. Blackstone's *Commentaries on the laws of England* (first published in four volumes from 1765–9)

Dalison Dalison's *Common Pleas Reports*, in *English Reports* (q.v.), vol. 123 (The reports cover the years 1486–1580)

Dyer *Dyer's King's Bench Reports*, in *English Reports* (q.v.), vol. 73 (The reports cover the years 1513–82)

English Reports *The English Reports*, 176 volumes (Edinburgh and London, 1900–30)

Fitz. *Abr.* Fitzherbert's *La Graunde Abridgement* (first published in 1514)

History of tithes Selden's *History of tythes* (first published in 1617)

Hob. Hobart's *Common Pleas Reports and King's Bench Reports*, in *English Reports* (q.v.), vol. 80 (The reports cover the years 1603–25)

Kirchenrecht F. K. P. Hinschius, *Das Kirchenrecht der Katholiken und Protestanten in Deutschland* (published in 6 volumes from 1869–97)

Lib. Ass. *Liber Assisarum* or *Le livre des assizes et plees del corone*, a compilation of selected cases from the yearbooks of Edward III

Lit. Littleton's *Tenures* (first known edition from 1481, later published as *Littleton's tenures in English*)

L.Q.R. *Law Quarterly Review*

L. R. *Law Reports* (sometimes followed by Q. B. for Queen's Bench, H. L. for House of Lords, etc.)

Placit Abbrev. *Placitorum Abbreviatio*, published in 1811 by the Records Commission. A selection of reports of cases held before itinerant justices from Richard I to Edward II

Plowden Plowden's *Commentaries*, available in *English Reports* (q.v.) vol. 75 (The commentaries cover the years 1550–79)

Q.B. Queen's Bench

Rep. Coke's *King's Bench Reports*, available in *English Reports* (q.v.), vols. 76–7 (The reports cover the years 1572–1616)

Rot. Parl. *Rotuli parliamentorum*, or parliamentary rolls (published in six volumes from 1778–83, containing the extant records of parliament from 1278–1503)

Salk. Salkeld's *King's Bench Reports*, available in *English Reports* (q.v.), vol. 91 (The reports cover the years 1689–1712)

Stat. Statute (followed by the year of the reign of the monarch in question)

Y.B. Year Book (followed by the year of the reign of the monarch in question)

The publishing history of the essays

'The corporation sole' first appeared in the *Law Quarterly Review* (16, 1900), pp. 335–54.

'The Crown as corporation' first appeared in the *Law Quarterly Review* (17, 1901), pp. 131–46.

'The unincorporate body' was not published before its appearance in the *Collected papers* of 1911. The original manuscript is in the library of The Institute of Advanced Legal Studies in London, and states that it was first delivered as a paper to the Eranus Club in Cambridge. (The Eranus Club was a secret debating society, modelled on the Apostles, which numbered Henry Sidgwick and Arthur Balfour among its members.) The manuscript is not dated but the material it contains indicates it must have been written between late 1901 and 1903.

'Moral personality and legal personality' was first delivered as the Sidgwick lecture at Newnham College, Cambridge, in 1904. (The *Collected papers* list it as the Sidgwick lecture for 1903, which was the year Maitland was invited to deliver it, but a substantial amount of the material in the lecture refers to events and literature dating from 1904. It is also listed as that year's Sidgwick lecture in the *Newnham College Newsletter* of 1904.) It was subsequently published in *The Journal of the Society for Comparative Legislation*, (ns 14, 1905), pp. 192–200.

'Trust and corporation', though written by Maitland in English, was first published in German as 'Trust und Korporation' in *Grünhut's Zeitschrift für das Privat- und öffentliche Recht* (33, 1904). The translation was made by Josef Redlich, and Maitland suggests in a letter to him that it was never intended to appear in English, despite his having had it privately printed. ('Dr Grünhut will understand that I am not publishing the essay in English – the print is only for your eyes and those of a few advising friends and the type will be "broken up" when it has served its purpose' (letter to Redlich of 30 April 1904, in *Letters of F. W. Maitland*, vol. II, p. 281)).

The essays were first published together in H. A. L. Fisher's Cambridge University Press edition of Maitland's *Collected papers* in 1911. Fisher's edition uses the manuscript version of 'The unincorporate body' and the printed versions of the other essays (including the privately printed English version of 'Trust and corporation').

The essays were republished by Cambridge University Press in 1936 as *Maitland: Selected essays* ed. H. D. Hazeltine, G. Lapsley and P. H. Winfield. This 1936 edition uses Fisher's earlier edition, but adds a series of editorial notes, designed to keep the reader 'abreast of later research' (p. vii). These footnotes consist mainly of references to legal and historical articles published between 1900 and 1936 that address some of the legal controversies that Maitland discusses (but do not in most cases discuss Maitland himself). The edition also translates the longer passages of German in 'Trust and corporation' but nothing else. It appears to have been targeted at a specialist audience of lawyers and historians, and includes alongside the five essays collected here Maitland's introduction to his edition of the parliament roll of 1305, written in 1893. It also includes another unpublished paper Maitland delivered to the Eranus Club entitled 'The body politic', which appeared in the *Collected papers* of 1911, and which contains a critique of the increasing use of naturalistic and scientific analogies in the study of politics. The essay concludes with an expression of regret at the 'title . . . political science'.

'Trust and corporation' has more recently been published in an abridged form in *Group rights: perspectives since 1900* ed. Julia Stapleton (Bristol: Thoemmes Press, 1996). This edition contains a translation of all German terms and passages by D. P. O'Brien.

We have made our own translations throughout this current edition and these occasionally differ substantially from those made by the editors of earlier editions. However, we have also drawn on these earlier editions when appropriate.

Other works by Maitland

Maitland's oeuvre is extensive. Listed below are a small number of his writings, either directly relevant to the content of the essays collected here, or likely to be of interest to the non-specialist.

'The corporation aggregate: the history of a legal idea' (Liverpool [privately printed], 1893; IALS Library, London; All Souls' Library, Oxford; The Bodleian, Oxford). This is a version of the lecture Maitland delivered 'under the auspices of the Liverpool Board of Legal Studies', in which he first addresses some of the questions relating to the doctrine of the *persona ficta* and its role in the evolution of English law. The lecture contains some treatment of broadly political themes (including a brief discussion of the frontispiece of Hobbes's *Leviathan*). But its main concern is local government and 'the question of village communities', and it does not make many of the larger connections between moral and legal personality that characterise the later essays collected here.

Letters of F. W. Maitland, vol. 1 ed. C. H. S. Fifoot, vol. 2 ed. P. N. R. Zutshi (London: Selden Society, 1965 and 1995). Both volumes contain letters that discuss the writing of these essays, and some more limited references to their reception.

Collected Papers, 3 volumes, ed. H. A. L. Fisher (Cambridge: Cambridge University Press, 1911). The essays that Fisher takes to be of interest to the non-specialist (including 'Moral personality and legal personality') are marked in the contents page of each volume by an asterisk.

The constitutional history of England: a course of lectures (Cambridge: Cambridge University Press, 1908). Some of the more overtly political ideas alluded to in these essays are also discussed in this posthumous work. (See in particular 'The "Crown" and the "Government"' in the section entitled 'Sketch of public law at the present day (1887–8)', pp. 387–421.)

A Historical Sketch of Liberty and Equality, as Ideals of English Political Philosophy from the Time of Hobbes to the Time of Coleridge (Indianapolis: The Liberty Fund, 2000). This is Maitland's rejected fellowship dissertation printed here with 'The body politic'.

Works about Maitland

Biography

There are three very different book-length accounts of Maitland's life and thought. Shortly after his death, his friend H. A. L. Fisher published *Frederick William Maitland: A biographical sketch* (Cambridge: Cambridge University Press, 1910). This is essentially a personal reminiscence, and draws heavily on Maitland's correspondence. A semi-official biography is C. H. S. Fifoot, *Frederic William Maitland: a life* (Cambridge, Mass:

Harvard University Press, 1971). This is a narrative account of Maitland's life and the evolution of his career, drawing mainly on published evidence, but also on some personal knowledge obtained from Maitland's daughter, Ermengard. (The Selden Society published a biographical sketch by Ermengard entitled *F. W. Maitland: a child's-eye view* in 1957.) More idiosyncratic is G. R. Elton, *F. W. Maitland* (London: Weidenfeld and Nicolson, 1985). This contains a brief account of Maitland's life, but is more of an attempt to describe and explain the phenomenon of Maitland's posthumous reception, and the 'continued devotion' he inspires among historians. Elton is not particularly interested in the essays collected in this volume, which he describes (incorrectly) as primarily 'legal' rather than 'historical'.

The essays

Though Maitland's work continues to be widely cited by lawyers and historians, the particular essays collected in this edition have not been the subject of much detailed scholarly or critical analysis since they were written. They do, however, in different ways form the basis of much of what is discussed in the following:

J. N. Figgis, *Churches in the modern state* [originally published 1913] (Bristol; Thoemmes Press, 1997) is perhaps the best-known attempt to turn some of the insights offered by Maitland and Gierke into a coherent and distinctive political philosophy, often labelled political pluralism. H. J. Laski, *Studies in the problem of sovereignty* (New Haven: Yale University Press, 1917) and *Authority in the modern state* (New Haven: Yale University Press, 1919), are two more well-known works of political pluralism. Both draw on Maitland, but use him in an intellectual setting that is both socialist and American. A second English language edition of an extract from Gierke's *Das Deutsche Genossenschaftsrecht* was published as O. von Gierke, *Natural law and the theory of society 1500–1800*, ed. E. Barker (Cambridge: Cambridge University Press, 1934). Barker's edition and introduction were designed as a companion to Maitland's earlier edition of Gierke, though Barker is critical in his introduction of the idea of 'real group personality' that he takes to have been extrapolated from Maitland's earlier work. Maitland also features heavily in E. Barker, 'Maitland as a sociologist' *The Sociological Review*, 29 (1937), 121–35. This was Barker's Presidential Address to the Institute of Sociology in London, in which he describes these essays as containing the 'quintessence' of Maitland as a sociologist, because of 'the light [they] shed on the social growth of our people'. The essays on 'The corporation sole' and 'The Crown as corporation' form part of the inspiration behind E. H. Kantorowicz, *The king's two bodies: a study in medieval political theology* (Princeton: Princeton University Press, 1957). They are specifically discussed in the 'Introduction' and in chapter VII, entitled 'The king never dies'. Some of the philosophical presuppositions behind Maitland's arguments for group personality are assessed in R. Scruton, 'Corporate persons', *Aristotelian Society*, supplementary volume (LXIII (1989), pp. 239–66). Scruton also discusses the essays briefly in *England: an elegy* (London: Chatto and Windus, 2000). The continuing historical relevance of Maitland's treatment of the legal and political origins of the Crown are the subject of G. Garnett, 'The origins of the Crown', in *The history of English law: centenary essays on Pollock and Maitland*, ed. J. Hudson (Oxford: Oxford University Press, 1996), pp. 171–214. The broader connections between the subject of these essays and the development of pluralist ideas in twentieth century Britain are discussed in D. Runciman, *Pluralism and the personality of the state* (Cambridge: Cambridge University Press, 1997).

Biographical notes

These notes include all the names cited by Maitland as authorities in their own right. It does not include all the various royal justices whom Maitland mentions when referring to particular judgments (e.g. Danby, Fineux, Keble etc.). These names are often followed in the text by 'J.' or 'C. J.'. These refer to 'Justice' and 'Chief Justice' respectively.

ALEXANDER III (d. 1181), pope from 1159. Driving force in the expansion of papal jurisdiction and consequently of canon law. Staunch opponent of the Emperor Frederick I over their respective jurisdictions in Northern Italy. The northern Italian town of Alessandria is named after him.

SIR WILLIAM ANSON (1843–1914), jurist. Warden of All Souls 1881–1904. Author of *The principles of the English laws of contract* (1879) and *The law and custom of the constitution* (1886–92). Like Dicey (q.v.) a staunch Unionist who left the Liberal party over the question of Home Rule.

JOHN AUSTIN (1790–1859), legal philosopher. Professor of Jurisprudence and the Law of Nations, University of London from 1826–35. He resigned the Chair because of poor attendances at his lectures, though his audience included John Stuart Mill, whom Austin had previously tutored in Roman Law. The first ten lectures of his course on jurisprudence were published as *The province of jurisprudence determined* in 1832. The remainder were published after his death, edited by his wife, the well-known author and translator, Sarah Austin.

ARTHUR BALFOUR (1848–1930), 1st Earl Balfour, philosopher and statesman. Brother-in-law of Henry Sidgwick (q.v.). Succeeded his uncle Salisbury as Conservative Prime Minister in 1902. Resigned December 1905. Remained in politics and as foreign secretary under Lloyd George was author of the so-called Balfour Declaration, in which he expressed the government's sympathy with 'the establishment in Palestine of a national home for the Jewish people'. He was also the author of *A defence of philosophic doubt* (1879), *The foundations of belief* (1895), *Theism and humanism* (1915) and *Theism and thought* (1923).

SIR WILLIAM BLACKSTONE (1723–80), legal writer and judge. First professor of English law at Oxford 1760–6, where he lectured to Jeremy Bentham. Author of *Commentaries on the laws of England* (1765–9), by far the best-known and most widely read of all synthetic summaries of English law. The later school of analytical jurisprudence associated with Bentham and Austin was in large part a reaction against this work.

HENRY BRACTON (d. 1268), ecclesiastic and judge. Long reputed to be the author of *De legibus et consuetudinibus angliae*, one of the first attempts to treat the law of England in a systematic and practical manner. In fact, it was almost certainly the work of more than one author. Maitland edited *Bracton's Note Book* in 1887 and *Select passages from the work of Bracton and Azo* in 1895 for the Selden Society.

SIR ROBERT BROKE (d. 1558), lawyer and judge. Speaker of the House of Commons and chief justice of common pleas 1554–8. His 'La Grande Abridgement', which was posthumously published in 1568, was an abstract of the year books down to his own time, and forms the basis of much of Maitland's discussion in 'The corporation sole'. It was based largely on the writing of Fitzherbert (q.v.).

WILLIAM BUCKLAND (1859–1946), jurist, scholar of Roman law. Regius Professor of Civil Law at Cambridge 1914–45. His *A text-book of Roman law from Augustus to Justinian* (1922) was seen as 'much the most important work on Roman law ever published in English' (P. W. Duff). A friend of Maitland's, who like Maitland suffered from ill-health (in his case tuberculosis) which took him to the Canary Islands in 1900 (Maitland wintered there from 1898 onwards).

SIR EDWARD COKE (1552–1634), judge, legal writer and politician. M.P. variously between 1589 and 1628 for Aldeburgh, Norfolk, Liskeard, Coventry and Buckinghamshire. He published his *Law reports* between 1600–15, during which time no other reports appeared. The first volume of his *Institutes of the laws of England* was published in 1628, comprising his commentaries on Littleton (q.v.). Though early in his career a defender of the royal prerogative, he became the leading champion of the common law.

ALBERT VENN DICEY (1835–1922), jurist. Vinerian Professor of English Law at Oxford 1882–1909. Author of *Lectures on the relation between law and public opinion in England during the nineteenth century* (1905), in which he staunchly defended the British constitutional settlement and the Union.

SIR ANTHONY FITZHERBERT (1470–1538), judge. Justice of the common pleas from 1522. Member of the tribunal that tried Sir Thomas More. He was the author of 'La Graunde Abridgement' (1514), which consisted of a digest of the Year Books and other cases not found in them, and came to be accepted as authoritative by Coke (q.v.) among others. It served as the basis for Sir Robert Broke's (q.v.) later 'Abridgement'.

OTTO VON GIERKE (1841–1921), jurist and intellectual historian. His *Das deutsche Genossenschaftsrecht* was published in four volumes between 1868 and 1913, and contains all the elements of what Maitland calls 'Germanism' as a legal and philosophical doctrine, broadly liberal in outlook. Gierke fought in the Franco-Prussian war of 1870–1, which helped shape his lifelong nationalism, and was closely involved in the drafting of the *Bürgerliches Gesetzbuch* of 1896, whose original draft of 1888 he criticised as being too 'Roman' and insufficiently 'social' in its treatment of private law.

THOMAS HILL GREEN (1832–86), idealist philosopher. Professor of Moral Philosophy at Oxford 1878–82. Among the works published posthumously were his *Lectures on the principles of political obligation*. He opposed positivist conceptions of the state, and influenced a generation of Oxford students (some of whom became 'New Liberals') with his demand for action on the part of the state to remedy obstacles to the moral life of the community.

SIR JAMES HALES (d. 1554), lawyer and judge. Counsel to the Corporation of Canterbury (1541–2). Became justice of the common pleas in 1549. In 1553 he refused to affix his name to the seal making Lady Jane Grey queen. Then in the same year, under the new Queen Mary, he refused at Kent assizes to relax laws of non-conformity in favour of Roman Catholics. He was imprisoned, and on his release the following year went mad and drowned himself in a stream near Canterbury (see separate endnote to 'The Crown as corporation').

THOMAS HOBBES (1588–1679), philosopher. Best known as a political philosopher, he also wrote extensively on mathematics, natural philosophy and history. His first publication was a translation of Thucydides and one of his last a translation of Homer. He nearly died in exile in France in 1647, but survived to write *Leviathan*, the most celebrated and most notorious of his various attempts to describe and justify the nature of sovereign political power. A lifetime servant of the Cavendish family, he experienced the workings of the Virginia Company, in which they were shareholders, at first-hand.

INNOCENT IV (*c.* 1200–54), pope from 1243. A trained lawyer and teacher of law at the University of Bologna, he was in Maitland's words 'the greatest lawyer who ever sat upon the chair of St Peter'. Best known for his role in the development of the concept of the *persona ficta*, though the nature of the doctrine itself remains much disputed. Gierke's (q.v.) *Das deutsche Genossenschaftsrecht*, particularly the section translated by Maitland, is in large part a modern contribution to that dispute.

JUSTINIAN I (reigned 527–65), Roman Emperor and promulgator of the *Corpus Juris Civilis*, the fullest surviving collection of Roman Law. Upon rediscovery in the West at the end of the eleventh century the *Corpus* was the inspiration for the legal renaissance of the twelfth century, and remains the most important source of Roman legal ideas. As Emperor, he oversaw the reconquest of Africa from the Vandals and Italy from Goths.

SIR THOMAS LITTLETON (1402–81), judge and legal author. Justice of the common pleas from 1466. Author of the 'Tenures', which he wrote for the instruction of his son Richard, and which he is thought to have left unfinished in 1474–5. It became, in combination with Coke's (q.v.)

commentary on it published in 1628, the principal authority on real property law.

JAMES MARTINEAU (1805–90), Unitarian minister and philosopher. Professor of Mental and Moral Philosophy and Political Economy at Manchester New College from 1840–57, becoming Professor of Mental and Moral Philosophy and Religious Philosophy, 1857–69. Later publications include *Ideal substitutes for God* (1879) and *Types of ethical theory* (1885), in which he attempted to establish an alternative to biblical authority in the workings of man's own conscience.

JAMES OTIS (1725–83), lawyer and politician. Leading member of the Massachusetts legislature from 1761–9 and polemicist on its behalf against British rule. Author of *The rights of the British Colonies asserted and proved* (1764). He was progressively incapacitated by mental illness, and following a head injury became harmlessly insane from 1769 until his death, which came when he was struck by lightning.

EDMUND PLOWDEN (1518–85), lawyer and jurist. Acknowledged by Coke (q.v.) to be one of the greatest lawyers of his age. Best-known for his *Commentaries* or *Reports* covering the years 1548–79. As a Roman Catholic high office was closed to him following the accession of Queen Elizabeth. Offered the Lord Chancellorship by Elizabeth on condition of his renouncing the Catholic faith, which he refused to do.

SIR FREDERICK POLLOCK (1845–1937), jurist and editor. Corpus Professor of Jurisprudence at Oxford 1883–1903. Editor of the *Law Quarterly Review* (in which 'The corporation sole' and 'Crown as corporation' first appeared) 1885–1919. Close friend of Maitland's, and founder of the 'Sunday Tramps' walking club to which both Maitland and Leslie Stephen (q.v.) belonged. Co-author of Maitland's best known book, *The history of English law before the time of Edward I* (1895), though it was primarily written by Maitland.

JOHN SELDEN (1584–1654), jurist, antiquary and politician. M.P. for Oxford University throughout the Long Parliament. Earlier one of the driving forces behind the petition of right (1628). Retired from public life in 1649. Author of *History of tythes* (1617), *Mare clausum* (1635), *De iure naturali* (1640), and the posthumously published *Table talk* (1689). As a practising lawyer he had specialised, like Maitland, in conveyancing.

HENRY SIDGWICK (1838–99), philosopher. The last of the great utilitarians, though utilitarianism became in his hands a complex and subtle doctrine. He taught Maitland at Cambridge. Author of *Methods of ethics* (1874), *Principles of political economy* (1883) and *The elements of politics* (1891). He helped to found Newnham College (then Newnham Hall) in Cambridge in 1876, where Maitland delivered 'Moral personality and legal personality' as the Sidgwick lecture in 1903.

HERBERT SPENCER (1820–1903), philosopher. Author, among many other works, of *Principles of sociology* (3 vols., 1876–96), in which he pursued an analogy between natural and social organisms. The leading Victorian proponent of social individualism and scientific materialism, he coined the phrase 'the survival of the fittest' in 1864. He was a close friend of both George Eliot and Beatrice Webb.

SIR LESLIE STEPHEN (1832–1904), man of letters. Author of *A history of English thought in the eighteenth century* (1876), and the first editor of the *Dictionary of national biography* 1882–91. He was also a leading mountaineer, and like his friends Maitland and Pollock (q.v.), a founder member of the 'Sunday Tramps' club. Maitland devoted a substantial part of the last years of his life to producing a biography of Stephen (*The life and letters of Leslie Stephen*, published in 1906).

Glossary of technical terms

Except where specified (i.e. in the case of terms derived from Roman or Germanic law), these are terms of English common law.

ACCRESCENCE Accrual (between, for example, co-owners, such that when one dies, his portion accrues to the survivor).

ACTIO IN PERSONAM (Lat.) A personal action, used to force a person or persons to fulfil their contractual or other ('delictal') obligations. (See *ius in personam.*)

ACTIO IN REM (Lat.) In the classification of legal remedies derived from Roman law, a 'real' action (from Latin *res*: 'object'), by which a plaintiff claimed a particular thing, as opposed to an *actio in personam* (q.v.). In the complex of issues discussed by Maitland in 'Trust and corporation', an *actio in rem* is used to claim a real right. (See *ius in rem.*)

ADVOWSON The right of presenting a priest to a bishop or other similarly qualified ecclesiastical officer for appointment to a vacant church or, more exactly, a benefice (q.v.). The canon law (q.v.) calls this right *ius patronatus*, the right of patronage. The person who has the advowson is therefore called the patron (q.v.).

AID When a tenant of land, or an incumbent of an ecclesiastical benefice (q.v.) was challenged in his possession, he could ask certain people who had an interest in the matter at issue to help him in court, in such a way that the latter became party to the suit. In the case Maitland cites, a parson prays the aid of the patron (q.v.) of his church.

xlvi

ANNATES A tax paid to the papacy by new incumbents of benefices (q.v.), amounting to the first year's income from the benefice. Liability was extended to most benefices in the course of the fourteenth century, having originally been restricted to those whose previous holder had died whilst at the papal court.

BAILEE See bailment.

BAILIFF 'A servant that hath administration and charge (q.v.) of lands, goods and chattels (q.v.), to make the best benefit for the owner' (*Coke on Littleton*).

BAILMENT The delivery of goods by one person to another for a certain purpose, on the understanding that the goods will either be returned or passed on to someone else once the purpose has been fulfilled. A bailee is the person to whom those goods are delivered.

BENEFICE Derived from *beneficium* (q.v.); the ensemble of office and emoluments held by a priest with an incumbency, often called a living.

BENEFICIAL OWNER The person entitled to property without being accountable to any other person for his enjoyment of it, as distinct from a trustee, who owns property in order to manage it for the benefit of someone else. (See also feoffment to uses.)

BENEFICIUM (Lat.) Originally, a temporary and conditional grant of land to soldiers and other royal servants such as counts as an adjunct to their office, to enable them to support themselves, first used in mid-eighth-century Francia.

BUNDESSTAAT (Ger.) Federal state i.e. a state with its own federal constitution (cf. *Staatenbund*).

CANON LAW The law of the church, regulating such things as ecclesiastical property, ecclesiastical persons and offices, the administration of the sacraments, marriage, and potentially everything else thought to touch upon the health of souls and thus to be beyond the competence of secular law.

CAPITIS DIMINUTIO Properly *deminutio*. Loss of legal status in Roman law, which at its most serious ('first degree') meant loss of freedom and Roman citizenship. Intermediate or second degree loss of status meant loss of citizenship only, whilst third degree loss of status was not a punishment but came about by operation of law when an independent person passed into the authority of another.

CASUAL EJECTOR   A fictional defendant in an action of ejectment (q.v.), so called because *casualiter* (or 'by accident') he was supposed to have come onto the land and ejected the plaintiff.

CESSAVIT   (Lat.) A writ (q.v.) allowing a landlord to confiscate land from a tenant whose rent or service had not been forthcoming for two years or more. (Latin for: "He/she has stopped . . .")

CESTUI QUE TRUST (Anglo-Norm.)   The beneficiary of a trust (originally *cestui que use* or 'he who has the use').

CHARGE   Most generally, a burden on property which has been earmarked as security for a debt.

CHATTEL   Movable property.

CHATTEL REAL   Property which is not technically real-estate but which is closely related to it, such as certain kinds of interest in land.

CHOSE IN ACTION   The right to go to law to obtain payment of money or damages.

CLAGE UP GUT   (Ger.) In modern spelling, *Klage auf Gut*, German for 'claim to a piece of property'. An action to obtain a particular thing, and thus translated in the text as real action. (See *actio in rem*.)

COLLUSIVE ACTION   An action in which the plaintiff and the defendant are in league together to the disadvantage of a third party.

COMMON VOUCHEE   In the procedure called common recovery used to turn a tenant's fee tail (q.v.) into a fee simple (q.v.), the fiction was required that the land in question had already been sold to the tenant. The seller was accordingly vouched, or cited, by the tenant to declare before the court that he had indeed sold him the land. Since the entire procedure was fictitious, this seller was obviously fictitious too. Such a seller was called a common vouchee.

CONSTRUCTIVE NOTICE   The notice a purchaser is deemed ('by construction') to have if he has neglected to carry out elementary investigations into the title of the seller and possible burdens on the property.

CONTINGENT REMAINDER A remainder (q.v.) which only comes into force upon the fulfilment of a certain condition, which may never happen.

CONVEYANCES Voluntary modes of transferring property.

COPYHOLD, COPYHOLDER A form of land tenure which arose in the later Middle Ages for villeins, that is, the unfree, so-called because it became the custom to give tenants a copy of the details of the tenure, regarding their unfree tenements, preserved in the records of the manor court.

CORPUS JURIS (CIVILIS) (Lat.) 'The Body of Civil Law': the name given in the later Middle Ages and ever since to the Roman law as promulgated by the emperor Justinian (regn. 528–65). It consists of the *Digest*, *Code* and *Institutes* (all in force by 535) and a collection of later imperial constitutions called the *Novels*. From the late eleventh century onwards, Roman law became the object of intense scholarly and ever-increasing practical interest, at first in Bologna but very soon all over Europe, including, by the late twelfth century, England.

DELIKTSFÄHIGKEIT (Ger.) The capacity to commit a delict (in English law a tort).

DEMISE Most commonly, to grant a lease in land and other immovable property.

DEVISE A gift made in a will.

DISCONTINUANCE If a man wrongfully alienated land and then died, his heir could not take possession of it immediately, but had to bring an action to recover it. This temporary obstacle or interruption to the heir's entry was called discontinuance.

DISTRAIN To impound goods so as to enforce the fulfilment of legal obligations.

EASEMENT The right of a property-owner to do something on adjacent property, or to prevent the owner of that property from doing certain things there. The right inheres in the property, such that a buyer of the dominant tenement benefits from the easement, and the buyer of the subservient tenement is bound to comply with it.

EJECTMENT An action for the recovery of possession of land and, at the same time, a claim for damages and costs caused by the wrongful detention of that land.

ELEEMOSYNARY Of or dependent on alms (Latin: *eleemosyna*; ultimately from Greek *eleos*: 'compassion').

ENFEOFFMENT The bestowal of a feudal tenure to be held by the recipient and his heirs in return for knight service.

ENTER, ENTRY The assertion of one's title to land by going on it, or by a number of other mechanisms regarded as equivalent to going on it.

ESCHEAT The reversion of a fief or fee (q.v.) to the lord from whom it was held upon the death of the tenant without heirs or as a result of his felony.

ESPLEES The produce from land including rents and other services owed for it.

ESTATE A word of vast application in the common law, frequently used as a synonym for assets or property. An estate is technically not property, but rather one's relationship with any immovable property in which one has an interest.

ESTOPPEL A rule preventing a party denying what he has previously asserted or implicitly recognised.

EXTRA COMMERCIUM (Lat.) Not vendible or purchasable, nor legally transferrable between private persons.

FEE Land granted heritably in return for knight service; a unit of account to express the value of such tenements; an estate (q.v.) of inheritance in land.

FEE SIMPLE The greatest and least restricted estate (q.v.) under English law, the closest approximation to absolute ownership in a country where only the Crown is an absolute owner of land.

FEE TAIL At its most general, the stipulation that an estate (q.v.) in land must pass to the recipient's descendants or heirs of his body. More precise restrictions (for example, to specific children, or children from a specific marriage) were also possible.

FEOFFEE The recipient of a grant in fee (an enfeoffment, q.v.).

FEOFFMENT TO USES The transfer of land by enfeoffment (q.v.) to a tenant such that the tenant has seisin (q.v.), but somebody other than the tenant enjoys the beneficial ownership (q.v) of the land as *cestui que use*. (See *cestui que trust*.)

FIDEICOMMISSUM (Lat.) A Roman law mechanism by which a testator asked his heir, and later other people apart from the heir, to do something for the benefit of a third party, such as handing over money or property, an appeal to the good faith of the heir which only became legally enforceable at a comparatively late stage (under Augustus).

FIDUCIA (Lat.) Roman law. Typically, an agreement constraining the new owner after a transfer of property to retransfer it to the original owner upon the original owner's repayment of a debt to him. There were other uses of fiduciary agreement, including transfer of property between friends for safekeeping, and transfers of slaves on the understanding that the transferee would then emancipate them. Of interest to Maitland because it implied a restraint on the exercise of ownership, comparable to the terms of trusteeship.

FIEF Typically a piece of land held of a lord by a vassal in return for military service, supposedly derived from the *beneficium* (q.v.).

FRANKALMOIN (from Norm.) Perpetual tenure in free alms, for which the tenant (an ecclesiastical foundation) performed no secular service to the lord.

GLEBE The land pertaining to an ecclesiastical benefice (q.v.).

GROSS A thing in gross exists in its own right and not as an appendage to some other thing.

HAEREDITATES IACENTES (Lat.) Plural of *haereditas iacens*, the things belonging to an inheritance between the death of the person whose estate it is, and acquisition of the inheritance by the heir.

HEREDITAMENTS Any property which can be inherited.

IMPROPRIATED The practice, dating to the Reformation, whereby laymen took over rectories or tithes (q.v.).

IN MALLO (Lat.) 'In the *mallus*'. The *mallus* was the judicial assembly of the county throughout the Carolingian empire, to which Lombard Italy (here under discussion) belonged from 774.

INTESTATE Without leaving a will.

INVESTITURE (i) The ceremonial bestowal of an archbishopric, bishopric, or other high ecclesiastical office, a right hotly contested between the papacy and various secular powers in western Europe in the later eleventh- and twelfth centuries. (ii) Bestowal of any office or dignity on the new incumbent. (iii) The ceremonial delivery of land or rights which committed the grantor to make good on the grant or provide compensation. The most prominent example in medieval sources is investiture by a lord of his vassal with a fief.

IURATA UTRUM (Lat.) See below *utrum*.

IUS COMMUNE (Lat.) An amalgam of Roman law, canon law, and eventually feudal law, together with the standard-setting commentaries and glosses on such texts produced in the medieval schools from the twelfth century onwards. It was called *ius commune* or 'common law' because for many purposes it was taken to represent the normal state of affairs against which to interpret local laws and customs, especially in Italy. Not to be confused with English common law.

IUS IN PERSONAM (Lat.) Derived from Roman law but not part of it. The right to oblige a specific person or specific persons to do or not to do something. The most common German term for *ius in personam* used throughout Maitland's 'Trust and corporation' is 'obligatorisches Recht'.

IUS IN REM (Lat.) The right to have a particular thing, valid against the world at large rather than against specific persons. The German term for *ius in rem* used in 'Trust and corporation' is 'dingliches Recht', literally 'a *thingly* right', less literally 'an objective right'.

IUS PATRONATUS (Lat.) See advowson.

LIEN At common law, a right to retain possession pending satisfaction of some obligation, usually a debt due. In equity, a lien is imposed by the Chancellor as security for such repayments.

MANSE A clergyman's dwelling.

MERE DROIT (Anglo-Norm.) Bare or naked property right.

MISE The point at issue in proceedings initiated by a writ of right (q.v.).

MORTMAIN 'The dead hand', in allusion to impersonal ownership, used to describe the condition of inalienable possessions held by corporations, typically in the medieval period ecclesiastical corporations, prohibited by canon law (q.v.) from alienating their land.

OBITS An annual mass held for the repose of a deceased person's soul, often financed by grants of land to the church where the mass was to be celebrated.

OBLATIONS Offerings and customary payments to the priest of a church by his flock.

OBLIGATIONENRECHT (Ger.) The law of obligations (in contrast to *Sachenrecht*: the law of things).

OBVENTIONS The same as oblations (q.v.).

ORDINARY The holder of jurisdiction by right of office rather than special appointment or ad hoc delegation.

PAROL Parol agreements are those that are made by word of mouth or those that are written down but not under seal.

PATRON The holder of an advowson (q.v.).

PETITION OF RIGHT A means of gaining restitution of property or compensation from the Crown, which could not be made a defendant in a normal plea.

PRAECIPE QUOD REDDAT (Lat.) The first words of the writ (q.v.) meaning 'Order that he restores . . .', by which a sheriff was instructed to have someone return a thing or land to the person on whose behalf the writ was issued.

PRESCRIBE, PRESCRIPTION Roman law. A means of acquiring ownership of land by remaining in uninterrupted possession for a period which varied with circumstances. Just cause and good faith were necessary for valid prescription.

PRESENTATION, PRESENTMENT, PRESENTEE. See advowson.

QUASI-DELICT Roman law. Behaviour which was thought to be sufficiently similar to a real delict, strictly defined, for the perpetrator to become liable for compensation.

RELIEF (lat. *relevium*) The sum paid upon his succession by an heir of full age to the lord of the fief (q.v.).

REMAINDER The residual interest reserved to someone, specifically by his own or another's act, in an estate currently held by somebody else which takes effect when that second person's estate comes to an end.

REVERSION A remainder (q.v.) which is created automatically by operation of the law, rather than by any act of parties. The lord of a fief has the reversion of the fief (q.v.) when his tenant dies without heirs, not because he and the tenant have agreed that this shall be so, but because the law decrees it.

SALICA Properly *Lex Salica* (Lat.): the Salic law, or law of the Salian Franks, dating in its earliest part to the reign of Clovis (484–511).

SCHULDVERHÄLTNISSE (Ger.) Obligations (equivalent to the obligations of *Obligationenrecht* (q.v.)).

SCIRE FACIAS (Lat.) ('That you cause to know ...') A writ (q.v.) directing the sheriff to tell the defendant that he must explain why any official record or prior judgment supporting his title should not be either annulled or made over to the plaintiff who brings the writ.

SEISED, SEISIN 'In the history of our law there is no idea more cardinal than that of seisin' (Pollock and Maitland, *A history of English law*). A noun derived from the Anglo-Norman French verb 'saisire', to give into somebody's hand. As Maitland explains elsewhere: seisin was the only word available in English law to describe possession; to be seised with X meant something very like being in a position to enjoy X with prima facie good title. Henry II (1154–89) gave seisin such extensive legal protection that it became the fulcrum of the nascent common law.

SINGULARE BENEFICIUM (Lat.) A legal remedy or defence available to one category of person only.

STAATENBUND (Ger.) Confederation or league of states, lacking its own formal constitution (cf. *Bundesstaat*).

TENANT IN TAIL (after possibility of issue extinct) A tenant who continues to enjoy land which has been entailed (q.v.) to him and his issue from a particular marriage when no such children can now be born thanks to the death of the tenant's spouse.

TITHE A tenth of yearly increase or profit of various kinds paid by all Christians to their parish church.

TOLL AN ENTRY To bar or remove a right of entry (q.v.).

TRUSTIS (Lat.) In Salic law (see *Salica*), the fidelity sworn to the king of the Franks by his closest advisers and functionaries. It was also used to describe collectively all those who had sworn such an oath.

UTRUM (Lat.) A procedure formalised by Henry II to determine whether a tenement was held in frankalmoin (q.v.) or for secular service.

VEREIN (Ger.) Club, society, association.

WARDSHIP The lucrative right to act as guardian of minors upon the death of their father. Wardship of the person could be separated from wardship of lands, such that two guardians could have an interest in the same minority. Rights of wardship were hotly contested in twelfth-century England between the feudal lord of the deceased and the surviving adult relatives of the deceased, and were capable of extension to some non-feudal tenures.

WARRANT Etymologically related to 'guarantee'; the responsibility to guarantee the title of any person to whom one has transferred a piece of property (for example, by enfeoffment, sale, lease, etc.) by appearing before the court when that person is challenged.

WRIT A letter bearing the king's seal containing an order or notification, often but not always addressed to a royal officer such as a sheriff. The royal writ was one of the indispensible mechanisms in the growth of English common law in the twelfth century.

WRIT OF RIGHT The royal writ by which a plaintiff laid claim to the ownership of a free tenement.

Preface
Extract from Maitland's Introduction to *Political Theories of the Middle Age* by Otto von Gierke

Staats- und Korporationslehre – the Doctrine of State and Corporation. Such a title may be to some a stumbling-block set before the threshold. A theory of the State, so it might be said, may be very interesting to the philosophic few and fairly interesting to the intelligent many, but a doctrine of Corporations, which probably speaks of fictitious personality and similar artifices, can only concern some juristic speculators, of whom there are none or next to none in this country. On second thoughts, however, we may be persuaded to see here no rock of offence but rather a stepping-stone which our thoughts should sometimes traverse. For, when all is said, there seems to be a genus of which State and Corporation are species. They seem to be permanently organised groups of men; they seem to be group-units; we seem to attribute acts and intents, rights and wrongs to these groups, to these units. Let it be allowed that the State is a highly peculiar group unit; still it may be asked whether we ourselves are not the slaves of a jurist's theory and a little behind the age of Darwin if between the State and all other groups we fix an immeasurable gulf and ask ourselves no questions about the origin of species.[i] Certain it is that our medieval history will go astray, our history of Italy and Germany will go far astray, unless we can suffer communities to acquire and lose the character of States somewhat easily, somewhat insensibly, or rather unless we know and feel that we must not thrust our modern 'State-concept', as a German would call it, upon the reluctant material.

Englishmen in particular should sometimes give themselves this warning, and not only for the sake of the Middle Ages. Fortunate in littleness and insularity, England could soon exhibit as a difference in kind what elsewhere was a difference in degree, namely, to use medieval terms, the difference between a community or corporation (*universitas*) which does and one which does not recognise a 'superior'. There was no likelihood that the England which the Norman duke had subdued and surveyed would be either *Staatenbund* or *Bundesstaat*, and the aspiration of Londoners to have 'no king but the mayor' was fleeting. This, if it diminished our expenditure of blood and treasure – an expenditure that impoverishes – diminished also our expenditure of thought – an expenditure that enriches – and facilitated (might this not be said?) a certain thoughtlessness or poverty of ideas. The State that an Englishman knew was a singularly unicellular State, and at a critical time they were not too well equipped with tried and traditional thoughts which would meet the case of Ireland or of some communities, commonwealths, corporations in America which seemed to have wills – and hardly fictitious wills – of their own, and which became States and United States.[1] The medieval Empire laboured under the weight of an incongruously simple theory so soon as lawyers were teaching that the Kaiser was the Princeps of Justinian's law-books.[ii] The modern and multicellular British State – often and perhaps harmlessly called an Empire – may prosper without a theory, but does not suggest and, were we serious in our talk of sovereignty, would hardly tolerate, a theory that is simple enough and insular enough, and yet withal imperially Roman enough, to deny an essentially state-like character to those 'self-governing colonies', communities and commonwealths, which are knit and welded into a larger sovereign whole. The adventures of an English joint-stock company which happened into a rulership of the Indies,[iii] the adventures of another English company which while its charter was still very new had become the puritan commonwealth of Massachusett's Bay[iv] should be enough to show that our popular English *Staatslehre* if, instead of analysing the contents of a speculative jurist's mind,[v] it seriously grasped the facts of English history, would show some inclination to become a *Korporationslehre* also.

Even as it is, such a tendency is plainly to be seen in many zones. Standing on the solid ground of positive law and legal orthodoxy we confess the king of this country to be a 'corporation sole' and, if we

[1] See the remarks of Sir. C. Ilbert, *The government of India*, p. 55: 'Both the theory and the experience were lacking which are requisite for adapting English institutions to new and foreign circumstances. For want of such experience England was destined to lose her colonies in the Western hemisphere. For want of it mistakes were committed which imperilled the empire she was building up in the East.' The want of a theory about Ireland which would have mediated between absolute dependence and absolute independence was the origin of many evils.

have any curiosity, ought to wonder why in the sixteenth century the old idea that the king is the head of a 'corporation aggregate of many'[2] gave way before a thought which classed him along with the parish parson of decadent ecclesiastical law under one uncomfortable rubric. Deeply convinced though our lawyers may be that individual men are the only 'real' and 'natural' persons, they are compelled to find some phrase which places State and Man upon one level. 'The greatest of all artificial persons, politically speaking, is the State': so we may read in an excellent First Book of Jurisprudence.[3] Ascending from the legal plain, we are in the middle region where a sociology emulous of the physical sciences discourses of organs and organisms and social tissue,[vi] and cannot sever by sharp lines the natural history of the state-group from the natural history of other groups. Finally, we are among the summits of philosophy and observe how a doctrine, which makes some way in England, ascribes to the State, or, more vaguely, the Community, not only a real will, but 'the' real will,[vii] and it must occur to us to ask whether what is thus affirmed in the case of the State can be denied in the case of other organised groups: for example, that considerable group the Roman Catholic Church. It seems possible to one who can only guess, that even now-a-days a Jesuit may think that the real will of the Company to which he belongs is no less real than the will of any State, and, if the reality of this will be granted by the philosopher, can he pause until even the so-called one-man-company has a real will really distinct from the several wills of the one man and his six humble associates?[viii] If we pursue that thought, not only will our philosophic *Staatslehre* be merging itself in a wider doctrine, but we shall already be deep in *Genossenschaftstheorie*. In any case, however, the law's old habit of co-ordinating men and 'bodies politic' as two kinds of Persons seems to deserve the close attention of the modern philosopher, for, though it be an old habit, it has become vastly more important in these last years than it ever was before. In the second half of the nineteenth century corporate groups of the most various sorts have been multiplying all the world over at a rate that far outstrips the increase of 'natural persons',[ix] and a large share of all our newest law is law concerning corporations.[4] Something not unworthy of philosophic discussion would seem to lie in this quarter:

---

[2] A late instance of this old concept occurs in Plowden's *Commentaries* 254.

[3] Pollock, *First book of Jurisprudence*, 113.

[4] In 1857 an American judge went the length of saying 'It is probably true that more corporations were created by the legislature of Illinois at its last session than existed in the whole civilized world at the commencement of the present century.' Dillon, Municipal Corporations, §37 a.

either some deep-set truth which is always bearing fresh fruit, or else a surprisingly stable product of mankind's propensity to feign.

Notes

i The particular jurist Maitland has in mind is John Austin, whose *The province of jurisprudence determined* was published in 1832. This text contained the classic positivist definition of the state as an institution characterised by its unique sovereignty: 'The meanings of "state" or "the state" are numerous and disparate: of which numerous and disparate meanings the following are the most remarkable – 1. "The state" is usually synonymous with "the sovereign". It denotes the individual person or the body of individual persons, which bears the supreme power in an independent political society. This is the meaning which I annex to the term . . .' (J. Austin, *The province of jurisprudence determined*, ed. W. E. Rumble (Cambridge: Cambridge University Press [1832] 1995), p. 190 n.1).

ii This was axiomatic from 1158 at the latest, when the Emperor Frederick I convened the Diet of Roncaglia, at which he laid claim to all jurisdiction in the kingdom of Lombardy. Among other things, Justinian's law taught that the *Princeps* was the sole source of law and not subject himself to the law.

iii The East India Company received its first charter from Elizabeth I on 31 December 1600, to last for fifteen years. It became a joint stock company in 1657, and acquired quasi-sovereign rights over its affairs in a series of charters granted by Charles II beginning in 1661. In 1684, with the fortification of Bombay, it began to assume the military, administrative and fiscal character of a kind of state. Only in 1784 did the government of British India come under the jurisdiction of a British government department. In 1813, the Company lost its monopoly of trade in the territories it had controlled, and in 1858, following the Indian mutiny, its possessions were transferred to the Crown.

iv 'The Governor and Company of Massachusetts Bay in New England' received their charter in 1629, modelled on the earlier charter given to the Virginia Company in 1609. However, unlike the Virginia company, the Massachusetts company transferred its management and charter to the colony itself, from where it was able to establish strong religious rule under conditions of effective self-government. Massachusetts was given a new charter only in 1691, which provided the colony with a royal governor and reasserted rule from London, albeit of a more tolerant kind than the previous theocratic regime. The state of Massachusetts became the first state to describe itself as a commonwealth in its own constitution, which it acquired in 1780.

v The reference again is to Austin, of whom Maitland says at the end of his introduction to Gierke: 'It will be gathered also that the set of thoughts about Law and Sovereignty into which Englishmen were lectured by John Austin appears to Dr. Gierke as a past stage.' (O. von Gierke, *Political theories of the Middle Age*, ed. F. W. Maitland (Cambridge: Cambridge University Press, 1900), p. xliii.)

vi Maitland is alluding to the work of Herbert Spencer, particularly his *Principles of sociology*, the third volume of which had been published in 1896.

vii Maitland is referring to the work of Bernard Bosanquet, whose *The philosophical theory of the state* had been published a year previously in 1899, and became the dominant expression of idealist political philosophy in England.

viii The problem of the 'one-man company' had come to prominence in a famous case of 1895–7, *Salomon v. Salomon and Co*. Mr Salomon had sold his business to a limited company, the company consisting of himself, his wife and five children (the seven persons required by law). Mr Salomon also issued to himself additional shares and debentures forming a floating security. When the company was wound up, Mr Salomon claimed its assets as debenture holder, leaving nothing for unsecured creditors. In both Chancery and the Court of Appeal Mr Salomon was found liable, it being decided that the business was nothing but a name being used to screen him from liability. In other words, the company had no separate identity apart from the identity of its founder, and the other members of the company served only a nominal purpose (hence 'one-man company'). The early stages of this case, and the initial decision against Salomon are discussed in an article in the *Law Quarterly Review* (E. Manson, 'One man companies', *Law Quarterly Review* (XII, 1895), pp. 185–8) that is certain to have been read by Maitland. There it is argued that the law should not discriminate against enterprises that formally accord with the 1862 Companies Act, for risk of discrediting the whole enterprise of limiting liabilities: 'The giant growth of joint-stock enterprises is one of the marvels of the day . . . It has unlocked by the magic key of limited liability vast sums for useful industrial undertakings; it has made the poor man, by co-operation, a capitalist. Let us beware lest in gathering the tares we root up the wheat also.' (Ibid., p. 188.) Subsequently, the House of Lords found for Mr Salomon, insisting that in strict legal terms the company did exist in its own right. These were, though, technically legal arguments about 'personality' rather than philosophical arguments about 'will' or economic arguments about 'co-operation'. As P. W. Duff puts it in *Personality in Roman private law* (Cambridge: Cambridge University Press, 1938): 'Like most English cases and most Roman texts, *Salomon* v *Salomon and Co.* can be reconciled with any theory but is authority for none' (p. 215).

ix This process was of course to continue throughout the twentieth century. For example, the number of profit-making corporations increased five-fold in the United States between 1917 and 1969, and the number of limited companies ten-fold in the Netherlands between 1950 and 1994, rates of growth which far outstrip growths in population (see M. Bovens, *The quest for responsibility. Accountability and citizenship in complex organisations* (Cambridge: Cambridge University Press, 1998)).

The Essays

I

The Corporation Sole

Persons are either natural or artificial. The only natural persons are men. The only artificial persons are corporations. Corporations are either aggregate or sole. This, I take it, would be an orthodox beginning for a chapter on the English Law of Persons, and such it would have been at any time since the days of Sir Edward Coke.[1] It makes use, however, of one very odd term which seems to approach self-contradiction, namely, the term 'corporation sole', and the question may be raised, and indeed has been raised, whether our corporation sole is a person, and whether we do well in endeavouring to co-ordinate it with the corporation aggregate and the individual man. A courageous paragraph in Sir William Markby's *Elements of Law*[2] begins with the words, 'There is a curious thing which we meet with in English law called a corporation sole', and Sir William then maintains that we have no better reason for giving this name to a rector or to the king than we have for giving it to an executor. Some little debating of this question will do no harm, and may perhaps do some good, for it is in some sort prejudicial to other and more important questions.

A better statement of what we may regard as the theory of corporations that is prevalent in England could hardly be found than that which occurs in Sir Frederick Pollock's book on Contract.[3] He speaks of 'the Roman invention, adopted and largely developed in modern systems of law, of constituting the official character of the holders for the time being of the same office, or the common interest of the persons who for the time being are adventurers in the same undertaking, into an artificial person or ideal subject of legal capacities and duties'. There follows a comparison which is luminous, even though some would say that it suggests doubts touching the soundness of the theory that is being expounded. 'If it is allowable to

[1] *Co. Lit.* 2 a, 250 a.
[2] Markby, *Elements of Law*, §145.
[3] Pollock, *Contract*, ed. 6, p. 107.

9

illustrate one fiction by another, we may say that the artificial person is a fictitious substance conceived as supporting legal attributes.'

It will not be news to readers of this journal that there are nowadays many who think that the personality of the corporation aggregate is in no sense and no sort artificial or fictitious, but is every whit as real and natural as is the personality of a man.[i] This opinion, if it was at one time distinctive of a certain school of Germanists, has now been adopted by some learned Romanists, and also has found champions in France and Italy. Hereafter I may be allowed to say a little about it.[4,ii] Its advocates, if they troubled themselves with our affairs, would claim many rules of English law as evidence that favours their doctrine and as protests against what they call 'the Fiction Theory'. They would also tell us that a good deal of harm was done when, at the end of the Middle Ages, our common lawyers took over that theory from the canonists and tried, though often in a half-hearted way, to impose it upon the traditional English materials.

In England we are within a measurable distance of the statement that the only persons known to our law are men and certain organised groups of men which are known as corporations aggregate. Could we make that statement, then we might discuss the question whether the organised group of men has not a will of its own – a real, not a fictitious, will of its own – which is really distinct from the several wills of its members. As it is, however, the corporation sole stops, or seems to stop, the way. It prejudices us in favour of the Fiction Theory. We suppose that we personify offices.

Blackstone, having told us that 'the honour of inventing' corporations 'entirely belongs to the Romans', complacently adds that 'our laws have considerably refined and improved upon the invention, according to the usual genius of the English nation: particularly with regard to sole corporations, consisting of one person only, of which the Roman lawyers had no notion'.[5] If this be so, we might like to pay honour where honour is due, and to name the name of the man who was the first and true inventor of the corporation sole.

Sir Richard Broke[iii] died in 1558, and left behind him a Grand Abridgement, which was published in 1568. Now I dare not say that he was the

---

[4] Dr Otto Gierke, of Berlin, has been its principal upholder.
[5] 1 *Comm.* 469.

father of 'the corporation sole'; indeed I do not know that he ever used precisely that phrase; but more than once he called a parson a 'corporation',
and, after some little search, I am inclined to believe that this was an
unusual statement. Let us look at what he says:

> *Corporations et Capacities*, pl. 41: Vide Trespas in fine ann. 7 E. 4 fo. 12
> per Danby: one can give land to a parson and to his successors, and
> so this is a corporation by the common law, and elsewhere it is agreed
> that this is mortmain.

> *Corporations et Capacities*, pl. 68: Vide tithe *Encumbent* 14, that a
> parson of a church is a corporation in succession to prescribe, to take
> land in fee, and the like, 39 H. 6, 14 and 7 E. 4, 12.

> *Encumbent et Glebe*, pl. 14 [Marginal note: *Corporacion en le person*:]
> a parson can prescribe in himself and his predecessor, 39 H. 6, fo. 14;
> and per Danby a man may give land to a parson and his successors, 7
> E. 4, fo. 12; and the same per Littleton in his chapter of Frankalmoin.

The books that Broke vouches will warrant his law, but they will not
warrant his language. In the case of Henry VI's reign[6] an action for an
annuity is maintained against a parson on the ground that he and all his
predecessors have paid it; but no word is said of his being a corporation.
In the case of Edward IV's reign we may find Danby's dictum.[7] He says
that land may be given to a parson and his successors, and that when
the parson dies the donor shall not enter; but there is no talk of the
parson's corporateness. So again we may learn from Littleton's chapter
on frankalmoin[8] that land may be given to a parson and his successors;
but again there is no talk of the parson's corporateness.

There is, it is true, another passage in what at first sight looks like
Littleton's text which seems to imply that a parson is a body politic, and
Coke took occasion of this passage to explain that every corporation is
either 'sole or aggregate of many', and by so doing drew for future times
one of the main outlines of our Law of Persons.[9] However, Butler has duly
noted the fact that just the words that are important to us at the present

---

[6] 39 Hen. VI, f. 13 (Mich. pl. 17).
[7] 7 Edw. IV, f. 12 (Trin. pl. 2).
[8] Lit. sec. 134.
[9] Lit. sec. 413; *Co. Lit.* 250 a. Other classical passages are *Co. Lit.* 2 a; *Sutton's Hospital* case,
10 *Rep.* 29 b.

moment are not in the earliest editions of the Tenures, and I believe that we should be very rash if we ascribed them to Littleton.[10]

Still the most that I should claim for Broke would be that by applying the term 'corporation' to a parson, he suggested that a very large number of corporations sole existed in England, and so prepared the way for Coke's dogmatic classification of persons. Apparently for some little time past lawyers had occasionally spoken of the chantry priest as a corporation. So early as 1448 a writ is brought in the name of 'John Chaplain of the Chantry of B. Mary of Dale'; objection is taken to the omission of his surname; and to this it is replied that the name in which he sues may be that by which he is corporate.[11] Then it would appear that in 1482 Bryan C. J. and Choke J. supposed the existence of a corporation in a case in which an endowment was created for a single chantry priest. Fitzherbert, seemingly on the authority of an unprinted Year Book, represents them as saying that 'if the king grants me licence to make a chantry for a priest to sing in a certain place, and to give to him and his successors lands to the value of a certain sum, and I do this, that is a good corporation without further words'.[12] Five years later some serjeants, if I understand them rightly, were condemning as void just such licences as those which Bryan and Catesby had discussed, and thereby were proposing to provide the lately crowned Henry VII with a rich crop of forfeitures. Keble opines that such a licence does not create a corporation (apparently because the king cannot delegate his corporation-making power), and further opines that the permission to give land to a corporation that does not already exist must be invalid.[13] Whether more came of this threat – for such it seems to be – I do not know.[14] Bullying the chantries was not a new practice in the days of Henry VII's son and grandson. In 1454 Romayn's Chantry, which had been confirmed by Edward III and Richard II, stood in need of a private Act of Parliament because a new generation of lawyers

[10] Littleton is telling us that no dying seised tolls an entry if the lands pass by 'succession'. He is supposed to add: 'Come de prelates, abbates, priours, deans, ou parson desglyse [ou dauter corps politike].' But the words that are here bracketed are not in the Cambridge MS.; nor in the edition by Lettou and Machlinia; nor in the Rouen edition; nor in Pynson's. On the other hand they stand in one, at least, of Redman's editions.

[11] 27 Hen. VI, f. 3 (Mich. pl. 24): 'poet estre entende que il est corporate par tiel nom'.

[12] Fitz. *Abr.* Graunt, pl. 30, citing T. 22 Edw. IV and M. 21 Edw. IV, 56. The earlier part of the case stands in Y. B. 21 Edw. IV, f. 55 (Mich. pl. 28). The case concerned the municipal corporation of Norwich, and the dictum must have been gratuitous.

[13] 2 Hen. VII, f. 13 (Hil. pl. 16).

[14] 20 Hen. VII, f. 7 (Mich. pl. 17): Rede J. seems to say that such a licence would make a corporation.

was not content with documents which had satisfied their less ingenious predecessors.[15]

Now cases relating to endowed chantry priests were just the cases which might suggest an extension of the idea of corporateness beyond the sphere in which organised groups of men are active. Though in truth it was the law of mortmain, and not any law touching the creation of fictitious personality, which originally sent the founders of chantries to seek the king's licence, still the king was by this time using somewhat the same language about the single chantry priest that he had slowly learned to use about bodies of burgesses and others. The king, so the phrase went, was enabling the priest to hold land to himself and his successors. An investigation of licences for the formation of chantries might lead to some good results. At present, however, I cannot easily believe that, even when the doom of the chantries was not far distant, English lawyers were agreed that the king could make, and sometimes did make, a corporation out of a single man or out of that man's official character. So late as the year 1522, the year after Richard Broke took his degree at Oxford, Fineux, C. J. B. R., was, if I catch the sense of his words, declaring that a corporation sole would be an absurdity, a nonentity. 'It is argued', he said, 'that the Master and his Brethren cannot make a gift to the Master, since he is the head of the corporation. Therefore let us see what a corporation is and what kinds of corporations there are. A corporation is an aggregation of head and body: not a head by itself, nor a body by itself; and it must be consonant to reason, for otherwise it is worth nought. For albeit the king desires to make a corporation of J. S., that is not good, for common reason tells us that it is not a permanent thing and cannot have successors.'[16] The Chief Justice goes on to speak of the Parliament of King, Lords, and Commons as a corporation by the common law. He seems to find the essence of corporateness in the permanent existence of the organised group, the 'body' of 'members', which remains the same body though its particles change, and he denies that this phenomenon can exist where only one man is concerned. This is no permanence. The man dies and,

---

[15] *Rot. Parl.* v. 258. It had been supposed for a hundred and twenty years that there had been a chantry sufficiently founded in law and to have stood stable in perpetuity 'which for certain diminution of the form of making used in the law at these days is not held sufficient'.

[16] 14 Hen. VIII, f. 3 (Mich. pl. 2): 'Car coment que le roy veut faire corporacion a J. S. ceo n'est bon, pur ceo que comon reson dit que n'est chose permanente et ne peut aver successor.' Considering the context, I do not think that I translate this unfairly, though the words 'faire corporacion a J. S.' may not be exactly rendered or renderable. The king, we may say, cannot make a corporation which shall have J. S. for its basis.

if there is office or benefice in the case, he will have no successor until time has elapsed and a successor has been appointed. That is what had made the parson's case a difficult case for English lawyers. Fineux was against feigning corporateness where none really existed. At any rate, a good deal of his judgment seems incompatible with the supposition that 'corporation sole' was in 1522 a term in current use.

That term would never have made its fortune had it not been applied to a class much wider and much less exposed to destructive criticism than was the class of permanently endowed chantry priests. That in all the Year Books a parochial rector is never called a corporation I certainly dare not say. Still, as a note at the end of this paper may serve to show, I have unsuccessfully sought the word in a large number of places where it seemed likely to be found if ever it was to be found at all. Such places are by no means rare. Not unfrequently the courts were compelled to consider what a parson could do and could not do, what leases he could grant, what charges he could create, what sort of estate he had in his glebe. Even in Coke's time what we may call the theoretical construction of the parson's relation to the glebe had hardly ceased to be matter of debate. 'In whom the fee simple of the glebe is', said the great dogmatist, 'is a question in our books.'[17] Over the glebe, over the parson's freehold, the parson's see, the parson's power of burdening his church or his successors with pensions or annuities, there had been a great deal of controversy; but I cannot find that into this controversy the term 'corporation' was introduced before the days of Richard Broke.

If now we turn from the phrase to the legal phenomena which it is supposed to describe, we must look for them in the ecclesiastical sphere. Coke knew two corporations sole that were not ecclesiastical, and I cannot find that he knew more. They were a strange pair: the king[18] and the chamberlain of the city of London.[19] As to the civic officer, a case from 1468 shows us a chamberlain suing on a bond given to a previous chamberlain 'and his successors'. The lawyers who take part in the argument say nothing of any corporation sole, and seem to think that obligations could be created in favour of the Treasurer of England and his successors or the Chief Justice and his successors.[20] As to the king, I strongly suspect that Coke himself was living when men first called the king a corporation

[17] *Co. Lit.* 340 b, 341 a.
[18] *Sutton's Hospital* case, 10 *Rep.* 29 b.
[19] *Fulwood's* case, 4 *Rep.* 65 a.
[20] 8 Edw. IV, f. 18 (Mich. pl. 29).

sole, though many had called him the head of a corporation. But of this at another time. The centre of sole corporateness, if we may so speak, obviously lies among ecclesiastical institutions. If there are any, there are thousands of corporations sole within the province of church property law. But further, we must concentrate our attention upon the parish parson. We may find the Elizabethan and Jacobean lawyers applying the new term to bishops, deans, and prebendaries; also retrospectively to abbots and priors. Their cases, however, differed in what had been a most important respect from the case of the parochial rector. They were members, in most instances they were heads, of corporations aggregate. As is well known, a disintegrating process had long been at work within the ecclesiastical groups, more especially within the cathedral groups.[21] Already when the Year Books began their tale this process had gone far.[iv] The bishop has lands that are severed from the lands of the cathedral chapter or cathedral monastery; the dean has lands, the prebendary has lands or other sources of revenue. These partitions have ceased to be merely matters of internal economy; they have an external validity which the temporal courts recognise.[22] Still, throughout the Middle Ages it is never forgotten that the bishop who as bishop holds lands severed from the lands of the chapter or the convent holds those lands as head of a corporation of which canons or monks are members. This is of great theoretical importance, for it obviates a difficulty which our lawyers have to meet when they consider the situation of the parochial rector. In the case of the bishop a permanent 'body' exists in which the ownership, the full fee simple, of lands can be reposed. 'For', as Littleton says, 'a bishop may have a writ of right of the tenements of the right of his church, for that the right is in his chapter, and the fee simple abideth in him and in his chapter.'[23] The application of the term 'corporation sole' to bishops, deans, and prebendaries marked the end of the long disintegrating process, and did some harm to our legal theories. If the episcopal lands belong to the bishop as a 'corporation sole', why, we may ask, does he require the consent of the chapter if he is to alienate them? The 'enabling statute' of Henry VIII and the 'disabling statutes'

---

[21] *Lib. Ass.* f. 117, ann. 25, pl. 8: 'All the cathedral churches and their possessions were at one time a gross.'

[22] For instance, *Chapter v. Dean of Lincoln*, 9 Edw. III, f. 18 (Trin. pl. 3) and f. 33 (Mich. pl. 33).

[23] Lit. sec. 645. 6 Edw. III, f. 10, 11 (Hil. pl. 28), it is said in argument, 'The right of the church [of York] abides rather in the dean and chapter than in the archbishop, car ceo ne mourt pas [because it does not die].' This case is continued in 6 Edw. III, f. 50 (Mich. pl. 50).

of Elizabeth deprived this question of most of its practical importance.[v] Thenceforward in the way of grants or leases the bishop could do little with that he could not do without the chapter's consent.[24] It is also to be remembered that an abbot's powers were exceedingly large; he ruled over a body of men who were dead in the law, and the property of his 'house' or 'church' was very much like his own property. Even if without the chapter's consent he alienated land, he was regarded, at least by the temporal courts, much rather as one who was attempting to wrong his successors than as one who was wronging that body of 'incapables' of which he was the head. It is to be remembered also that in England many of the cathedrals were monastic. This gave our medieval lawyers some thoughts about the heads of corporations aggregate and about the powerlessness of headless bodies which seem strange to us. A man might easily slip from the statement that the abbey is a corporation into the statement that the abbot is a corporation, and I am far from saying that the latter phrase was never used so long as England had abbots in it;[25] but, so far as I can see, the 'corporation sole' makes its entry into the cathedral along with the royal supremacy and other novelties. Our interest lies in the parish church.[26]

Of the parish church there is a long story to be told. Dr Stutz is telling it in a most interesting manner[27]. Our own Selden, however, was on the true track; he knew that the patron had once been more than a patron,[28] and we need go no further than Blackstone's Commentaries to learn that Alexander III did something memorable in this matter.[29] To be brief: in

---

[24] See Coke's exposition, *Co. Lit.* 44 a, ff; and Blackstone's 2 Com. 319.

[25] Apparently in 1487 (3 Hen. VII, f. 11, Mich. pl. 1), Vavasor J. said 'every abbot is a body politic ["corps politique"], because he can take nothing except to the use of the house'.

[26] Is the idea of the incapacity of a headless corporation capable of doing harm at the present day? Grant, *Corporations*, 110, says that 'if a master of a college devise lands to the college, they cannot take, because at the moment of his death they are an incomplete body'. His latest authority is *Dalison*, 31. In 1863 Dr Whewell or his legal adviser was careful about this matter. A devise was made 'unto the Master, Fellows, and Scholars of Trinity College aforesaid and their successors for ever, or, in case that devise would fail of effect in consequence of there being no Master of the said College at my death, then to the persons who shall be the Senior Fellows of the said College at my decease and their heirs until the appointment of a Master of such College, and from and after such appointment (being within twenty-one years after my death) to the Master, Fellows, and Scholars of the said College and their successors for ever'. Thus international law was endowed while homage was paid to the law of England. But perhaps I do wrong in attracting attention to a rule that should be, if it is not, obsolete.

[27] Ulrich Stutz, *Geschichte des kirchlichen Benefizialwesens*. Only the first part has yet appeared, but Dr Stutz sketched his programme in *Die Eigenkirche*, Berlin, 1895.

[28] *History of Tithes*, c. 12.

[29] 2 Bl. Com. 23.

the twelfth century we may regard the patron as one who has been the owner of church and glebe and tithe, but an owner from whom ecclesiastical law has gradually been sucking his ownership. It has been insisting with varying success that he is not to make such profit out of his church as his heathen ancestor would have made out of a god-house. He must demise the church and an appurtenant manse to an ordained clerk approved by the bishop. The ecclesiastical 'benefice' is the old Frankish *beneficium*, the old land-loan of which we read in all histories of feudalism.[30] In the eleventh century occurred the world-shaking quarrel about investitures. Emperors and princes had been endeavouring to treat even ancient cathedrals as their 'owned churches'. It was over the investiture of bishops that the main struggle took place; nevertheless, the principle which the Hildebrandine papacy asserted was the broad principle, 'No investiture by the lay-hand.' Slowly in the twelfth century, when the more famous dispute had been settled, the new rule was made good by constant pressure against the patrons or owners of the ordinary churches. Then a great lawyer, Alexander III (1159–81), succeeded, so we are told, in finding a new 'juristic basis' for that right of selecting a clerk which could not be taken away from the patron. That right was to be conceived no longer as an offshoot of ownership, but as an outcome of the Church's gratitude towards a pious founder. Thus was laid the groundwork of the classical law of the Catholic Church about the *ius patronatus*; and, as Dr Stutz says, the Church was left free to show itself less and less grateful as time went on.

One part of Pope Alexander's scheme took no effect in England. Investiture by the lay hand could be suppressed. The parson was to be instituted and inducted by his ecclesiastical superiors. Thus his rights in church and glebe and tithe would no longer appear as rights derived out of the patron's ownership, and the patron's right, if they were to be conceived – and in England they certainly would be conceived – as rights of a proprietary kind, would be rights in an incorporeal thing, an 'objectified' advowson. But with successful tenacity Henry II and his successors asserted on behalf of the temporal forum no merely concurrent, but an absolutely exclusive jurisdiction over all disputes, whether possessory or petitory, that touched the advowson. One consequence of this most important assertion was that the English law about this matter strayed away from the jurisprudence of the Catholic Church. If we compare what we have learned as to the old English law of advowsons with the *ius commune* of the Catholic Church as

[30] Stutz, 'Lehen und Pfründe', *Zeitschrift der Savigny-Stiftung*, Germ. Abt. xx. 213.

it is stated by Dr Hinschius we shall see remarkable differences, and in all cases it is the law of England that is the more favourable to patronage.[31] Also in England we read of survivals which tell us that the old notion of the patron's ownership of the church died hard.[32]

But here we are speaking of persons. If the patron is not, who then is the owner of the church and glebe? The canonist will 'subjectify' the church. The church (subject) owns the church (object). Thus he obtains temporary relief.[33] There remains the question how this owning church is to be conceived; and a troublesome question it is. What is the relation of the *ecclesia particularis* (church of Ely or of Trumpington) to the universal church? Are we to think of a *persona ficta*, or of a patron saint, or of the Bride of Christ, or of that vast corporation aggregate the *congregatio omnium fidelium*, or of Christ's vicar at Rome, or of Christ's poor throughout the world; or shall we say that walls are capable of retaining possession? Mystical theories break down: persons who can never be in the wrong are useless in a court of law. Much might be and much was written about these matters, and we may observe that the extreme theory which places the ownership of all church property in the pope was taught by at least one English canonist.[34] Within or behind a subjectified church lay problems which English lawyers might well endeavour to avoid.

On the whole it seems to me that a church is no person in the English temporal law of the later Middle Ages. I do not mean that our lawyers

---

[31] *Kirchenrecht*, vol. III, pp. I ff. In particular, English law regards patronage as normal. When the ordinary freely chooses the clerk, this is regarded as an exercise of patronage; and so we come by the idea of a 'collative advowson'. On the other hand, the catholic canonist should, so I understand, look upon patronage as abnormal, should say that when the bishop selects a clerk this is an exercise not of patronage but of 'jurisdiction', and should add that the case in which a bishop as bishop is patron of a benefice within his own diocese, though not impossible, is extremely rare (Hinschius, *Kirchenrecht*, pp. 35–7). To a king who was going to exercise the 'patronage' annexed to vacant bishoprics, but could not claim spiritual jurisdiction, this difference was of high importance.

[32] See Pike, 'Feoffment and Livery of Incorporeal Hereditaments', *Law Quarterly Review*, v. 29, 35 ff. 43 Edw. III, f. I (Hil. pl. 4): advowson conveyed by feoffment at church door. 7 Edw. III, f. 5 (Hil. pl. 7): Herle's dictum that not long ago men did not know what an advowson was, but granted churches. II Hen. VI, f. 4 (Mich. pl. 8): per Martin, an advowson will pass by livery, and in a writ of right of advowson the summons must be made upon the glebe. 38 Edw. III, f. 4 (scire facias): per Finchden, perhaps in old time the law was that patron without parson could charge the glebe. 9 Hen. VI, f. 52 (Mich. pl. 35): the advowson of a church is assets, for it is an advantage to advance one's blood or one's friend. 5 Hen. VII, f. 37 (Trin. pl. 3): per Vavasour and Danvers, an advowson lies in tenure, and one may distrain [for the services] in the churchyard.

[33] See Gierke, *Genossenschaftsrecht*, vol. III. *passim*.

[34] J. de Athon (ed. 1679), p. 76, gl. ad v. *summorum pontificum*.

maintain one consistent strain of language. That is not so. They occasionally feel the attraction of a system which would make the parson a guardian or curator of an ideal ward. *Ecclesia fungitur vice minoris* ('The church is taken to be a minor') is sometimes on their lips.[35] The thought that the 'parson' of a church was or bore the 'person' of the church was probably less distant from them than it is from us, for the two words long remained one word for the eye and for the ear. Coke, in a theoretical moment, can teach that in the person of the parson the church may sue for and maintain 'her' right.[36] Again, it seems that conveyances were sometimes made to a parish church without mention of the parson, and when an action for land is brought against a rector he will sometimes say, 'I found my church seised of this land, and therefore pray aid of patron and ordinary.'[37]

We may, however, remember at this point that in modern judgments and in Acts of Parliament lands are often spoken of as belonging to 'a charity'. Still, our books do not teach us that charities are persons. Lands that belong to a charity are owned, if not by a corporation, then by some man or men. Now we must not press this analogy between medieval churches and modern charities very far, for medieval lawyers were but slowly elaborating that idea of a trust which bears heavy weights in modern times and enables all religious bodies, except one old-fashioned body, to conduct their affairs conveniently enough without an apparatus of corporations sole. Still, in the main, church and charity seem alike. Neither ever sues, neither is ever sued. The parson holds land 'in right of his church'. So the king can hold land or claim a wardship or a presentation, sometimes 'in right of his crown', but sometimes 'in right of' an escheated honour or a vacant bishopric. So too medieval lawyers were learning to say that an executor will own some goods in his own right and others *en autre droit* ('in right of another').

The failure of the church to become a person for English temporal lawyers is best seen in a rule of law which can be traced from Bracton's day to Coke's through the length of the Year Books. A bishop or an abbot can bring a writ of right, a parson cannot. The parson requires a special action, the *iurata utrum*; it is a *singulare beneficium*[38] provided to suit his peculiar needs. The difficulty that had to be met was this: You can conceive ownership, a full fee simple, vested in a man 'and his heirs', or in an

---

[35] Pollock and Maitland, *Hist. Eng. Law*, ed. 2, 1. 503.
[36] *Co. Lit.* 300 b.
[37] 11 Hen. IV, f. 84 (Trin. pl. 34). But see 8 Hen. V, f. 4 (Hil. pl. 15).
[38] Bracton, f. 286 b.

organised body of men such as a bishop and chapter, or abbot and convent, but you cannot conceive it reposing in the series, the intermittent series, of parsons. True, that the *iurata utrum* will be set to inquire whether a field 'belongs' (*pertinet*) to the plaintiff's 'church'. But the necessity for a special action shows us that the *pertinet* of the writ is thought of as the *pertinet* of appurtenancy, and not as the *pertinet* of ownership. As a garden belongs to a house, as a stopper belongs to a bottle, not as house and bottle belong to a man, so the glebe belongs to the church.

If we have to think of 'subjectification' we have to think of 'objectification' also. Some highly complex 'things' were made by medieval habit and perceived by medieval law. One such thing was the manor; another such thing was the church. Our pious ancestors talked of their churches much as they talked of their manors. They took esplees of the one and esplees of the other; they exploited the manor and exploited the church. True, that the total sum of right, valuable right, of which the church was the object might generally be split between parson, patron, and ordinary. Usually the claimant of an advowson would have to say that the necessary exploitation of the church had been performed, not by himself, but by his presentee. But let us suppose the church impropriated by a religious house, and listen to the head of that house declaring how to his own proper use he has taken esplees in oblations and obventions, great tithes, small tithes, and other manner of tithes.[39] Or let us see him letting a church to farm for a term of years at an annual rent.[40] The church was in many contexts a complex thing, and by no means *extra commercium*. I doubt if it is generally known how much was done in the way of charging 'churches' with annuities or pensions in the days of Catholicism. On an average every year seems to produce one law-suit that is worthy to be reported and has its origin in this practice. In the Year Books the church's objectivity as the core of an exploitable and enjoyable mass of wealth is, to say the least, far more prominent than its subjectivity.[41]

---

[39] 5 Edw. III, f. 18 (Pasch. pl. 18).

[40] 9 Hen. V, f. 8 (Mich. pl. 1).

[41] Sometimes the thing that is let to farm is called, not the church, but the rectory. This, however, does not mean merely the rectory house. 21 Hen. VII, f. 21 (Pasch. pl. 11): 'The church, the churchyard, and the tithe make the rectory, and under the name of rectory they pass by parol.' See *Greenslade* v. *Darby*, L.R. 3 Q.B. 421: The lay impropriator's right to the herbage of the churchyard maintained against a perpetual curate: a learned judgment by Blackburn J. See also Lyndwood, *Provinciale*, pp. 154 ff, as to the practice of letting churches. 30 Edw. III, f. 1: Action of account against bailiff of the plaintiff's church; unsuccessful objection that defendant should be called bailiff, not of the church, but of a rectory: car esglise est a les

'If', said Rolfe Serj., in 1421, 'a man gives or devises land to God and the church of St Peter of Westminster, his gift is good, for the church is not the house nor the walls, but is to be understood as the *ecclesia spiritualis*, to wit, the abbot and convent, and because the abbot and convent can receive a gift, the gift is good . . . but a parish church can only be understood as a house made of stones and walls and roof which cannot take a gift or feoffment.'[42]

We observe that God and St Peter are impracticable feoffees, and that the learned serjeant's 'spiritual church' is a body of men at Westminster. It seems to me that throughout the Middle Ages there was far more doubt than we should expect to find as to the validity of a gift made to 'the [parish] church of *X*', or to 'the parson of *X* and his successors', and that Broke was not performing a needless task when he vouched Littleton and Danby to warrant a gift that took the latter of these forms. Not much land was, I take it, being conveyed to parish churches or parish parsons, while for the old glebe the parson could have shown no title deeds. It had been acquired at a remote time by a slow expropriation of the patron.

The patron's claim upon it was never quite forgotten. Unless I have misread the books, a tendency to speak of the church as a person grows much weaker as time goes on. There is more of it in Bracton than in Littleton or Fitzherbert.[43] English lawyers were no longer learning from civilians and canonists, and were constructing their grand scheme of estates in land. It is with their heads full of 'estates' that they approach the problem of the glebe, and difficult they find it. At least with the consent of patron and ordinary, the parson can do much that a tenant for life cannot do;[44] and, on the other hand, he cannot do all that can be done by a tenant in fee simple. It is hard to find a niche for the rector in our system of

---

parochiens, et nemy le soen [the parson's]. This is the only instance that I have noticed in the Year Books of any phrase which would seem to attribute to the parishioners any sort of proprietary right in the church.

[42] 8 Hen. V, f. 4 (Hil. pl. 15). I omit some words expressing the often recurring theory that the conventual church cannot accept a gift made when there is no abbot. Headless bodies cannot act, but they can retain a right.

[43] 21 Edw. IV, f. 61 (Mich. pl. 32): per Pigot, fines were formerly received which purported to convey *Deo et ecclesiae*, but the judges of those days were ignorant of the law. 9 Hen. VII, f. 11 (Mich. pl. 6): conveyances to God and the church are still held valid if made in old time; they would not be valid if made at the present day.

[44] Even without the active concurrence of patron and ordinary, who perhaps would make default when prayed in aid, the parson could do a good deal in the way of diminishing his successor's revenue by suffering collusive actions. See e.g. 4 Hen. VII, f. 2 (Hil. fol. 4), where the justices in Cam. Scac. ['Exchequer'] were divided, four against three.

tenancies. But let us observe that this difficulty only exists for men who are not going to personify churches or offices.

There is an interesting discussion in 1430.[45] The plaintiff's ancestor had recovered land from a parson, the predecessor of the defendant, by writ of *Cessavit*; he now sues by *Scire facias*, and the defendant prays aid of the patron; the question is whether the aid prayer is to be allowed.

Cottesmore J. says:

> I know well that a parson has only an estate for the term of his life; and it may be that the plaintiff after the judgement released to the patron, and such a release would be good enough, for the reversion of the church is in him [the patron], and this release the parson cannot plead unless he has aid. And I put the case that a man holds land of me for the term of his life, the reversion being in me; then if one who has right in the land releases to me who am in reversion, is not that release good? So in this case.

Paston J. takes the contrary view:

> I learnt for law that if *Praecipe quod reddat* is brought against an abbot or a parson, they shall never have aid, for they have a fee simple in the land, for the land is given to them and their successors, so that no reversion is reserved upon the gift . . . If a writ of right is brought against them they shall join the mise upon the *mere droit*, and that proves that they have a better estate than for term of life. And I have never seen an estate for life with the reversion in no one; for if the parson dies the freehold of the glebe is not in the patron, and no writ for that land is maintainable against any one until there is another parson. So it seems to me that aid should not be granted.

Then speaks Babington C. J., and, having put an ingenious case in which, so he says, there is a life estate without a reversion, he proceeds to distinguish the case of the abbot from that of the parson:

> When an abbot dies seised the freehold always remains in the house (*meason*) and the house cannot be void . . . but if a parson dies, then the church is empty and the freehold in right is in the patron, notwithstanding that the patron can take no advantage of the land; and if a recovery were good when the patron was not made party, then the patronage would be diminished, which would be against reason. So it seems to me that [the defendant] shall have aid.

---

[45] 8 Hen. VI, f. 24 (Hil. pl. 10).

Two other judges, Strangways and Martin, are against the aid prayer; Martin rejects the theory that the parson is tenant for life, and brings into the discussion a tenant in tail after possibility of issue extinct. On the whole the case is unfavourable to the theory which would make the parson tenant for life and the patron reversioner, but that this theory was held in 1430 by a Chief Justice of the Common Pleas seems plain and is very remarkable. The weak point in the doctrine is the admission that the patron does not take the profits of the vacant church. These, it seems settled, go to the ordinary[46] so that the patron's 'reversion' (if any) looks like a very nude right. But the Chief Justice's refusal to repose a right in an empty 'church', while he will place one in a 'house' that has some monks in it, should not escape attention.

Nearly a century later, in 1520, a somewhat similar case came before the court,[47] and we still see the same diversity of opinion. Broke J. (not Broke of Abridgement[vi]) said that the parson had the fee simple of the glebe *in iure ecclesiae* ('in right of his church'). 'It seems to me', said Pollard J.

> that the fee simple is in the patron; for [the parson] has no inheritance in the benefice and the fee cannot be in suspense, and it must be in the patron, for the ordinary only has power to admit a clerk. And although all parsons are made by the act of the ordinary, there is nothing in the case that can properly be called succession. For if land be given to a parson and his successor, that is not good, for he [the parson] has no capacity to take this; but if land be given *Priori et Ecclesiae* ('to the prior and the church') that is good, because there is a corporation . . . And if the parson creates a charge, that will be good only so long as he is parson, for if he dies or resigns, his successor shall hold the land discharged; and this proves that the parson has not the fee simple. But if in time of vacation patron and ordinary charge the land, the successor shall hold it charged, for they [patron and ordinary] had at the time the whole interest.[48]

Eliot J. then started a middle opinion:

---

[46] 11 Hen. VI, f. 4 (Mich. pl. 8): per Danby, the ordinary shall have the occupation and all the profit. 9 Hen. V, f. 14 (Mich. pl. 19) accord. See Stat. 28 Hen. VIII, c. 11, which gives the profits to the succeeding parson.

[47] 12 Hen. VIII, f. 7 (Mich. pl. 1).

[48] Apparently Belknap J. had said that such a charge would be good: Fitz. *Abr.* Annuitie, pl. 53 (8 Ric. II).

It seems to me that the parson has the fee *in iure ecclesiae*, and not the patron – as one is seised in fee *in iure uxoris suae* ('in right of his wife') – and yet for some purposes he is only tenant for life. So tenant in tail has a fee tail, and yet he has only for the term of his life, for if he makes a lease or grants a rent charge, that will be only for the term of his life . . . As to what my brother Pollard says, namely, that in time of vacation patron and ordinary can create a charge, that is not so.

Then Brudenel C. J. was certain that the parson has a fee simple: 'He has a fee simple by succession, as an heir [has one] by inheritance, and neither the ordinary nor the patron gives this to the parson.'

Pollard's opinion was belated; but we observe that on the eve of the Reformation it was still possible for an English judge to hold that the ownership, the fee simple, of the church is in the patron. And at this point it will not be impertinent to remember that even at the present-day timber felled on the glebe is said to belong to the patron.[49]

In the interval between these two cases Littleton had written. He rejected the theory which would place the fee simple in the patron; but he also rejected that which would place it in the parson. Of any theory which would subjectify the church or the parson's office or dignity he said nothing; and nothing of any corporation sole. Let us follow his argument.

He is discussing 'discontinuance' and has to start with this, that if a parson or vicar grants land which is of the right of his church and then dies or resigns, his successor may enter.[50] In other words, there has been no discontinuance. 'And', he says, 'I take the cause to be for that the parson or vicar that is seised as in right of his church hath no right of the fee simple in the tenements, and the right of the fee simple doth not[51] abide in another person.' That, he explains, is the difference between the case of the parson and the case of a bishop, abbot, dean, or master of a hospital; their alienations may be discontinuances, his cannot; 'for a bishop may have a writ of right of the tenements of the right of the church, for that the right is in his chapter, and the fee simple abideth in him and his chapter . . . And a master of a hospital may have a writ of right because the

---

[49] *Sowerby* v. *Fryer* (1869), *L.R.* 8 Eq. 417, 423: James V. C.: 'I never could understand why a vicar who has wrongfully cut timber should not be called to account for the proceeds after he has turned it into money, in order that they may be invested for the benefit of the advowson; *it being conceded that the patron is entitled to the specific timber.*'

[50] Litt. sec. 643.

[51] There are various readings, but the argument seems plainly to require this 'not'.

right remaineth in him and in his *confreres*, &c.; and so in other like cases. But a parson or vicar cannot have a writ of right, &c.' A discontinuance, if I rightly understand the matter, involves the alienation of that in which the alienor has some right, but some right is vested in another person. In the one case the bishop alienates what belongs to him and his chapter; in the other case the parson alienates what belongs to no one else.

Then we are told[52] that the highest writ that a parson or vicar can have is the *Utrum*, and that this 'is a great proof that the right of fee is not in them, nor in others. But the right of the fee simple is in abeyance; that is to say, that it is only in the remembrance, intendment, and consideration of law, for it seemeth to me that such a thing and such a right which is said in divers books to be in abeyance is as much as to say in Latin, *Talis res, vel tale rectum, quae vel quod non est in homine adtunc superstite, sed tantummodo est et consistit in consideratione et intelligentia legis, et, quod alii dixerunt, talem rem aut tale rectum fore in nubibus* ['Such a thing or right, which is not in a man now living, but exists and consists solely in the consideration and intendment of law, and, as others have said, such a thing or right will be in the clouds.'] Yes, rather than have any dealings with fictitious persons, subjectified churches, personified dignities, corporations that are not bodies, we will have a subjectless right, a fee simple in the clouds.'[53]

Then in a very curious section Littleton[54] has to face the fact that the parson with the assent of patron and ordinary can charge the glebe of the parsonage perpetually. Thence, so he says, some will argue that these three persons, or two or one of them, must have a fee simple. Littleton must answer this argument. Now this is one of those points at which a little fiction might give us temporary relief. We might place the fee simple in a fictitious person, whose lawfully appointed guardians give a charge on the property of their imaginary ward. We might refer to the case of a town council which sets the common seal to a conveyance of land which belongs to the town. But, rather than do anything of the kind, Littleton has recourse to a wholly different principle.

The charge has been granted by parson, patron, and ordinary, and then the parson dies. His successor cannot come to the church but by the presentment of the patron and institution of the ordinary, 'and for this cause he ought to hold himself content and agree to that which his patron

---

[52] Lit. sec. 646.

[53] Apparently the talk about a fee simple *in nubibus* began in debates over contingent remainders: 11 Hen. IV, f. 74 (Trin. pl. 14).

[54] Lit. sec. 648.

and the ordinary have lawfully done before'. In other words, the parson is debarred by decency and gratitude from examining the mouth of the gift horse. No one compelled him to accept the benefice. Perhaps we might say that by his own act he is estopped from quarrelling with the past acts of his benefactors. Such a piece of reasoning would surely be impossible to any one who thought of the church or the rector's office as a person capable of sustaining proprietary rights.

Before Littleton's Tenures came to Coke's hands, Broke or some one else had started the suggestion that a parson was a corporation, or might be likened to a corporation. Apparently that suggestion was first offered by way of explaining how it came about that a gift could be made to a parson and his successors. Now it seems to me that a speculative jurist might have taken advantage of this phrase in order to reconstruct the theory of the parson's relation to the glebe. He might have said that in this case, as in the case of the corporation aggregate, we have a *persona ficta*, an ideal subject of rights, in which a fee simple may repose; that the affairs of this person are administered by a single man, in the same way in which the affairs of certain other fictitious persons are administered by groups of men; and that the rector therefore must be conceived not as a proprietor but as a guardian, though his powers of administration are large, and may often be used for his own advantage. And Coke, in his more speculative moments, showed some inclination to tread this path. Especially is this the case when he contrasts 'persons natural created of God, as J. S., J. N., &c., and persons incorporate and politic created by the policy of man', and then adds that the latter are 'of two sorts, viz. aggregate or sole.'[55] But to carry that theory through would have necessitated a breach with traditional ideas of the parson's estate and a distinct declaration that Littleton's way of thinking had become antiquated.[56] As it is, when the critical point is reached and we are perhaps hoping that the new-found corporation sole will be of some real use, we see that it gives and can give Coke no help at all, for, after all, Coke's corporation sole is a man: a man who fills an office and can hold land 'to himself and his successors', but a mortal man.

When that man dies the freehold is in abeyance. Littleton had said that this happened 'if a parson of a church dieth'. Coke adds:[57] 'So it is

---

[55] *Co. Litt.* 2 a.

[56] In *Wythers v. Iseham*, Dyer, f. 70 (pl. 43), the case of the parson had been noticed as the only exception to the rule that the freehold could not be in abeyance.

[57] *Co. Litt.* 342 b.

of a bishop, abbot, dean, archdeacon, prebend, vicar, and of every other sole corporation or body politic, presentative, elective, or donative, which inheritances put in abeyance are by some called *haereditates iacentes*.' So here we catch our corporation sole 'on the point of death' (*in articulo mortis*). If God did not create him, then neither the inferior not yet the superior clergy are God's creatures.

So much as to the state of affairs when there is no parson: the freehold is in abeyance, and 'the fee and right is in abeyance'. On the other hand, when there is a parson, then, says Coke,[58] 'for the benefit of the church and of his successor he is in some cases esteemed in law to have a fee qualified; but, to do anything to the prejudice of his successor, in many cases the law adjudgeth him to have in effect but an estate for life'. And again, 'It is evident that to many purposes a parson hath but in effect an estate for life, and to many a qualified fee simple, but the entire fee and right is not in him.'

This account of the matter seems to have been accepted as final. Just at this time the Elizabethan statutes were giving a new complexion to the practical law. The parson, even with the consent of patron and ordinary, could no longer alienate or charge the glebe, and had only a modest power of granting leases. Moreover, as the old real actions gave place to the action of ejectment, a great deal of the old learning fell into oblivion. Lawyers had no longer to discuss the parson's aid prayer or his ability or inability to join the mise on the *mere droit*, and it was around such topics as these that the old indecisive battles had been fought. Coke's theory, though it might not be neat, was flexible: for some purposes the parson has an estate for life, for others a qualified fee. And is not this the orthodoxy of the present day? The abeyance of the freehold during the vacancy of the benefice has the approval of Mr Challis;[59] the 'fee simple qualified' appears in Sir H. Elphinstone's edition of Mr Goodeve's book.[60]

Thus, so it seems to me, our corporation sole refuses to perform just the first service that we should require at the hands of any reasonably useful *persona ficta*. He or it refuses to act as the bearer of a right which threatens to fall into abeyance or dissipate itself among the clouds for want of a 'natural' custodian. I say 'he or it'; but which ought we to

[58] *Ibid.*, 341 a.
[59] Challis, *Real Property*, ed. 2, p. 91.
[60] Goodeve, *Real Property*, ed. 4, pp. 85, 133. See the remarks of Jessel M. R. in *Mulliner v. Midland Railway Co.*, 11 Ch. D. 622.

say? Is a beneficed clergyman – for instance, the Rev. John Styles – a corporation sole, or is he merely the administrator or representative of a corporation sole? Our Statute Book is not very consistent. When it was decreeing the Disestablishment of the Irish Church it declared that on January 1, 1871, every ecclesiastical corporation in Ireland, whether sole or aggregate, should be dissolved,[61] and it were needless to say that this edict did not contemplate a summary dissolution of worthy divines. But turn to a carefully worded Statute of Limitations. 'It shall be lawful for any archbishop, bishop, dean, prebendary, parson, master of a hospital, or other spiritual or eleemosynary corporation sole to make an entry or distress, or to bring an action or suit to recover any land or rent within such period as hereinafter is mentioned next after the time at which *the right of such corporation sole or of his predecessor . . .* shall have first accrued.'[62] Unquestionably for the draftsman of this section the corporation sole was, as he was for Coke, a man, a mortal man.

If our corporation sole really were an artificial person created by the policy of man we ought to marvel at its incompetence. Unless custom or statute aids it, it cannot (so we are told) own a chattel, not even a chattel real.[63] A different and an equally inelegant device was adopted to provide an owning 'subject' for the ornaments of the church and the minister thereof – adopted at the end of the Middle Ages by lawyers who held themselves debarred by the theory of corporations from frankly saying that the body of parishioners is a corporation aggregate. And then we are also told that in all probability a corporation sole 'cannot enter into a contract except with statutory authority or as incidental to an interest in land.'[64] What then can this miserable being do? It cannot even hold its glebe tenaciously enough to prevent the freehold falling into abeyance whenever a parson dies.

When we turn from this mere ghost of a fiction to a true corporation, a corporation aggregate, surely the main phenomenon that requires explanation, that sets us talking of personality and, it may be, of fictitious personality, is this, that we can conceive and do conceive that legal transactions, or acts in the law, can take place and do often take place between

[61] 32 and 33 Vict. c. 42, sec. 13.
[62] 3 and 4 Will. IV, c. 27, sec. 29.
[63] *Fulwood's* case, 4 *Rep.* 65 a; *Arundel's* case, *Hob.* 64.
[64] Pollock, *Contract*, ed. 6, p. 109. The principal modern authority is *Howley* v. *Knight*, 14 Q.B. 240.

the corporation of the one part and some or all of the corporators of the other part. A beautiful modern example[65] shows us eight men conveying a colliery to a company of which they are the only members; and the Court of Appeal construes this as a 'sale' by eight persons to a ninth person, though the price consists not in cash, but in the whole share capital of the newly formed corporation. But to all appearance there can be no legal transaction, no act in the law, between the corporation sole and the natural man who is the one and only corporator. We are told, for example, that 'a sole corporation, as a bishop or a parson, cannot make a lease to himself, because he cannot be both lessor and lessee.'[66] We are told that 'if a bishop hath lands in both capacities he cannot give or take to or from himself.'[67] Those who use such phrases as these show plainly enough that in their opinion there is no second 'person' involved in the cases of which they speak: 'he' is 'himself', and there is an end of the matter.[68] I can find no case in which the natural man has sued the corporation sole or the corporation sole has sued the natural man.

When a man is executor, administrator, trustee, bailee, or agent, we do not feel it necessary to speak of corporateness or artificial personality, and I fail to see why we should do this when a man is a beneficed clerk. Whatever the Romans may have done – and about this there have been disputes enough – we have made no person of the *hereditas iacens*. On an intestate's death we stopped the gap with no figment, but with a real live bishop, and in later days with the Judge of the Probate Court: English law has liked its persons to be real. Our only excuse for making a fuss over the parson is that, owing to the slow expropriation of the patron, the parson has an estate in church and glebe which refuses to fit into any of the ordinary categories of our real property law; but, as we have already seen, our talk of corporations sole has failed to solve or even to evade the difficulty. No one at the present day would dream of introducing for the first time the scheme of church property law that has come down to us, and I think it not rash to predict that, whether the Church of England remains established or no, churches and glebes will some day find their

---

[65] *Foster & Son, Lim.* v. *Com. of Inland Rev.* [1894] 1 Q.B. 156.

[66] *Salter* v. *Grosvenor*, 8 Mod. 303, 304.

[67] *Wood* v. *Mayor, &c., of London, Salk.* 396, 398. See also Grant, *Corporations*, 635.

[68] The matter was well stated by Broke J. in 14 Hen. VIII, f. 30 (Pasch. pl. 8): a parson cannot grant unto or enfeoff himself, 'because howeverso he has two aspects, he is still the one person'.

owners in a corporation aggregate or in many corporations aggregate.[69] Be that as it may, the ecclesiastical corporation sole is no 'juristic person'; he or it is either natural man or juristic abortion. The worst of his or its doings we have not yet considered. He or it has persuaded us to think clumsy thoughts or to speak clumsy words about King and Commonwealth.[70]

Notes

i This controversy was formally aired in the pages of the *Law Quarterly Review* between the publication of 'The corporation sole' there (October 1900) and 'Crown as corporation' (April 1901). In the edition of January 1901, the editor Frederick Pollock reviewed Maitland's edition of Gierke's *Political theories of the Middle Age* (*Law Quarterly Review* (XVII, 1901), pp. 95–6). Pollock applauds the appearance of the volume, the scholarship of the edition and the lucidity of Maitland's introduction, but he does not approve the theory of the 'real personality' of corporations that he takes both Maitland and Gierke to share and the book to champion. He argues that proponents of the 'fiction theory' do suppose that corporate personality has no bearing on the reality of corporate life and should not be caricatured as though they do. Moreover, he claims that it was precisely the 'fiction theory' that gave life to corporate identity in ways that both German and English conceptions of law were unlikely to do on their own: 'Now we may doubt whether the courts left to themselves in the light of merely Germanic principles would ever have recognized a person where there was not a physical body . . . Without the Roman *universitas* and its accompanying "fiction theory" we should perhaps have had no corporation at all, but some device like the equity method of an individual plaintiff suing "on behalf of himself and all others" in the same interest.' [*Ibid.*, p. 96.]

ii Maitland cites some of the French literature on these questions in his final footnote to 'Moral personality and legal personality' (see below, p. 71, n. 9), in which he makes particular reference to the work of Michoud as an introduction to Germanism (see L. Michoud, *La théorie de la personnalité morale* (Paris, 1899)).

iii Maitland means Sir Robert Broke.

---

[69] See *Eccl. Com. v. Pinney* [1899] 1 Ch. 99, a case prophetic of the ultimate fate of the glebe.

[70] In looking through the Year Books for the corporation sole, I took note of a large number of cases in which this term is not used, but might well have been used had it been current. I thought at one time of printing a list of these cases, but forbear, as it would fill valuable space and only points to a negative result. The discussion of the parson's rights in F.N.B. 109–112 is one of the places to which we naturally turn, but turn in vain.

iv The Year Books were reports, probably first taken down by apprentices, of cases heard by royal justices. They date back to 1291. The publication of scholarly editions of these reports was one of the purposes for which the Selden Society was founded by Maitland.

v The 'enabling statute' referred to here is the statute of 1540 which allowed for the leasing of ecclesiastical property. The 'disabling' statute is the statute of 1559 which restrained this practice.

vi Sir Robert Broke, referred to by Maitland above (see Biographical notes).

2

The Crown as Corporation

The greatest of artificial persons, politically speaking, is the State. But it depends on the legal institutions and forms of every commonwealth whether and how far the State or its titular head is officially treated as an artificial person. In England we now say that the Crown is a corporation: it was certainly not so when the king's peace died with him, and 'every man that could forthwith robbed another'.[1]

I quote these words from Sir F. Pollock's *First Book of Jurisprudence*.[i] They may serve to attract a little interest to that curious freak of English law, the corporation sole. In a previous paper I have written something concerning its history.[2] I endeavoured to show that this strange conceit originated in the sixteenth century and within the domain of what we may call 'church property law'. It held out a hope, which proved to be vain, that it would provide a permanent 'subject' in which could be reposed that fee simple of the parochial glebe which had been slowly abstracted from the patron and was not comfortable in those clouds to which Littleton had banished it. Then, following in the steps of Sir William Markby, I ventured to say that this corporation sole has shown itself to be no 'juristic person', but is either a natural man or a juristic abortion.

If the corporation sole had never trespassed beyond the ecclesiastical province in which it was native, it would nowadays be very unimportant. Clearly it would have no future before it, and the honour of writing its epitaph would hardly be worth the trouble. Unfortunately, however, the thought occurred to Coke – or perhaps in the first instance to some other lawyer of Coke's day – that the King of England ought to be brought into one class with the parson: both were to be artificial persons and both were to be corporations sole.

[1] Pollock, *First Book of Jurisprudence*, p. 113.
[2] *L.Q.R.* XVI. 335.

Whether the State should be personified, or whether the State, being really and naturally a person, can be personified, these may be very interesting questions. What we see in England, at least what we see if we look only at the surface, is, not that the State is personified or that the State's personality is openly acknowledged, but (I must borrow from one of Mr Gilbert's operas[ii]) that the king is 'parsonified'. Since that feat was performed, we have been, more or less explicitly, trying to persuade ourselves that our law does not recognise the personality or corporate character of the State or Nation or Commonwealth, and has no need to do anything of the sort if only it will admit that the king, or, yet worse, the Crown, is not unlike a parson.

It would be long to tell the whole story of this co-ordination of king and parson, for it would take us deep into the legal and political thoughts of the Middle Ages. Only two or three remarks can here be hazarded.[3]

The medieval king was every inch a king, but just for this reason he was every inch a man and you did not talk nonsense about him. You did not ascribe to him immortality or ubiquity or such powers as no mortal can wield. If you said that he was Christ's Vicar, you meant what you said, and you might add that he would become the servant of the devil if he declined towards tyranny. And there was little cause for ascribing to him more than one capacity. Now and then it was necessary to distinguish between lands that he held in right of his crown and lands which had come to him in right of an escheated barony or vacant bishopric. But in the main all his lands were his lands, and we must be careful not to read a trusteeship for the nation into our medieval documents. The oftrepeated demand that the king should 'live of his own' implied this view of the situation. I do not mean that this was at any time a complete view. We may, for example, find the lawyers of Edward II's day catching up a notion that the canonists had propagated, declaring that the king's crown is always under age, and so co-ordinating the *corona* with the *ecclesia*.[4,iii] But English lawyers were not good at work of this kind; they liked their persons to be real, and what we have seen of the parochial glebe has shown us that even the church (*ecclesia particularis*) was not for them a person.[5] As to the king, in all the Year Books I have seen very little said of him that was not meant to be strictly and literally true of a man, of an Edward or a Henry.

---

[3] The theme of this paper was suggested by Dr Gierke's *Genossenschaftsrecht*, a portion of which I have lately published in English: *Political Theories of the Middle Age*. Cambridge, 1900.
[4] *Placit. Abbrev.* p. 339 (15 Edw. II).
[5] *L.Q.R.* XVI. 344.

Then, on the other hand, medieval thought conceived the nation as a community and pictured it as a body of which the king was the head. It resembled those smaller bodies which it comprised and of which it was in some sort composed. What we should regard as the contrast between State and Corporation was hardly visible. The 'commune of the realm' differed rather in size and power than in essence from the commune of a county or the commune of a borough. And as the *comitatus* or county took visible form in the *comitatus* or county court, so the realm took visible form in a parliament. 'Every one', said Thorpe C. J. in 1365, 'is bound to know at once what is done in Parliament, for Parliament represents the body of the whole realm.'[6] For a time it seems very possible, as we read the Year Books, that so soon as lawyers begin to argue about the nature of corporations or bodies politic and clearly to sever the Borough, for example, from the sum of burgesses, they will definitely grasp and formulate the very sound thought that the realm is 'a corporation aggregate of many'. In 1522 Fineux C. J., after telling how some corporations are made by the king, others by the pope, others by both king and pope, adds that there are corporations by the common law, for, says he, 'the parliament of the king and the lords and the commons are a corporation'.[7] What is still lacking is the admission that the corporate realm, besides being the wielder of public power, may also be the 'subject' of private rights, the owner of lands and chattels. And this is the step that we have never yet formally taken.[8]

The portrait that Henry VIII painted of the body politic of which he was the sovereign head will not be forgotten:[9]

> Where by divers sundry old authentic histories and chronicles it is manifestly declared and expressed that this realm of England is an Empire, and so hath been accepted in the world, governed by One supreme Head and King, having the dignity and royal estate of the Imperial Crown of the same, unto whom a Body Politick, compact of all sorts and degrees of people and by names of Spirituality and Temporalty been bounden, and owen to bear, next to God, a natural and humble obedience . . .

---

[6] Y.B. 39 Edw. III, f. 7.

[7] Y.B. 14 Hen. VIII, f. 3 (Mich. pl. 2).

[8] The mistake, so I think, of Allen's memorable treatise on the Royal Prerogative [1830] consists in the supposition that already in very old days the Folk could be and was clearly conceived as a person: a single 'subject' of ownership and other rights.

[9] 25 Hen. VIII, c. 12 (For the Restraint of Appeals).

It is stately stuff into which old thoughts and new are woven. 'The body spiritual' is henceforth to be conceived as 'part of the said body politick' which culminates in King Henry. The medieval dualism of Church and State is at length transcended by the majestic lord who broke the bonds of Rome. The frontispiece of the Leviathan is already before our eyes. But, as for Hobbes, so also for King Henry, the personality of the corporate body is concentrated in and absorbed by the personality of its monarchical head.[iv] His reign was not the time when the king's lands could be severed from the nation's lands, the king's wealth from the common wealth, or even the king's power from the power of the State. The idea of a corporation sole which was being prepared in the ecclesiastical sphere might do good service here. Were not all Englishmen incorporated in King Henry? Were not his acts and deeds the acts and deeds of that body politic which was both Realm and Church?

A certain amount of disputation there was sure to be over land acquired by the king in divers ways. Edward VI, not being yet of the age of twenty-one years, purported to alienate land which formed part of the duchy of Lancaster. Did this act fall within the doctrine that the king can convey while he is an infant? Land had been conveyed to Henry VII 'and the heirs male of his body lawfully begotten'. Did this give him an estate tail or a fee simple conditional? Could the head of a body politic beget heirs? A few cases of this kind came before the Court soon after the middle of the sixteenth century. In Plowden's reports of these cases we may find much curious argumentation about the king's two 'bodies', and I do not know where to look in the whole series of our law books for so marvellous a display of metaphysical – or we might say metaphysiological – nonsense.[10] Whether this sort of talk was really new about the year 1550, or whether it had gone unreported until Plowden arose, it were not easy to say; but the Year Books have not prepared us for it. Two sentences may be enough to illustrate what I mean:

> So that he [the king] has a body natural adorned and invested with the estate and dignity royal, and he has not a body natural distinct and divided by itself from the office and dignity royal, but a body natural and a body politic together indivisible, and these two bodies are incorporated in one person and make one body and not divers, that is, the body corporate in the body natural *et e contra* the body natural in

---

[10] *Case of the Duchy of Lancaster, Plowden*, 212; *Willion v. Berkley, Ibid.* 223; *Sir Thomas Wroth's case, Ibid.* 452.

the body corporate. So that the body natural by the conjunction of the body politic to it (which body politic contains the office, government and majesty royal) is magnified and by the said consolidation hath in it the body politic.[11]

'Which faith', we are inclined to add, 'except every man keep whole and undefiled, without doubt he shall perish everlastingly.' However, a gleam of light seems sometimes to penetrate the darkness. The thought that in one of his two capacities the king is only the 'head' of a corporation has not been wholly suppressed.

> The king has two capacities, for he has two bodies, the one whereof is a body natural . . . the other is a body politic, and the members thereof are his subjects, and he and his subjects together compose the corporation, as Southcote said, and he is incorporated with them and they with him, and he is the head and they are the members, and he has the sole government of them.[12]

Again, in that strange debate occasioned by the too sudden death of Sir James Hales,[v] Brown J. says that suicide is an offence not only against God and Nature, but against the King, for 'he, being the Head, has lost one of his mystical members.'[13] But, for reasons that lie for the more part outside the history of law, this thought fell into the background. The king was left with 'two bodies'; one of them was natural, the other non-natural. Of this last body we can say little; but it is 'politic,' whatever 'politic' may mean.

Meanwhile the concept of a corporation sole was being fashioned in order to explain, if this were possible, the parson's relation to the glebe. Then came Coke and in his masterful fashion classified Persons for the coming ages. They are natural or artificial. Kings and parsons are artificial persons, corporations sole, created not by God but by the policy of man.[14]

Abortive as I think the attempt to bring the parson into line with corporations aggregate – abortive, for the freehold of the glebe persists in falling into abeyance whenever a parson dies – the attempt to play the same trick with the king seems to me still more abortive and infinitely more mischievous. In the first place, the theory is never logically formulated even by those who are its inventors. We are taught that the king is two

[11] *Plowden*, 213.
[12] *Ibid.* 234.
[13] *Ibid.* 261.
[14] *Co. Lit.* 2 a, 250 a; *Sutton's Hospital* case, 10 *Rep.* 26 b.

'persons', only to be taught that though he has 'two bodies' and 'two capacities' he 'hath but one person'.[15] Any real and consistent severance of the two personalities would naturally have led to 'the damnable and damned opinion', productive of 'execrable and detestable consequences', that allegiance is due to the corporation sole and not to the mortal man.[16] In the second place, we are plunged into talk about kings who do not die, who are never under age, who are ubiquitous, who do no wrong and (says Blackstone[17]) think no wrong; and such talk has not been innocuous. Readers of Kinglake's *Crimea*[vi] will not have forgotten the instructive and amusing account of 'the two kings' who shared between them control of the British army: 'the personal king' and 'his constitutional rival'. But in the third place, the theory of the two kings or two persons stubbornly refuses to do any real work in the cause of jurisprudence.

We might have thought that it would at least have led to a separation of the land that the king held as king from the land that he held as man, and to a legal severance of the money that was in the Exchequer from the money that was in the king's pocket. It did nothing of the sort.[vii] All had to be done by statute, and very slowly and clumsily it was done. After the king's lands had been made inalienable, George III had to go to Parliament for permission to hold some land as a man and not as a king, for he had been denied rights that were not denied to 'any of His Majesty's subjects'.[18] A deal of legislation, extending into Queen Victoria's reign, has been required in order to secure 'private estates' for the king. 'Whereas it is doubtful', says an Act of 1862.[19] 'And whereas it may be doubtful,' says an Act of 1873.[20] Many things may be doubtful if we try to make two persons of one man, or to provide one person with two bodies.

The purely natural way in which the king was regarded in the Middle Ages is well illustrated by the terrible consequences of what we now call a demise of the Crown, but what seemed to our ancestors the death of a man who had delegated many of his powers to judges and others. At the delegator's death the delegation ceased. All litigation not only came to a stop but had to be begun over again. We might have thought that the introduction of phrases which gave the king an immortal as well as

---

[15] *Calvin's* case, 7 *Rep.* 10 a.
[16] *Ibid.* 11 a, b.
[17] 1 *Comm.* 246.
[18] 39 & 40 Geo. III, c. 88.
[19] 25 & 26 Vict. c. 37.
[20] 36 & 37 Vict. c. 61.

a mortal body would have transformed this part of the law. But no. The consequences of the old principle had to be picked off one after another by statute.[21] At the beginning of Queen Victoria's reign it was discovered that 'great inconvenience had arisen on occasion of the demise of the Crown from the necessity of renewing all military commissions under the royal sign manual'.[22] When on a demise of the Crown we see all the wheels of the State stopping or even running backwards, it seems an idle jest to say that the king never dies.

But the worst of it is that we are compelled to introduce into our legal thinking a person whose personality our law does not formally or explicitly recognise. We cannot get on without the State, or the Nation, or the Commonwealth, or the Public, or some similar entity, and yet that is what we are professing to do. In the days when Queen Elizabeth was our Prince – more often Prince than Princess – her secretary might write in Latin *De republica Anglorum*, and in English *Of the Commonwealth of England*: Prince and Republic were not yet incompatible. A little later Guy Fawkes and others, so said the Statute Book, had attempted the destruction of His Majesty and 'the overthrow of the whole State and Common wealth'.[23] In 1623 the Exchequer Chamber could speak of the inconvenience that 'remote limitations' had introduced 'in the republic'.[24] But the great struggle that followed had the effect of depriving us of two useful words. 'Republic' and 'Commonwealth' implied kinglessness and therefore treason. As to 'the State', it was a late comer – but little known until after 1600 – and though it might govern political thought, and on rare occasions make its way into the preamble of a statute, it was slow to find a home in English law-books. There is wonderfully little of the State in Blackstone's *Commentaries*.[25] It is true that 'The people' exists, and 'the liberties of the People' must be set over against 'the prerogatives of the King'; but just because the King is no part of the People, the People cannot be the State or Commonwealth.

But 'the Publick' might be useful. And those who watch the doings of this Publick in the Statute Book of the eighteenth century may feel inclined to say that it has dropped a first syllable. After the rebellion of 1715 an Act of Parliament declared that the estates of certain traitors were

---

[21] 1 Edw. VI, begins the process.
[22] 7 Will. IV & 1 Vict. c. 31.
[23] 3 Jac. I, c. 3, pr.
[24] *Child* v. *Baylie*, Palm. 335, 336.
[25] Such phrases as 'when the danger of the state is great' (1, 135) are occasionally used.

to be vested in the king 'to the use of the Publick'.[26] Whether this is the first appearance of 'the Publick' as *cestui que trust* of a part of those lands of which the king is owner I do not know; but it is an early example. Then we come upon an amusing little story which illustrates the curious qualities of our royal corporation sole. One of the attainted traitors was Lord Derwentwater, and the tenants of his barony of Langley had been accustomed to pay a fine when their lord died – such a custom was, I believe, commoner elsewhere than in England. But, says an Act of 1738, the said premises 'being vested in His Majesty, his heirs and successors in his politick capacity, which in consideration of law never dies, it may create a doubt whether the tenants of the said estates ought . . . to pay such fines . . . on the death of His present Majesty (whom God long preserve for the benefit of his People) or on the death of any future King or Queen'. So the tenants are to pay as they would have paid 'in case such King or Queen so dying was considered as a private person only and not in his or her politick capacity'.[27] Thus that artificial person, the king in his politick capacity, who is a trustee for the Publick, must be deemed to die now and then for the benefit of *cestui que trust*.

But it was of 'the Publick' that we were speaking, and I believe that 'the Publick' first becomes prominent in connexion with the National Debt. Though much might be done for us by a slightly denaturalized king, he could not do all that was requisite. Some proceedings of one of his predecessors, who closed the Exchequer and ruined the goldsmiths, had made our king no good borrower.[viii] So the Publick had to take his place. The money might be 'advanced to His Majesty,' but the Publick had to owe it. This idea could not be kept off the statute book. 'Whereas', said an Act of 1786, 'the Publick stands indebted to' the East India Company in a sum of four millions and more.[28]

What is the Publick which owes the National Debt? We try to evade that question. We try to think of that debt not as a debt owed by a person, but as a sum charged upon a pledged or mortgaged thing, upon the Consolidated Fund.[ix] This is natural, for we may, if we will, trace the beginnings of a national debt back to days when a king borrows money and charges the repayment of it upon a specific tax; perhaps he will even appoint his creditor to collect that tax, and so enable him to repay himself. Then

---

[26] I Geo. I, stat. 2, c. 50. We must distinguish this Public from the Public (*quilibet de populo* ['any one of the people']) to whom a highway is dedicated.

[27] 11 Geo. II, c. 30, pr. and sec. 1.

[28] 26 Geo. III, c. 62.

there was the long transitional stage in which annuities were charged on the Aggregate Fund, the General Fund, the South Sea Fund, and so forth. And now we have the Consolidated Fund; but even the most licentious 'objectification' (or, as Dr James Ward says, 'reification') can hardly make that Fund 'a thing' for jurisprudence. On the one hand, we do not conceive that the holders of Consols would have the slightest right to complain if the present taxes were swept away and new taxes invented, and, on the other hand, we conceive that if the present taxes will not suffice to pay the interest of the debt more taxes must be imposed. Then we speak of 'the security of an Act of Parliament', as if the Act were a profitbearing thing that could be pledged. Or we introduce 'the Government' as a debtor. But what, we may ask, is this Government? Surely not the group of Ministers, not the Government which can be contrasted with Parliament. I am happy to think that no words of mine can affect the price of Bank Annuities, but it seems to me that the national debt is not a 'secured debt' in any other than that loose sense in which we speak of 'personal security', and that the creditor has nothing to trust to but the honesty and solvency of that honest and solvent community of which the King is the head and 'Government' and Parliament are organs.

One of our subterfuges has been that of making the king a trustee (*vel quasi* ('of sorts')) for unincorporated groups. Another of our subterfuges has been that of slowly substituting 'the Crown' for King or Queen. Now the use which has been made in different ages of the crown – a chattel now lying in the Tower and partaking (so it is said[29]) of the nature of an heirloom – might be made the matter of a long essay. I believe, however, that an habitual and perfectly unambiguous personification of the Crown – in particular, the attribution of acts to the Crown – is much more modern than most people would believe. It seems to me that in fully half the cases in which Sir William Anson writes 'Crown', Blackstone would have written 'King'. In strictness, however, 'the Crown' is not, I take it, among the persons known to our law, unless it is merely another name for the King. The Crown, by that name, never sues, never prosecutes, never issues writs or letters patent. On the face of formal records the King or Queen does it all. I would not, if I could, stop the process which is making 'the Crown' one of the names of a certain organised community; but in the meantime that term is being used in three or four different, though closely related, senses. 'We all know that the Crown is an

---

[29] *Co. Lit.* 18 b.

abstraction', said Lord Penzance.[30] I do not feel quite sure of knowing even this.[31]

The suggestion that 'the Crown' is very often a suppressed or partially recognised corporation aggregate is forced upon us so soon as we begin to attend with care to the language which is used by judges when they are freely reasoning about modern matters and are not feeling the pressure of old theories. Let us listen, for example, to Blackburn J., when in a famous opinion he was explaining why it is that the Postmaster-General or the captain of a man-of-war cannot be made to answer in a civil action for the negligence of his subordinates. 'These cases were decided upon the ground that *the government* was the principal and the defendant merely the servant. . . . All that is decided by this class of cases is that the liability of a servant of *the public* is no greater than that of the servant of any other principal, though the recourse against the principal, *the public*, cannot be by an action'.[32] So here the Government and the Public are identified, or else the one is an organ or agent of the other. But the Postmaster-General or the captain of a man-of-war is assuredly a servant of the Crown, and yet he does not serve two masters. A statute of 1887 tells us that 'the expressions "permanent civil service of the State", "permanent civil service of Her Majesty", and "permanent civil service of the Crown", are hereby declared to have the same meaning'.[33] Now as it is evident that King Edward is not (though Louis XIV may have been) the State, we seem to have statutory authority for the holding that the State is 'His Majesty'. The way out of this mess, for mess it is, lies in a perception of the fact, for fact it is, that our sovereign lord is not a 'corporation sole', but is the head of a complex and highly organised 'corporation aggregate of many' – of very many. I see no great harm in calling this corporation a Crown. But a better word has lately returned to the statute book. That word is Commonwealth.

Even if the king would have served as a satisfactory debtor for the national debt, some new questions would have been raised in the course of that process which has been called the expansion of England; for colonies came into being which had public debts of their own. At this point it is well for us to remember that three colonies which were exceptionally important

[30] *Dixon* v. *London Small Arms Co.*, L.R. 1 App. Cas. 632, at 652.

[31] The Acts which enable the king to hold 'private estates' are officially indexed under 'Crown Private Estates'. It is hard to defend this use of the word unless the Crown is to give garden parties.

[32] *Mersey Docks Trustees* v. *Gibbs*, L.R. 1 H. L. 93, III. The italics, it need hardly be said, are mine.

[33] Pensions (Colonial Service) Act, 1887, 50 & 51 Vict. c. 13, s. 8.

on account of their antiquity and activity, namely Massachusetts, Rhode Island, and Connecticut, were corporations duly created by charter with a sufficiency of operative and inoperative words. Also we may notice that the king was no more a corporator of Rhode Island than he was a corporator of the city of Norwich or of the East India Company, and that the Governor of Connecticut was as little a deputy of the king as was the Governor of the Bank of England. But even where there was a royal governor, and where there was no solemnly created corporation, there was a 'subject' capable of borrowing money and contracting debts. At least as early as 1709, and I know not how much earlier, bills of credit were being emitted which ran in this form:

> This indented bill of – shillings due from the Colony of New York to the possessor thereof shall be in value equal to money and shall be accepted accordingly by the Treasurer of this Colony for the time being in all public payments and for any fund at any time in the Treasury. Dated, New York the first of November, 1709, by order of the Lieutenant Governor, Council and General Assembly of the said Colony.[34]

In 1714 the Governor, Council and General Assembly of New York passed a long Act 'for the paying and discharging the several debts and sums of money claimed as debts of this Colony'. A preamble stated that some of the debts of the Colony had not been paid because the Governors had misapplied and extravagantly expended 'the revenue given by the loyal subjects aforesaid to Her Majesty and Her Royal Predecessors, Kings and Queens of England, sufficient for the honourable as well as necessary support of their Government here'. 'This Colony,' the preamble added, 'in strict justice is in no manner of way obliged to pay many of the said claims'; however, in order 'to restore the Publick Credit', they were to be paid.[35] Here we have a Colony which can be bound even in strict justice to pay money. What the great colonies did the small colonies did also. In 1697 an Act was passed at Montserrat 'for raising a Levy or Tax for defraying the Publick Debts of this His Majesty's Island'.

The Colonial Assemblies imitated the Parliament of England. They voted supplies to 'His Majesty'; but they also appropriated those supplies. In Colonial Acts coming from what we may call an ancient date and from places which still form parts of the British Empire, we may see a good

[34] Act of 12 Nov. 1709 (8 Anne).
[35] Act of 1714 (13 Anne).

deal of care taken that whatever is given to the king shall be marked with a trust. For instance, in the Bermudas, when in 1698 a penalty is imposed, half of it is given to the informer, 'and the remainder to His Majesty, His Heirs and Successors, to be imployed for and towards the support of the Government of these Islands and the contingent charges thereof'.[36] If 'the old house and kitchen belonging to their Majesties [William and Mary] and formerly inhabited by the Governors of these Islands' is to be sold, then the price is to be paid 'into the Publick Stock or Revenue for the Publick Uses of these Islands and the same to be paid out by Order of the Governor, Council and a Committee of Assembly'.[37] It would, I believe, be found that in some colonies in which there was no ancestral tradition of republicanism, the Assemblies were not far behind the House of Commons in controlling the expenditure of whatever money was voted to the king. In 1753 the Assembly of Jamaica resolved 'that it is the inherent and undoubted right of the Representatives of the People to raise and apply monies for the services and exigencies of government and to appoint such person or persons for the receiving and issuing thereof as they shall think proper, which right this House hath exerted and will always exert in such manner as they shall judge most conducive to the service of His Majesty and the interest of his People'. In many or most of the colonies the treasurer was appointed, not by the Governor but by an Act of Assembly; sometimes he was appointed by a mere resolution of the House of Representatives. In the matter of finance, 'responsible government' (as we now call it) or 'a tendency of the legislature to encroach upon the proper functions of the executive' (as some modern Americans call it) is no new thing in an English colony.[38]

We deny nowadays that a Colony is a corporation. The three unquestionably incorporated colonies have gone their own way and are forgotten of lawyers. James L. J. once said that it seemed to him an abuse of language to speak of the Governor and Government of New Zealand as a corporation.[39] So be it, and I should not wish to see a 'Governor' or a

---

[36] Act of 11 Nov. 1698. Acts of the British Parliament (e.g. 6 Geo. II, c. 13, s. 3) sometimes give a penalty to the use of the king 'to be applied for the support of the government of the colony or plantation in which the same shall be recovered'. See Palfrey, *New England*, IV. 302. Apparently it was over a clause of this kind that James Otis first came to the front in Massachusetts.

[37] Act of 29 Sept. 1693.

[38] See Mr E. B. Greene's very interesting book on the Provincial Governor, Harvard Historical Series; especially p. 177 ff. The Jamaican resolution stands on p. 172.

[39] *Sloman v. Government of New Zealand*, 1 C.P.D. 563.

'Government' incorporated. But can we – do we really and not merely in words – avoid an admission that the Colony of New Zealand is a person? In the case that was before the Court a contract for the conveyance of emigrants had professedly been made between 'Her Majesty the Queen for and on behalf of the Colony of New Zealand' of the first part, Mr Featherston, 'the agent-general in England for the Government of New Zealand', of the second part, and Sloman and Co. of the third part. Now when in a legal document we see those words 'for and on behalf of' we generally expect that they will be followed by the name of a person; and I cannot help thinking that they were so followed in this case. I gather that some of the colonies have abandoned the policy of compelling those who have aught against them to pursue the ancient, if royal, road of a petition of right. Perhaps we may not think wholly satisfactory the Australian device of a 'nominal defendant' appointed to resist an action in which a claim is made 'against the Colonial Government', for there is no need for 'nominal' parties to actions where real parties (such, for example, as a Colony or State) are forthcoming.[40] But it is a wholesome sight to see 'the Crown' sued[41] and answering for its torts.[42] If the field that sends cases to the Judicial Committee is not narrowed, a good many old superstitions will be put upon their trial.

In the British North America Act, 1867, there are courageous words.[43] 'Canada shall be liable for the debts and liabilities of each Province existing at the Union. Ontario and Quebec conjointly shall be liable to Canada . . . The assets enumerated in the fourth schedule . . . shall be the property of Ontario and Quebec conjointly. Nova Scotia shall be liable to Canada . . . New Brunswick shall be liable to Canada . . . The several Provinces shall retain all their respective public property . . . New Brunswick shall receive from Canada . . . The right of New Brunswick to levy the lumber duties . . . No lands or property belonging to Canada or any Province shall be liable to taxation . . .' This is the language of statesmanship, of the statute book, and of daily life. But then comes the lawyer with theories in his head, and begins by placing a legal estate in what he calls the Crown or Her Majesty. 'In construing these enactments, it must always be kept in view that wherever public land with its incidents is described as "the property of" or as "belonging to" the Dominion or a Province, these expressions

---

[40] *Farnell* v. *Bowman*, 12 App. Cas. 643 (N. S. Wales).
[41] *Hettihewage Siman Appu* v. *The Queen's Advocate*, 9 App. Cas. 571 (Ceylon).
[42] *A. G. of the Straits Settlement* v. *Wemyss*, 13 App. Cas. 192 (Penang).
[43] 30 Vict. c. 3, ss. 110–25.

merely import that the right to its beneficial use, or to its proceeds, has been appropriated to the Dominion or the Province, as the case may be, and is subject to the control of its legislature, the land itself being vested in the Crown'.[44] And so we have to distinguish the lands vested in the Crown 'for' or 'in right of' Canada from the lands vested in the Crown 'for' or 'in right of' Quebec or Ontario or British Columbia, or between lands 'vested in the Crown as represented by the Dominion' and lands 'vested in the Crown as represented by a Province'. Apparently 'Canada' or 'Nova Scotia' is person enough to be the Crown's *cestui que trust* and at the same time the Crown's representative, but is not person enough to hold a legal estate. It is a funny jumble, which becomes funnier still if we insist that the Crown is a legal fiction.

'Although the Secretary of State [for India] is a body corporate, or in the nature of a body corporate, for the purpose of contracts, and of suing and being sued, yet he is not a body corporate for the purpose of holding property. Such property as formerly vested, or would have vested, in the East India Company now vests in the Crown'.[45] So we sue Person No. 1, who has not and cannot have any property, in order that we may get at a certain part of the property that is owned by Person No. 2. It is a strange result; but not perhaps one at which we ought to stand amazed, if we really believe that both these Persons, however august, are fictitious: fictitious like the common vouchee and the casual ejector.[46]

We are not surprised when we read the following passage in an American treatise:

> Each one of the United States in its organized political capacity, although it is not in the proper use of the term a corporation, yet it has many of the essential faculties of a corporation, a distinct name, indefinite succession, private rights, power to sue, and the like. Corporations, however, as the term is used in our jurisprudence, do not include States, but only derivative creations, owing their existence

---

[44] *St Catharine's Milling and Lumber Co.* v. *The Queen*, 14 App. Cas. 46. esp. p. 56; *A.–G. of Brit. Columbia* v. *A.–G. of Canada*, 14 App. Cas. 295; *A.–G. of Ontario* v. *Mercer*, 8 App. Cas. 767; *A.–G. of Canada* v. *As.–Gs. of Ontario, Quebec, Nova Scotia* [1898], App. Cas. 700.

[45] Ilbert, *Government of India*, p. 173.

[46] In *Kinlock* v. *Secretary of State for India in Council*, 15 Ch. D. 1, 8, James L. J. said that 'there really is in point of law, no such person or body politic whatever as the Secretary of State for India in Council'. Apparently in his view this is only a name by which 'the Government of India' is to sue and be sued. But this only has the effect of making 'the Government of India' a person, real or fictitious. [The report of the final appeal to the House of Lords, 7 App. Cas. 619, adds nothing on this head.]

and powers to the State, acting through its legislative department. Like corporations, however, a State, as it can make contracts and suffer wrongs, so it may, for this reason and without express provision, maintain in its corporate name actions to enforce its rights and redress its injuries.[47]

There are some phrases in this passage which imply a disputable theory.[x] However, the main point is that the American State is, to say the least, very like a corporation: it has private rights, power to sue and the like. This seems to me the result to which English law would naturally have come, had not that foolish parson led it astray. There is nothing in this idea that is incompatible with hereditary kingship. 'The king and his subjects together compose the corporation, and he is incorporated with them and they with him, and he is the head and they are the members.'[48]

There is no cause for despair when 'the people of New South Wales, Victoria, South Australia, Queensland and Tasmania, humbly relying on the blessing of Almighty God, have agreed to unite in one indissoluble Federal Commonwealth under the Crown of the United Kingdom of Great Britain and Ireland'. We may miss the old words that were used of Connecticut and Rhode Island: 'one body corporate and politic in fact and name'; but 'united in a Federal Commonwealth under the name of the Commonwealth of Australia' seems amply to fill their place.[49] And a body politic may be a member of another body politic.

But we must return from an expanding Empire, or rather Commonwealth, to that thin little thought the corporation sole, and we may inquire whether it has struck root, whether it has flourished, whether it is doing us any good.

Were there at the beginning of the nineteenth century more than two corporations sole that were not ecclesiastical? Coke had coupled the Chamberlain of the City of London with the King.[50] But the class of corporations sole was slow to grow, and this seems to me a sure proof that the idea was sterile and unprofitable. It is but too likely that I have missed some instances,[51] but provisionally I will claim the third place in the list

---

[47] Dillon, *Municipal Corporations*, ed. 4, § 31.
[48] *Plowden*, p. 234.
[49] 63 & 64 Vict. c. 12.
[50] *Fulwood's* case, 4 *Rep.* 64 b.
[51] The Master of the Rolls (who, however, as a matter of history, was not quite free from an ecclesiastical taint) must have been not unlike a corporation sole, for he held land in right of his office. 12 Car. II, c. 36; 20 Geo. II, c. 34 (Sir J. Jekyll granted leases to a trustee for himself).

for the Postmaster-General. In 1840 the Postmaster-General and his successors 'is and are' made 'a body corporate' for the purpose of holding and taking conveyances and leases of lands and hereditaments for the service of the Post Office. From the Act that effected this incorporation we may learn that the Postmaster as a mere individual had been holding land in trust for the Crown.[52] One of the main reasons, I take it, for erecting some new corporations sole was that our 'Crown', being more or less identifiable with the King, it was difficult to make the Crown a leaseholder or copyholder in a direct and simple fashion. The Treasurer of Public Charities was made a corporation sole in 1853.[53] Then in 1855 the Secretary of State intrusted with the seals of the War Department was enabled to hold land as a corporation sole.[54] Perhaps if there were a Lord High Admiral he would be a corporation sole *vel quasi* ('of sorts').[55] The Solicitor to the Treasury was made a corporation sole in 1876, and this corporation sole can hold 'real and personal property of every description'.[56] All this – and there is more to be said of Boards such as the Board of Trade and the Board of Agriculture and so forth – seems to me to be the outcome of an awkward endeavour to ignore the personality of the greatest body corporate and politic that has ever existed. And after all, we must ask whether this device does its work. The throne, it is true, is never vacant, for the kingship is entailed and inherited. But we have yet to be taught that the Solicitor to the Treasury never dies. When a Postmaster-General dies, what becomes of the freehold of countless post offices? If we pursue the ecclesiastical analogy – and it is the only analogy – we must let the freehold fall into abeyance, for, when all is said, our corporation sole is a man who dies.[57]

Suppose that a prisoner is indicted for stealing a letter being the proper goods of 'the Postmaster-General', and suppose that he objects that at the time in question there was no Postmaster-General, he can be silenced; but this is so, not because the Postmaster is a corporation sole, but because a statute seems to have said with sufficient clearness that the indictment is good.[58] So long as the State is not seen to be a person, we must either make an unwarrantably free use of the King's name, or else we must for ever be

---

[52] 3 & 4 Vict. c. 96, s. 67.
[53] 16 & 17 Vict. c. 137, s. 47.
[54] 18 & 19 Vict. c. 117, s. 2.
[55] 27 & 28 Vict. c. 57, s. 9.
[56] 39 & 40 Vict. c. 18, s. 1.
[57] See *L.Q.R.* XVI. 352.
[58] 7 Will. IV & 1 Vict. c. 36, s. 40; and see 11 & 12 Vict. c. 88, s. 5.

laboriously stopping holes through which a criminal might glide. A critical question would be whether the man who is Postmaster for the time being could be indicted for stealing the goods of the Postmaster, or whether the Solicitor to the Treasury could sue the man who happened to be the Treasury's Solicitor. Not until some such questions have been answered in the affirmative have we any reason for saying that the corporation sole is one person and the natural man another.[59]

I am aware of only one instance in which a general law, as distinguished from *privilegia* for this or that officer of the central government, has conferred the quality of sole-corporateness or corporate-soleness upon a class of office-holders. The exceptional case is that of the clerks of the peace.[60] This arrangement, made in 1858, was convenient because we did not and do not regard the justices of the peace as a corporation. But then so soon as the affairs of the counties were placed upon a modern footing by the Act of 1888,[xi] a corporation aggregate took the place of the corporation sole, and what had been vested in the clerk of the peace became vested in the county council. Such is the destined fate of all corporations sole.[61]

Notes

i In the sixth edition of Pollock's *First book of jurisprudence* (1929), he amended the last sentence of this quotation to run as follows: 'In England we now say that the Crown is a corporation, thought this is an innovation made in an age of pedantry, and seems to be of no real use. The conception of this or any other permanent representation of the State had not been formed at all in the earlier Middle Ages, when the king's peace died with him and "every man that could forthwith robbed another".' (pp. 121–2.) This change is evidence that Pollock had taken on board some of the arguments of 'The Crown as corporation'.

ii You shall quickly be parsonified,
 Conjugally matrimonified,
 By a doctor of Divinity
 Who is located in this vicinity . . .

        Gilbert and Sullivan, *The Pirates of Penzance.*

[59] See *L.Q.R. XVI.* 355.
[60] 21 & 22 Vict. c. 92. But this Act does not use the term *corporation sole.*
[61] 51 & 52 Vict. c. 41, s. 64. We do not find it necessary to use mysterious language about the corporateness of every public accountant. But when such an accountant dies the balance to his credit at the bank where the public account is kept is not 'in any manner subject to the control of his legal representative'. See 29 & 30 Vict. c. 39, s. 18.

iii Treating the Crown as 'under age' or as though a 'minor' is comparable to the doctrine that the 'The church is always taken to be a minor' (*Ecclesia fungitur vice minoris*) discussed in 'The corporation sole' [see above, p. 19].

iv In fact Hobbes's text does not entirely follow the logic of the frontispiece of *Leviathan* and describes the sovereign not as the head but as the 'soul' of the body politic: 'For the Soveraign, is the publique Soule, giving Life and Motion to the Commonwealth; which expiring, the Members are governed by it no more, than the Carcasse of a man, by his departed (though Immortall) Soule.' (T. Hobbes, *Leviathan*, ed. R. Tuck (Cambridge: Cambridge University Press [1651], 1996), p. 230.)

v The controversy revolved around the question of whether Hales's estate was forfeit at the moment he took his life or only from the point at which the estate was granted by the king to another person (as the forfeit of a suicide). It therefore became a question of whether the punishment was of the living man or of the dead. This was the point at issue in the action *Hales v. Petit* brought by his widow, concerning trespass on his estate after his death but before the official regranting of his land. Plowden discussed the case in his *Commentaries*: 'Sir James Hales was dead, and how came he to his death? It may be answered by drowning; and who drowned him? – Sir James Hales; and when did he drown him? – in his lifetime. So that Sir James Hales being alive caused Sir James Hales to die; and the act of a living man was the death of a dead man. And then after this offence it is reasonable to punish the living man who committed the offence and not the dead man. But how can he be said to be punished alive when the punishment comes after his death? Sir, this can be done no other way but by divesting out of him, from the time of the act done in his life which was the cause of his death, the title and property of those things which he had in his lifetime.' This case was almost certainly the point of reference in Shakespeare's use of 'crowner' and 'crowner's-quest law' in *Hamlet*, Act V, Scene I:

> 1st CLOWN Is she to be buried in Christian burial that willfully seeks her own salvation?
>
> 2nd CLOWN I tell thee, she is; and therefore make her grave straight: the crowner hath sate on her, and finds it Christian burial.
>
> 1st CLOWN How can that be, unless she drowned herself in her own defence?
>
> 2nd CLOWN Why, 'tis found so.
>
> 1st CLOWN It must be *se offendendo*; it cannot be else. For here lies the point: If I drown myself wittingly, it argues an act: an act hath three branches; it is, to act, to do and to perform: argal, she drowned herself wittingly.

49

2st CLOWN Nay, but hear you, goodman delver.

1st CLOWN Give me leave. Here lies the water; good: here stands the man; good: If the man go to this water, and drown himself, it is, will he, nill he, he goes; mark you that? but if the water come to him, and drown him, he drowns not himself; argal, he, that is not guilty of his own death, shortens his own life.

2st CLOWN But is this law?

1st CLOWN Ay, marry is't; crowner's-quest law.

The question of whether and how Shakespeare would have been familiar with Plowden is discussed in chapter 2 of E. H. Kantorowicz, *The king's two bodies. A study in medieval political theology* (Princeton: Princeton University Press, 1957).

vi A. W. Kinglake, *The invasion of the Crimea*, 8 volumes (London, 1863–87).

vii Hobbes's *Leviathan*, which exemplifies many of the ambiguities of the theory of the king's two persons – 'And whereas every man, or assembly that hath Soveraignty, representeth two persons, or (as the more common phrase is) has two Capacities, one Naturall, and another Politique' (Hobbes, *Leviathan*, p. 166) – is adamant on this point. 'The setting forth of Publique Land', Hobbes writes, 'or of any certain revenue for the Commonwealth, is in vaine; and tendeth to the dissolution of Government' (*ibid.*, p. 173). Hobbes's reasoning illustrates the tenuousness of the theory of the two persons: 'And whereas in *England*, there were by the Conqueror, divers Lands reserved to his own use, (besides Forests, and Chases, either for his recreation, or for the preservation of Woods,) and divers services reserved on the Land he gave his Subjects; yet it seems they were not reserved for his Maintenance as in his Publique, but as in his Naturall capacity; For he, and his Successors did for all that lay Arbitrary Taxes on all the Subjects Land, when they judged it necessary. Or if those publique Lands, and Services, were ordained as a sufficient maintenance of the Common-wealth, it was contrary to the scope of the Institution; being (as it appeared by those ensuing Taxes) insufficient, and (as it appears by the late small Revenue of the Crown) Subject to Alienation, and Diminuition. It is therefore in vaine, to assign a portion to the Common-wealth; which may sell, or give it away; and does sell, and give it away when tis done by their Representative.' (*Ibid.*)

viii This is a reference to Charles II's 'Stop of the Exchequer' of 1672. He had borrowed £13,000 from the goldsmiths and pledged the security of royal revenue. In shutting the Exchequer to them Charles was refusing to repay the principal debt and would only pay the interest. This is discussed by Maitland in more detail in *The constitutional history of England* (Cambridge: Cambridge University Press, 1908), pp. 438–9.

ix The 'Consolidated Fund' came into existence after the creation of Consolidated Annuities in 1751 (usually known as 'consols'). These bonds, in contrast to those that had preceded them, were perpetual (the longest previous bonds had been issued on a ninety-nine year term). The Consolidated Fund brought together the funds needed to service these bonds in perpetuity, and did this with sufficient efficiency and transparency to make the consol a benchmark of financial security for much of its history. By the First World War consols made up 90 per cent of Britain's national debt. However, by the end of the war that figure had fallen to 5% as the government fell back on the necessary expedient of short-term loans. The consol re-established some of its status during the inter-war years, but after the Second World War, consols counted for less than one percent of the total debt that the British state owed.

x That is, the phrases 'Corporations . . . as the term is used in our jurisprudence, do not include States, but only derivative creations, owing their existence and powers to the State, acting through its legislative department', imply not only the 'Fiction theory' but also the 'Concession theory', which is a variant of it, and which insists that corporate personality depends in each instance on the explicit sanction of the sovereign. The Concession theory was particularly associated with the German Romanist Friedrich Karl von Savigny (1779–1861), against whose work the Germanism of Gierke and others was in part a reaction.

xi The Local Government Act of 1888 established county councils for England and Wales.

3

The Unincorporate Body

Of the Taff Vale Case we are likely to hear a good deal for some time to come. The trade unions are not content; there will be agitation; perhaps there will be legislation.[i]

To one reader of English history and of English law it seems that certain broad principles of justice and jurisprudence are involved in and may be evolved from the debate: certain broad principles which extend far beyond the special interests of masters and workmen. Will he be able to persuade others that this is so? Can he assign to this Taff Vale Case its place in a long story?

Of late years under American teaching we have learned to couple together the two terms 'corporations' and 'trusts'. In the light of history we may see this as a most instructive conjunction. And yet an apprentice of English law might well ask what the law of trusts has to do with the law of corporations. Could two topics stand farther apart from each other in an hypothetical code? Could two law-books have less in common than Grant on Corporations and Lewin on Trusts?[ii]

To such questions English history replies that, none the less, a branch of the law of trusts became a supplement for the law of corporations, and some day when English history is adequately written one of the most interesting and curious tales that it will have to tell will be that which brings trust and corporation into intimate connexion with each other.

A few words about the general law of trusts may not be impertinent even though they say nothing that is new. The idea of trust is so familiar to us all that we never wonder at it. And yet surely we ought to wonder. If we were asked what is the greatest and most distinctive achievement performed by Englishmen in the field of jurisprudence I cannot think that we should have any better answer to give than this, namely, the development from century to century of the trust idea.

'I do not understand your trust', these words have been seen in a letter written by a very learned German historian familiar with law of all sorts and kinds.

Where lies the difficulty? In the terms of a so-called 'general jurisprudence' it seems to lie here: – A right which in ultimate analysis appears to be *ius in personam* (the benefit of an obligation) has been so treated that for practical purposes it has become equivalent to *ius in rem* and is habitually thought of as a kind of ownership, 'equitable ownership.' Or put it thus: – If we are to arrange English law as German law is arranged in the new code[iii] we must present to our law of trust a dilemma: it must place itself under one of two rubrics; it must belong to the Law of Obligations or to the Law of Things. In sight of this dilemma it reluctates and recalcitrates. It was made by men who had no Roman law as explained by medieval commentators in the innermost fibres of their minds.

To say much of the old feoffment to uses would be needless. Only we will note that for a long time the only and for a longer time the typical subject-matter of a trust is a piece of land or some incorporeal thing, such as an advowson, which is likened to a piece of land. For trusts of movable goods there was no great need. The common law about bailments was sufficient. We may indeed see these two legal concepts deriving from one source: the source that is indicated in Latin by *ad opus*, in old French by *al oes*, in English by 'to the use'. In the one case however a channel is cut by the Courts of Common Law and the somewhat vague *al oes* explicates itself in a law of bailments and agency, while in the other the destined channel must be cut, if at all, by a new court since the law of rights in land has already attained a relatively high stage of development and finds its expression in an elaborate scheme of writs and formal actions. For the purposes of comparative jurisprudence it is of some importance to observe that though for a long time past our trust idea – the idea of trust strictly and technically so called – has been extended to things of all sorts and kinds, still were it not for trusts of land we should hardly have come by trusts of other things. The ideas of bailment, agency, guardianship, might have shown themselves capable of performing all that was reasonably necessary. Foreigners manage to live without trusts. They must.

In the fourteenth century when feoffments to uses were becoming common, the most common of all instances seems to have been the feoffment to the feoffor's own use. The landowner enfeoffed some of his friends as joint tenants hoping for one thing that by keeping the legal ownership in joint tenants and placing new feoffees in vacant gaps no demand could ever be made by the feudal lord for wardship or marriage, relief or escheat, and hoping for another thing that the feoffees would observe his last will and that so in effect he might acquire that testamentary power which the law denied him and which the eternal interest of his sinful soul made an object of keen desire.

Now between feoffor and feoffee in such a case there is agreement. We have only to say that there is contract and then the highly peculiar character of our trust will soon display itself. For let us suppose that we treat this relationship as a contract and ask what will follow.

Well (1) as between feoffor and feoffee how shall we enforce that contract? Shall we just give damages if and when the contract is broken or shall we decree specific performance on pain of imprisonment? Perhaps this difficulty was hardly felt, for it can, so I think, be amply shown that the idea of compelling a man specifically to perform a contract relating to land was old, and that what was new was the effectual pressure of threatened imprisonment. But (2) think of the relationship as contractual and how are we to conceive the right of the feoffor? It is the benefit of a contract. It is a chose in action at a time when a chose in action is inalienable. Also if we held tight by this conception there would be much to be said for holding that the use or trust is in all cases personal property. Then (3) there is great difficulty in holding that a contract can give rights to a third person. We in England feel that difficulty now-a-days. Foreign lawyers and legislatures are surmounting it. We should have had to surmount it, had it not been for our trust. But from an early time, we find that the action, or rather the suit, is given to the destinatory, the beneficiary, the *cestui que use* as we call him, and indeed if the trustor can enforce the trust this will only be so because in the particular case he is the destinatory. And then (4) arises the all important question as to the validity of the beneficiary's right against purchasers from the trustee and against the trustee's creditors. Think steadily of that right as the benefit of a contract and you will find it hard to say why it should be enforced against one who was no party to the contract.

We know what happened. No sooner has the Chancellor got to work than he seems bent on making these 'equitable' rights as unlike mere *iura in personam* and as like *iura in rem* as he can possibly make them. The ideas that he employs for this purpose are not many; they are English; certainly they are not derived from any knowledge of Roman law with which we may think fit to equip him. On the one hand as regards what we might call the internal character of these rights, the analogies of the common law are to be strictly pursued. A few concessions may be made in favour of greater 'flexibility' but on the whole there is to be a law of equitable estates in land which is a mere replica of the law of legal estates. There are to be estates in fee simple, estates in fee tail, terms of years, remainders, reversions and the rest of it: the equitable estate tail (this is a good example) is to be barred by an equitable recovery.[iv] Then as regards the external side of the matter, 'good conscience' becomes the active principle; a conscience that can be opposed to strict law. The trust is to be enforced against all whose conscience is to be 'affected' by it. Class after class of persons is brought within the range of this idea. The purchaser who for value obtains ownership from the trustee must himself become a trustee if at the time of the purchase he knew of the trust, for it is unconscionable to buy what you know to be another's 'in equity.' Then the purchaser who did not know of the trust must be bound by it if he ought to have known of it: that is to say, if he would have known of it had he made such investigation of his vendor's title as a prudent purchaser makes in his own interest. It remains to screw up this standard of diligence higher and higher, until the purchaser who has obtained a legal estate *bona fide* for value and without notice, express or implied, of the equitable right, is an extremely rare and extremely lucky person. And apparently he is now the only person who can hold the land and yet ignore the trust. It was not so always. The lord who came to the land by escheat came to it with a clear conscience. Also we read in our old books that a use cannot be enforced against a corporation because a corporation has no conscience. But in the one case a statute has come to the rescue and in the other we have rejected the logical consequence of a certain speculative theory of corporations to which we still do lip-service.[v] The broad result is that we habitually think of the beneficiary's right as practically equivalent to full ownership, and the instances of rare occurrence in which a purchaser can ignore it seem almost anomalous. And in passing it may be noticed that such danger as there is falls to absolute zero in a class of cases of which we are to speak hereafter. No one will ever be heard to say that he has purchased without notice of a trust a building that was vested in trustees but was fitted up as a club-house, a Jewish synagogue, a Roman catholic cathedral.

Even that is not quite all. Even when the Court of Equity could not give the *cestui que trust* the very thing that was the original subject-matter of the trust it has struggled hard to prevent its darling from falling into the ruck of unsecured creditors of a defaulting trustee. It has allowed him to pursue a 'reified' trust-fund from investment to investment: in other words, to try to find some thing for which the original thing has been exchanged by means of a longer or shorter series of exchanges. That idea of the trust-fund which is dressed up (invested) now as land and now as current coin, now as shares and now as debentures seems to me one of the most remarkable ideas developed by modern English jurisprudence. How we have worked that metaphor! May not one have a vested interest in a fund that is vested in trustees who have invested it in railway shares. Even a Philosophy of Clothes stands aghast.[vi] However, the main point is that *cestui que trust* is magnificently protected.

Now I cannot but think that there is one large part of this long story of the trust that ordinarily goes untold. The student is expected to learn something about feoffments to uses and the objects that were gained thereby, something about the Chancellor's interposition, something about the ambitious statute that added three words to a conveyance;[vii] but no sooner is King Henry outwitted, no sooner is the Chancellor enforcing the secondary use, than the law of uses and trusts becomes a highly technical matter having for its focus the family settlement with its trustees to preserve contingent remainders, its name and arms clauses, its attendant terms and so forth. Very curious and excellent learning it all is, and in some sort still necessary to be known at least in outline; still we are free to say that some of the exploits that the trust performed in this quarter are not admirable in modern eyes, and at any rate it seems to me a misfortune that certain other and much less questionable exploits pass unnoticed by those books whence beginners obtain their first and their most permanent notions of legal history.

First and last the trust has been a most powerful instrument of social experimentation. To name some well-known instances: It (in effect) enabled the landowner to devise his land by will until at length the legislature had to give way, though not until a rebellion had been caused and crushed.[viii] It (in effect) enabled a married woman to have property that was all her own until at length the legislature had to give way. It (in effect) enabled men to form joint-stock companies with limited liability, until at length the legislature had to give way. The case of the married woman is specially instructive. We see a prolonged experiment. It is deemed a great success. And at last it becomes impossible to maintain (in effect) one law for the poor and another for the rich, since, at least in general estimation, the tried and well-known 'separate use' has been working well. Then on the other hand let us observe how impossible it would have been for the most courageous Court of Common Law to make or to suffer any experimentation in this quarter.

Just to illustrate the potency of the trust in unexpected quarters we might mention an employment of it which at one time threatened radically to change the character of the national church. Why should not an advowson be vested in trustees upon trust to present such clerk as the parishioners shall choose? As a matter of fact this was done in a not inconsiderable number of cases and we may even see Queen Elizabeth herself taking part in such a transaction.[1] Had a desire for ministers elected by their congregations become general among conformists, the law was perfectly ready to carry out their wishes. The fact that parishioners are no corporation raised no difficulty.

But there are two achievements of the trust which in social importance and juristic interest seem to eclipse all the rest. The trust has given us a liberal substitute for a law about personified institutions. The trust has given us a liberal supplement for a necessarily meagre law of corporations. The social importance of these movements will appear by and by. The juristic interest might perhaps escape us if we could not look abroad.

We in England say that persons are natural or artificial, and that artificial persons are corporations aggregate or corporations sole. A foreign lawyer would probably tell us that such a classification of persons will hardly cover the whole ground that in these days has to be covered: at all events he would tell us this if he knew how little good we get out of our corporation sole – a queer creature that is always turning out to be a mere mortal man just when we have need of an immortal person. We should be asked by a German friend where we kept our *Anstalt* or *Stiftung*, our Institution or Foundation. And then we should be told that, though in particular cases it may be difficult to draw the line between the corporation and the institute, we certainly in modern times require some second class of juristic persons. This necessity we should see if, abolishing in thought our law of trusts, we asked what was to become of our countless 'charities'. Unless some feat of personification can be performed they must perish. Let the "charitable" purpose of Mr Styles be, for example, the distribution of annual doles among the deserving poor of Pedlington, an incorporation of the deserving poor is obviously out of the question, and therefore we must either tell Mr Styles that he cannot do what he wants to do or else we must definitely admit "Styles's Charity" into the circle of "persons

[1] *In re* St Stephen, Coleman Street, 39 Ch. Div. 492.

known to the law." In the latter case what will follow? What is likely to follow among men who have been taught the orthodox and cosmopolitan lore of the fictitious person? Surely this, that without the cooperation of the State no charitable institution can be created. And this doctrine is likely to endure even in days when the State is relaxing its hold over the making of corporations and learned men are doubting the fictitiousness of the corporation's personality. Hear the new German Code: – "Zur Entstehung einer rechtsfähigen Stiftung ist ausser dem Stiftungsgeschäfte die Genehmigung des Bundesstaats erforderlich, in dessen Gebiete die Stiftung ihren Sitz haben soll". Translate that into English ("An endowed institution, having legal status, is created by the act of endowment together with its confirmation by that state of the confederation within which the endowed institution is to be located"[ix]) and suppose it to have been always law in England. How the face of England is changed!

Our way of escape was the trust. Vest the lands, vest the goods in some man or men. The demand for personality is satisfied. The lands, the goods, have an owner: an owner to defend them and recover them: an owner behind whom a Court of Common Law will never look. All else is mere equity.

Apparently we slid quite easily into our doctrine of charitable trusts. We may represent the process as gradual; we might call it the evanescence of *cestui que trust*. Observe the following series of directions given to trustees of land: (1) to sell and divide the proceeds among the twelve poorest women of the parish: (2) to sell and divide the proceeds among the twelve women of the parish who in the opinion of my trustees shall be the most deserving: (3) annually to divide the rents and profits among the twelve poorest for the time being: (4) annually to divide the rents and profits among the twelve who are most deserving in the opinion of the trustees. The bodily "owners in equity" who are apparent enough in the first of these cases seem to fade out of sight as small changes are made in the wording of the trust. When they disappear from view, what, let us ask, do they leave behind them?

Well, they leave "a charity" and perhaps no more need be said. If we must have a theory I do not think that any good will come of introducing the Crown or the Attorney-General, the State or the Public, for, although it be established in course of time that the Attorney-General is a necessary party to suits concerning the administration of the trust, still we do not think of Crown or Attorney-General, State or Public as "beneficial owner" of the lands that are vested in the trustees of Nokes's charity, and trustees are not to be multiplied *praeter necessitatem* ("beyond necessity"). Nor do I think that we personify the "charity": it cannot sue or be sued. Apparently our thought would be best expressed by saying that in these cases there is no 'equitable owner' and that the accomplishment of a purpose has taken the place of *cestui que trust*. Our rule that the place of *cestui que trust* cannot be taken by a "non-charitable" purpose – a rule that has not been always rigorously observed[2] – has not acted as a very serious restraint upon the desires of reasonable persons, so exceedingly wide from first to last has been our idea of "charity".

Now no doubt our free foundation of charitable institutions has had its dark side, and no doubt we discovered that some supervision by the State of the administration of charitable trust funds had become necessary, but let us observe that Englishmen in one generation after another have had open to them a field of social experimentation such as could not possibly have been theirs, had not the trustee met the law's imperious demand for a definite owner. Even if we held the extreme opinion that endowed charities have done more harm than good, it might well be said of us that we have learned this lesson in the only way it could be learnt.

And so we came by our English *Anstalt* or *Stiftung* without troubling the State to concede or deny the mysterious boon of personality. That was not an inconsiderable feat of jurisprudence. But a greater than that was performed. In truth and in deed we made corporations without troubling king or parliament though perhaps we said that we were doing nothing of the kind.

Probably as far back as we can trace in England any distinct theory of the corporation's personality or any assertion that this personality must needs have its origin in some act of sovereign power, we might trace also the existence of an unincorporated group to whose use land is held by feoffees. At any rate a memorable and misunderstood statute tells us that this was a common case in 1532. "Where by reason of feoffments . . . and assurances made of trusts of manors . . . and hereditaments to the use of parish churches, chapels, church-wardens, guilds, fraternities, comminalties, companies or brotherhoods erected or made of devotion or by common assent of the people without any corporation . . . there groweth and issueth to the King our Sovereign Lord, and to other lords and subjects of this realm the same like losses and inconveniences, and is [*sic*] as

---

[2] See *In re* Dean, 41 Ch. Div. 559: a trust for the comfortable maintenance of specific dogs and horses adjudged valid, though not charitable and not enforceable by any one. See however an article by J. C. Gray, 15 *Harv. L. Rev.* 509 on 'Gifts for a non-charitable purpose'.

much prejudicial to them as doth and is in case where lands be aliened into mortmain." Upon this recital follows a declaration that "all and every such uses, intents and purposes" that shall be declared or ordained after the 1st of March in 28 Henry VIII shall be utterly void in law if they extend beyond a term of twenty years. We know how Elizabethan lawyers construed this statute. They said that it struck at uses that were superstitious and not at such as were good and godly. We are better able than they are to trace the evolution of King Henry's abhorrence of superstition. In 1532 he was beginning to threaten the pope with a retention of annates, but he was no heretic and not even a schismatic; and indeed this very statute clearly contemplates the continued creation of obits provided that the trust does not exceed the limit of twenty years. The voice that speaks to us is not that of the Supreme Head upon earth of a purified church but that of a supreme landlord who is being done out of escheats and other commodities. I will not say but that there were some words in the Act which in the eyes of good and godly lawyers might confine its effect within narrow limits, but I also think that good and godly lawyers belonging as they did to certain already ancient and honourable societies for which lands were held in trust[x] must have felt that this statute had whistled very near their ears.

Notes

i The Taff Vale case is discussed in the Introduction (see above, p. xxiii). The legislation that did in the end follow was the Trades Disputes Act of 1906, which might or might not have surprised Maitland in the concessions it offered the trades unions, essentially cementing their identity as unincorporate bodies, whose agents did not incur the liability of the union when acting on its behalf. These immunities were secured following the general election of 1906, during the campaign for which the consequences of the Taff Vale judgment, generally seen as deleterious for the labour movement, were much ventilated, particularly by candidates for the ILP. The subsequent act would have confirmed Maitland in his view that in England *sozialpolitische* take precedence over *rechtswissenschaftliche* considerations [see below, 'Trust and corporation', p. 114]. The act of 1906 was a source of much controversy right up to the Thatcher years [see for example, A.V. Dicey, *Law and public opinion in Britain*, 2nd edition (London: Macmillan, 1914), Sidney and Beatrice Webb, *The history of trade unionism*, 2nd edition (London: Longmans, 1920), C. G. Hanson, 'From Taff Vale to Tebbit' in *1980s unemployment and the unions* by F. A. Hayek, 2nd edition (London: IEA, 1984).]

ii J. Grant, *A practical treatise on the law of corporations in general: as well aggregate as sole* (London, 1850); T. Lewin, *Law of Trust*, 10th edition (London, 1898).

iii The reference is to Germany's newly published civil code, the *Bürgerliches Gesetzbuch* of 1896. Otto von Gierke was closely involved in the drafting of this code, and remained critical of the Romanism of some of its final contents (see M. John, *Politics and law in late nineteenth-century Germany: the origins of the civil code* (Oxford: Oxford University Press, 1989), esp. pp. 108–16).

iv This is the parallel remedy provided by the chancellor in equity to the common law procedure of common recovery (see Glossary: common vouchee); hence a good example of the replication of common law procedures in equity.

v The conscienceless corporation is the logical consequence of the 'Fiction theory', which supposes that corporations cannot have conscience because they do not think or act for themselves.

vi This is a pun on the terms 'vest' and 'invest', whose legal sense derives from the original Latin meaning of *vestire*: 'to clothe'.

vii The three words were '*al oeps de*' ('to the use of') which enabled conveyancers to circumvent the Statute of Uses of 1536, thereby re-establishing that idea of trusteeship which Henry VIII had undermined in his effort to guarantee royal revenue from reliefs and escheats (see Glossary).

viii This is a reference to the Pilgrimage of Grace of 1536, one of the causes of which was the fact that the Statute of Uses had abolished wills of land.

ix This is the version given in *The civil code of the German Empire*, trans. W. Lowy (Boston and London, 1909) § 80.

x The reference is to the Inns of Court, whose case Maitland discusses in more detail in 'Trust and Corporation' (see below, pp. 106–7).

4

Moral Personality and Legal Personality

THE memory of Henry Sidgwick is not yet in need of revival. It lives a natural life among us, and will live so long as those who saw and heard him draw breath. Still the generations, as generations must be reckoned in this place, succeed each other rapidly, and already I may be informing, rather than reminding, some of you when I say that among his many generous acts was the endowment of a readership in English Law, of which one of his pupils was fortunate enough to be the first holder. If that pupil ventures to speak here this afternoon, it will not be unnatural that he should choose his theme from the borderland where ethical speculation marches with jurisprudence.

Ethics and Jurisprudence   That such a borderland exists all would allow, and, as usually happens in such cases, each of the neighbouring powers is wont to assert, in practice, if not in theory, its right to define the scientific frontier. We, being English, are, so I fancy, best acquainted with the claims of ethical speculation, and in some sort prejudiced in their favour. We are proud of a long line of moralists, which has not ended in Sidgwick and Martineau and Green, in Herbert Spencer and Leslie Stephen, and we conceive that the 'jurist', if indeed such an animal exists, plays, and of right ought to play, a subordinate, if not subservient, part in the delimitation of whatever moral sciences there may happen to be. I am not sure, however, that the poor lawyer with antiquarian tastes might not take his revenge by endeavouring to explain the moral philosopher as a legal phenomenon, and by classing our specifically English addiction to ethics as a by-product of the specifically English history of English law. That statement, if it be more than the mere turning of the downtrodden worm, is obviously too large, as it is too insolent, a text for an hour's lecture. What I shall attempt will be to indicate one problem of a speculative sort, which (so it seems to me) does not get the attention that it deserves from speculative Englishmen, and does not get that attention because it is shrouded from their view by certain peculiarities of the legal system in which they live.

The Natural Person and the Corporation Texts, however, I will have. My first is taken from Mr Balfour. Lately in the House of Commons the Prime Minister spoke of trade unions as corporations. Perhaps, for he is an accomplished debater, he anticipated an interruption. At any rate, a distinguished lawyer on the Opposition benches interrupted him with 'The trade unions are not corporations.' 'I know that', retorted Mr Balfour, 'I am talking English, not law.' A long story was packed into that admirable reply.[1]

And my second text is taken from Mr Dicey, who delivered the Sidgwick lecture last year. 'When', he said, 'a body of twenty, or two thousand, or two hundred thousand men bind themselves together to act in a particular way for some common purpose, they create a body, which by no fiction of law, but by the very nature of things, differs from the individuals of whom it is constituted.'[2] I have been waiting a long while for an English lawyer of Professor Dicey's eminence to say what he said – to talk so much 'English'. Let me repeat a few of his words with the stress where I should like it to lie: 'they create a body, which *by no fiction of law, but by the very nature of things*, differs from the individuals of whom it is constituted'. So says Blackstone's successor. Blackstone himself would, I think, have inverted that phrase, and would have ascribed to a fiction of law that phenomenon – or whatever we are to call it – which Mr Dicey ascribes to the very nature of things.

Now for a long time past the existence of this phenomenon has been recognised by lawyers, and the orthodox manner of describing it has been somewhat of this kind. Besides men or 'natural persons', law knows persons of another kind. In particular it knows the corporation, and for a multitude of purposes it treats the corporation very much as it treats the man. Like the man, the corporation is (forgive this compound adjective) a right-and-duty-bearing unit. Not all the legal propositions that are true of a man will be true of a corporation. For example, it can neither marry nor be given in marriage; but in a vast number of cases you can make a

---

[1] The *Standard*, April 23, 1904. *Mr Balfour:* 'The mere fact that funds can be used, or are principally used, for benefit purposes, is surely not of itself a sufficient reason for saying that trade unions, and trade unions alone, out of all the corporations in the country, commercial –' *Sir R. Reid:* 'The trade unions are not corporations.' *Mr Balfour:* 'I know; I am talking English, not law' (*cheers and laughter*).

[2] Professor Dicey's lecture on the Combination Laws is printed in *Harvard Law Review*, xvii, 511. See p. 513.

legal statement about *x* and *y* which will hold good whether these symbols stand for two men or for two corporations, or for a corporation and a man. The University can buy land from Downing, or hire the guildhall from the Town, or borrow money from the London Assurance; and we may say that *exceptis excipiendis* ('with the appropriate exceptions') a court of law can treat these transactions, these acts in the law, as if they took place between two men, between Styles and Nokes. But further, we have to allow that the corporation is in some sense composed of men, and yet between the corporation and one of its members there may exist many, perhaps most, of those legal relationships which can exist between two human beings. I can contract with the University: the University can contract with me. You can contract with the Great Northern Company as you can with the Great Eastern, though you happen to be a shareholder in the one and not in the other. In either case there stands opposite to you another right-and-duty-bearing unit – might I not say another individual? – a single 'not-yourself' that can pay damages or exact them. You expect results of this character, and, if you did not get them, you would think ill of law and lawyers. Indeed, I should say that, the less we know of law, the more confidently we Englishmen expect that the organised group, whether called a corporation or not, will be treated as person: that is, as right-and-duty-bearing unit.

Legal Orthodoxy and the Fictitious Person Perhaps I can make the point clearer by referring to an old case. We are told that in Edward IV's day the mayor and commonalty – or, as we might be tempted to say, the municipal corporation – of Newcastle gave a bond to the man who happened to be mayor, he being named by his personal name, and that the bond was held to be void because a man cannot be bound to himself.[3] The argument that is implicit in those few words seems to us quaint, if not sophistical. But the case does not stand alone; far from it. If our business is with medieval history and our aim is to re-think it before we re-present it, here lies one of our most serious difficulties. Can we allow the group – guild, town, village, nation – to stand over against each and all of its members as a distinct person? To be concrete, look at Midsummer

---

[3] Year Book, 21 Edw. IV, f. 68: 'Come fuit ajudgé en le cas del Maior de Newcastle ou le Maior et le Cominalty fist un obligation a mesme le person que fuit Maior par son propre nosme, et pur ceo que il mesme fuit Maior, et ne puit faire obligation a luy mesme, il [=l'obligation] fuit tenus voide.' Maitland also discusses this case in 'The corporation aggregate: the history of a legal idea' (see above, pp. xxxvi–xxxvii). There, though, he identifies the town in question as Norwich.

Common. It belongs, and, so far as we know, has always in some sense belonged, to the burgesses of Cambridge. But in what sense? Were they co-proprietors? Were they corporators? Neither – both?

I would not trouble you with medievalism. Only this by the way: If once you become interested in the sort of history that tries to unravel these and similar problems, you will think some other sorts of history rather superficial. Perhaps you will go the length of saying that much the most interesting person that you ever knew was *persona ficta*. But my hour flies.

To steer a clear or any course is hard, for controversial rocks abound. Still, with some security we may say that at the end of the Middle Age a great change in men's thoughts about groups of men was taking place, and that the main agent in the transmutation was Roman Law. Now just how the classical jurists of Rome conceived their *corpora* and *universitates* became in the nineteenth century a much debated question. The profane outsider says of the Digest what some one said of another book:

> *Hic liber est in quo quaerit sua dogmata quisque*
> *Invenit et pariter dogmata quisque sua.*[i]

Where people have tried to make antique texts do modern work, the natural result is what Mr Buckland has happily called 'Wardour Street Roman Law'.[4,ii] Still, of this I suppose there can be no doubt, that there could, without undue pressure, be obtained from the Corpus Juris a doctrine of corporations, which, so far as some main outlines are concerned, is the doctrine which has ruled the modern world. Nor would it be disputed that this work was done by the legists and canonists of the Middle Age, the canonists leading the way. The group can be a person: co-ordinated, equiparated, with the man, with the natural person.

With the 'natural' person – for the personality of the *universitas*, of the corporation, is not natural – it is fictitious. This is a very important part of the canonical doctrine, first clearly proclaimed, so we are told, by the greatest lawyer that ever sat upon the chair of St Peter, Pope Innocent IV. You will recall Mr Dicey's words: 'not by fiction of law, but by the very nature of things'. Invert those words, and you will have a dogma that works like leaven in the transformation of medieval society.

If the personality of the corporation is a legal fiction, it is the gift of the prince. It is not for you and me to feign and to force our fictions upon our neighbours. 'Only the prince may create by fiction what does

---

[4] Buckland, 'Wardour Street Roman Law', *Law Quarterly Review*, xvii, 179.

not exist in reality.'⁵ An argument drawn from the very nature of fictions thus came to the aid of less questionably Roman doctrines about the illicitness of all associations, the existence of which the prince has not authorised. I would not exaggerate the importance of a dogma, theological or legal. A dogma is of no importance unless and until there is some great desire within it. But what was understood to be the Roman doctrine of corporations was an apt lever for those forces which were transforming the medieval nation into the modern State. The federalistic structure of medieval society is threatened. No longer can we see the body politic as *communitas communitatum* ('a community of communities'), a system of groups, each of which in its turn is a system of groups. All that stands between the State and the individual has but a derivative and precarious existence.

Do not let us at once think of England. English history can never be an elementary subject: we are not logical enough to be elementary. If we must think of England, then let us remember that we are in the presence of a doctrine which in Charles II's day condemns all – yes, all – of the citizens of London to prison for 'presuming to act as a corporation'. We may remember also how corporations appear to our absolutist Hobbes as troublesome entozoa.ⁱⁱⁱ But it is always best to begin with France, and there, I take it, we may see the pulverising, macadamising tendency in all its glory, working from century to century, reducing to impotence, and then to nullity, all that intervenes between Man and State.

The State and the Corporation In this, as in some other instances, the work of the monarchy issues in the work of the revolutionary assemblies. It issues in the famous declaration of August 18, 1792: "A State that is truly free ought not to suffer within its bosom any corporation, not even such as, being dedicated to public instruction, have merited well of the country."⁶ That was one of the mottoes of modern absolutism: the absolute State faced the absolute individual. An appreciable part of the interest of the French Revolution seems to me to be open only to those who will be at pains to give a little thought to the theory of corporations. Take, for example, those memorable debates touching ecclesiastical property. To whom belong these broad lands when you have pushed fictions aside, when you have become a truly philosophical jurist with a craving for the natural? To the nation, which has stepped into the shoes of

---

⁵ Lucas de Penna, cited in Gierke, *Das deutsche Genossenschaftsrecht*, iii, 371.

⁶ 'Considérant qu'un État vraiment libre ne doit souffrir dans son sein aucune corporation, pas même celles qui, vouées à l'enseignement public, ont bien mérité de la patrie.'

the prince. That is at least a plausible answer, though an uncomfortable suspicion that the State itself is but a questionably real person may not be easily dispelled. And as with the churches, the universities, the trade guilds, and the like, so also with the communes, the towns and villages. Village property – there was a great deal of village property in France – was exposed to the dilemma: it belongs to the State, or else it belongs to the now existing villagers. I doubt we Englishmen, who never clean our slates, generally know how clean the French slate was to be.

Associations in France Was to be, I say. Looking back now, French lawyers can regard the nineteenth century as the century of association, and, if there is to be association, if there is to be group-formation, the problem of personality cannot be evaded, at any rate if we are a logical people. Not to mislead, I must in one sentence say, that even the revolutionary legislators spared what we call partnership, and that for a long time past French law has afforded comfortable quarters for various kinds of groups, provided (but notice this) that the group's one and only object was the making of pecuniary gain. Recent writers have noticed it as a paradox that the State saw no harm in the selfish people who wanted dividends, while it had an intense dread of the comparatively unselfish people who would combine with some religious, charitable, literary, scientific, artistic purpose in view. I cannot within my few minutes be precise, but at the beginning of this twentieth century it was still a misdemeanour to belong to any unauthorised *association* having more than twenty members. A licence from the prefect, which might be obtained with some ease, made the *association* non-criminal, made it licit; but personality – 'civil personality', as they say in France – was only to be acquired with difficulty as the gift of the central government.

Now I suppose it to be notorious that during the last years of the nineteenth century law so unfavourable to liberty of association was still being maintained, chiefly, if not solely, because prominent, typically prominent, among the *associations* known to Frenchmen stood the *congrégations* – religious houses, religious orders. The question how these were to be treated divided the nation, and at last, in 1901, when a new and very important law was made about 'the contract of association',[iv] a firm line was drawn between the nonreligious sheep and the religious goats. With the step then taken and the subsequent woes of the congregations I have here no concern; but the manner in which religious and other groups had previously been treated by French jurisprudence seems to me exceedingly instructive. It seems to me to prove so clearly that in a country where people take their legal theories seriously, a country where a Prime Minister will often talk law without ceasing to talk agreeable French, the question whether the group is to be, as we say, 'a person in the eye of the law' is the question whether the group as group can enjoy more than an uncomfortable and precarious existence. I am not thinking of attacks directed against it by the State. I am thinking of collisions between it and private persons. It lives at the mercy of its neighbours, for a law-suit will dissolve it into its constituent atoms. Nor is that all. Sometimes its neighbours will have cause to complain of its legal impersonality. They will have been thinking of it as a responsible right-and-duty-bearing unit, while at the touch of law it becomes a mere many, and a practically, if not theoretically, irresponsible many.

Group-Personality During the nineteenth century (so I understand the case) a vast mass of experience, French, German, Belgian, Italian, and Spanish (and I might add, though the atmosphere is hazier, English and American), has been making for a result which might be stated in more than one way. (1) If the law allows men to form permanently organised groups, those groups will be for common opinion right-and-duty-bearing units; and if the law-giver will not openly treat them as such, he will misrepresent, or, as the French say, he will 'denature' the facts: in other words, he will make a mess and call it law. (2) Group-personality is no purely legal phenomenon. The law-giver may say that it does not exist, where, as a matter of moral sentiment, it does exist. When that happens, he incurs the penalty ordained for those who ignorantly or wilfully say the thing that is not. If he wishes to smash a group, let him smash it, send the policeman, raid the rooms, impound the minute-book, fine, and imprison; but if he is going to tolerate the group, he must recognise its personality, for otherwise he will be dealing wild blows which may fall on those who stand outside the group as well as those who stand within it. (3) For the morality of common sense the group is person, is right-and-duty-bearing unit. Let the moral philosopher explain this, let him explain it as illusion, let him explain it away; but he ought not to leave it unexplained, nor, I think, will he be able to say that it is an illusion which is losing power, for, on the contrary, it seems to me to be persistently and progressively triumphing over certain philosophical and theological prejudices.

You know that classical distribution of Private Law under three grand rubrics – Persons, Things, Actions. Half a century ago the first of these three titles seemed to be almost vanishing from civilised jurisprudence. No longer was there much, if anything, to be said of exceptional classes, of nobles, clerics, monks, serfs, slaves, excommunicates or outlaws. Children there might always be, and lunatics; but women had been freed from tutelage. The march of the progressive societies was, as we all know, from status to contract. And now? And now that forlorn old title is wont to introduce us to ever new species and new genera of persons, to vivacious controversy, to teeming life; and there are many to tell us that the line of advance is no longer from status to contract, but through contract to something that contract cannot explain, and for which our best, if an inadequate, name is the personality of the organised group.

Fact or Fiction? Theorising, of course, there has been. I need not say so, nor that until lately it was almost exclusively German. Our neighbours' conception of the province of jurisprudence[v] has its advantages as well as its disadvantages. On the one hand, ethical speculation (as we might call it) of a very interesting kind was until these last days too often presented in the unattractive guise of Wardour Street Roman Law, or else, raising the Germanistic cry of 'Loose from Rome!' it plunged into an exposition of medieval charters. On the other hand, the theorising is often done by men who have that close grasp of concrete modern fact which comes of a minute and practical study of legal systems. Happily it is no longer necessary to go straight to Germany. That struggle over 'the contract of association' to which I have alluded, those woes of the 'congregations' of which all have heard, invoked foreign learning across the border, and now we may read in lucid French of the various German theories. Good reading I think it; and what interests me especially is that the French lawyer, with all his orthodoxy (legal orthodoxy) and conservatism, with all his love of clarity and abhorrence of mysticism, is often compelled to admit that the traditional dogmas of the law-school have broken down. Much disinclined though he may be to allow the group a real will of its own, just as really real as the will of a man, still he has to admit that if *n* men unite themselves in an organised body, jurisprudence, unless it wishes to pulverise the group, must see *n* + 1 persons. And that for the mere lawyer should I think be enough. 'Of heaven and hell he has no power to sing', and he might content himself with a phenomenal reality – such reality, for example, as the lamp-post has for the idealistic ontologist. Still, we do not like to be told that we are dealing in fiction, even if it be added that we needs must feign, and the thought will occur to us that a fiction that we needs must feign is somehow or another very like the simple truth.

Why we English people are not interested in a problem that is being seriously discussed in many other lands, that is a question to which I have tried to provide some sort of answer elsewhere.[7] It is a long, and you would think it a very dreary, story about the most specifically English of all our legal institutes; I mean the trust. All that I can say here is that the device of building a wall of trustees enabled us to construct bodies which were not technically corporations and which yet would be sufficiently protected from the assaults of individualistic theory. The personality of such bodies – so I should put it – though explicitly denied by lawyers, was on the whole pretty well recognised in practice. That something of this sort happened you might learn from one simple fact. For some time past we have had upon our statute book the term 'unincorporate body'. Suppose that a Frenchman saw it, what would he say? 'Unincorporate body: inanimate soul! No wonder your Prime Minister, who is a philosopher, finds it hard to talk English and talk law at the same time.'

One result of this was, so I fancy, that the speculative Englishman could not readily believe that in this quarter there was anything to be explored except some legal trickery unworthy of exploration. The lawyer assured him that it was so, and he saw around him great and ancient, flourishing and wealthy groups – the Inns of Court at their head – which, so the lawyer said, were not persons. To have cross-examined the lawyer over the bodiliness of his "unincorporate body" might have brought out some curious results; but such a course was hardly open to those who shared our wholesome English contempt for legal technique.

The Ultimate Moral Unit Well, I must finish; and yet perhaps I have not succeeded in raising just the question that I wanted to ask. Can I do that in two or three last sentences? It is a moral question, and therefore I will choose my hypothetical case from a region in which our moral sentiments are not likely to be perplexed by legal technique. My organised group shall be a sovereign state. Let us call it Nusquamia. Like many other sovereign states, it owes money, and I will suppose that you are one of its creditors. You are not receiving the expected interest and there is talk of repudiation. That being so, I believe that you will be, and indeed I think that you ought to be, indignant, morally, righteously indignant. Now the question that I want to raise is this: Who is it that really owes you money? Nusquamia. Granted, but can you convert the proposition that Nusquamia owes you money into a series of propositions imposing duties on certain human beings that are now in existence? The task will not be easy. Clearly you do not think that every Nusquamian owes you some aliquot share of the debt.

---

[7] Maitland, 'Trust und Korporation', Wien, 1904 (from *Grünhut's Zeitschrift für das Privat- und öffentliche Recht*, vol. xxxii).

No one thinks in that way. The debt of Venezuela is not owed by Fulano y Zutano[vi] and the rest of them.[vii] Nor, I think, shall we get much good out of the word 'collectively', which is the smudgiest word in the English language, for the largest 'collection' of zeros is only zero. I do not wish to say that I have suggested an impossible task, and that the right-and-duty-bearing group must be for the philosopher an ultimate and unanalysable moral unit: as ultimate and unanalysable, I mean, as is the man. Only if that task can be performed, I think that in the interests of jurisprudence and of moral philosophy it is eminently worthy of circumspect performance. As to our national law, it has sound instincts, and muddles along with semi-personality and demi-semi-personality towards convenient conclusions. Still, I cannot think that Parliament's timid treatment of the trade unions has been other than a warning, or that it was a brilliant day in our legal annals when the affairs of the Free Church of Scotland were brought before the House of Lords, and the dead hand fell with a resounding slap upon the living body.[viii] As to philosophy, that is no affair of mine. I speak with conscious ignorance and unfeigned humility; only of this I feel moderately sure, that those who are to tell us of the very nature of things and the very nature of persons will not be discharging their duties to the full unless they come to close terms with that triumphant fiction, if fiction it be, of which I have said in your view more than too much, and in my own view less than too little.[8]

[8] In the following list will be found the titles of a few French books which (by way of historical retrospect or legal exposition or juristic speculation or political controversy) illustrate competing theories of legal personality and bring them into close relation with a recent and interesting chapter of French history, namely the campaign against the *congrégations*. Some of these works (see especially M. Michoud's articles) will also serve as an introduction to German speculation.

J. Brissaud, *Manuel d'histoire du droit français*, pp. 1769–85: Paris, 1899. M. Planiol, *Traité élémentaire de droit civil*, t. i, pp. 259–90 (*Les personnes fictives*); t. ii, pp. 618–23 (*Association*): Paris, 1901. G. Trouillot et F. Chapsal, *Du contrat d'association – Commentaire de la Loi du Ier juillet 1901*: Paris, 1902. M. Vauthier, *Études sur les personnes morales*: Bruxelles et Paris, 1887. Le Comte de Vareilles-Sommières, *Du contrat d'association, ou, La loi française permet-elle aux associations non reconnues de posséder?* Paris, 1903. Le Marquis de Vareilles-Sommières, *Les personnes morales*: Paris, 1902. L. Michoud, 'La notion de personnalité morale' (*Revue du droit public et de la science politique*, t. xi, pp. 1, 193: Paris, 1899). A. Mestre, *Les personnes morales et le problème de leur responsabilité pénale*: Paris, 1899. M. Hauriou, 'De la personnalité comme élément de la réalité sociale' (*Revue générale du droit, de la législation et de la jurisprudence*, t. xxii, pp. 1, 119: Paris, 1898). D. Négulesco, *Le problème juridique de la personnalité morale et son application aux sociétés civiles et commerciales*: Paris, 1900. A. Gouffre de Lapradelle, *Théorie et pratique des fondations perpétuelles*: Paris, 1895. F. Garcin, *La mainmorte, – de 1749 à 1901*. Paris et Lyon, 1903. J. Imbart de Latour, *Des biens communaux*: Paris, 1899. P. M. Waldeck-Rousseau, *Associations et congrégations*: Paris, 1901. E. Combes, *Une campagne laïque* (1902–1903), Préface par Anatole France: Paris, 1904.

Notes

i The author of this adage was Samuel Werenfels, the eighteenth-century Swiss Protestant Divine. It means: 'This is the book where each his dogma seeks; This is the book where each his dogma finds.'

ii 'Wardour Street English' was a phrase used to denote fake antique uses of English, especially in novels that drew on a kind of archaic dialect. It got its name from the fact that Wardour Street was known for its antique shops, selling both real and fake articles. 'Wardour Street Roman Law' means the use of ersatz Roman ideas in modern legal settings to add a false air of grandeur to contemporary proceedings.

iii 'Another infirmity of a Common-wealth [is] the great number of Corporations; which are as it were many lesser Common-wealths in the bowels of the greater, like wormes in the entrayles of a naturall man.' (Hobbes, *Leviathan*, p. 230.) In his introduction to Gierke, Maitland imagines a German commenting on the formation of English law as follows: 'There is much in your history that we can envy, much in your free and easy formation of groups that we can admire. That great "trust concept" of yours stood you in good stead when the days were evil: when your Hobbes, for example, was instituting unsavoury comparisons between corporations and *ascarides*.' (Gierke, *Political theories of the Middle Age*, p. xxxiii.)

iv The law of 1 July 1901 stated that: 'Associations of people will be able to be freely formed without preliminary authorization or declaration' (Article 2), provided only that they conformed with certain formal requirements of registration. But an exception was made for religious congregations, whose legal recognition continued to depend on authorization by decree from the Council of State (article 13).

v Cf. Austin, *The province of jurisprudence determined*.

vi A Spanish expression that is the equivalent of the English 'Smith and Jones'.

vii Maitland chooses the example of Venezuela because that country had just reneged on its debts, resulting in the blockade of its coastline by a joint British-Italian-German fleet in 1902–3, and the impounding of the Venezuelan navy ('four little boats smelling of rust, bananas, stew and mestizo sweat' in the words of one of the Britons who impounded it (quoted in G. Moron, *A history of Venezuela* (London: Allen and Unwin, 1964)). The example of Venezuela would have been in the minds of Maitland's audience, but the problem was less a matter of moral or legal doctrine than of pure politics. The servicing of all national and international debts had been suspended on 1 March 1902 by the dictator Castro, who had come to power in 1899 and whose rule had been marked by violence and instability. The European blockade 'represented a challenge to United

States hegemony in the Caribbean more than it did a sincere attempt to settle claims' (J. Ewell, *Venezuela. A century of change* (London: Hurst, 1984), p. 40). It provoked President Theodore Roosevelt to enunciate a corollary to the Monroe Doctrine which stipulated that the United States would deal with the misbehaviour of any Latin American states in financial and other affairs, and European powers were not to intervene directly. Under pressure from the Americans, the blockade was lifted and some of the debts were settled. Among Latin American countries only Argentina protested against the use of European and then American force to collect debts.

viii In 1900 the Assembly of the Free Church of Scotland had elected by 643 votes to 27 to enter into a Union with the United Presbyterians. The minority of 27 (who became known as the 'Wee Frees') opposed the Union (on the grounds that the United Presbyterians were more liberal in their interpretation of Calvinism than had been the founders of the Free Church of Scotland in 1843) and took their case to law, claiming that the decision of the Assembly had been ultra vires. The case eventually reached the House of Lords where, after much deliberation on what were often obscure questions of theology, the Lords decided in favour of the Wee Frees, and awarded them the name of the Free Church, along with the whole of its property and all of its buildings. It is this decision that Maitland is referring to. The decision caused a considerable outcry and proved more or less unworkable in practice, as the majority continued to claim to embody the ongoing life of the Church. Eventually an act of parliament was required to sort out the mess. This was the Churches (Scotland) Act of 1905, which vested the funds of the Free Church in a Parliamentary Commission, whose job it was to distribute those funds as nearly as possible in accordance with the spirit in which they had been raised, and in broad accordance with the proportional interests of the divided parties.

The Scottish Church case was of considerable interest to the 'pluralists' who followed Maitland and took up many of the themes of the essays collected here. J. N. Figgis, in particular, was scathing about the decision of the House of Lords, which he took to confirm the absurdity of the 'Fiction theory', with its presupposition that group life is simply a construct of law rather than the result of the 'real personality' of a collective entity like the Free Church, which can to all intents and purposes be taken to have a life of its own (and therefore be taken to be capable of evolving and altering its identity, as happened in the Assembly decision of 1900). As Figgis writes: 'Does [the Church] exist by some inward living force, with powers of self-development? Or is she a mere aggregate, a fortuitous concourse of ecclesiastical atoms, treated it may be as one for the purposes of commonsense, but with no real claim to a mind or will of her own, except so far as the civil power sees good to invest her for the nonce with the portion of unity?' (Figgis, *Churches in the modern state* (London: Longmans, 1913), p. 40). The case of the Free Church of Scotland and the Wee Frees is also discussed by Harold Laski in his *Studies in the problem of sovereignty* (New Haven: Yale University Press, 1917).

5

Trust and Corporation

Not very long ago, in the pages of this Review, Dr Redlich,[i] whose book
on English Local Government we in England are admiring,[ii] did me the
honour of referring to some words that I had written concerning our
English Corporations and our English Trusts.[1] I have obtained permission
to say with his assistance a few more words upon the same matter, in the
hope that I may thereby invite attention to a part of our English legal
history which, so far as my knowledge goes, has not attracted all the
notice that it deserves.

Perhaps I need hardly say that we on this side of the sea are profoundly
grateful to those foreign explorers who have been at pains to investigate our insular arrangements. Looking at us from the outside, it has
been possible for them to teach us much about ourselves. Still we cannot
but know that it is not merely for the sake of England that English law,
both ancient and modern, has been examined. Is it not true that England
has played a conspicuous, if a passive, part in that development of historical jurisprudence which was one of the most remarkable scientific
achievements of the nineteenth century? Over and over again it has happened that our island has been able to supply just that piece of evidence,
just that link in the chain of proof, which the Germanist wanted but
could not find at home. Should I go too far if I said that no Germanistic
theory is beyond dispute until it has been tested upon our English
material?

Now I know of nothing English that is likely to be more instructive
to students of legal history, and in particular to those who are concerned
with Germanic law, than that legal *Rechtsinstitut* [legal institution] of ours
which Dr Redlich described in the following well chosen words: 'The
legal institution known as the trust, which arose originally out of certain
requirements of English land law, was developed by and by into a general

[1] *Grünhut's Zeitschrift für das Privat- und Öffentliche Recht*, Bd. xxx, S. 167.

legal institution and obtained practical importance and an extraordinarily sophisticated juristic form in all areas of legal life.'

It is a big affair our Trust. This must be evident to anyone who knows – and who does not know? – that out in America the mightiest trading corporations that the world has ever seen are known by the name of 'Trusts.'[iii] And this is only the Trust's last exploit. Dr Redlich is right when he speaks of it as an 'allgemeines Rechtsinstitut' [general legal institution]. It has all the generality, all the elasticity of Contract. Anyone who wishes to know England, even though he has no care for the detail of Private Law, should know a little of our Trust.

We may imagine an English lawyer who was unfamiliar with the outlines of foreign law taking up the new Civil Code of Germany.[iv] 'This', he would say, 'seems a very admirable piece of work, worthy in every way of the high reputation of German jurists. But surely it is not a complete statement of German private law. Surely there is a large gap in it. I have looked for the Trust, but I cannot find it; and to omit the Trust is, I should have thought, almost as bad as to omit Contract.' And then he would look at his book-shelves and would see stout volumes entitled 'Law of Trusts', and he would open his 'Reports' and would see trust everywhere, and he would remember how he was a trustee and how almost every man that he knew was a trustee.

Is it too bold of me to guess the sort of answer that he would receive from some German friend who had not studied England? 'Well, before you blame us, you might tell us what sort of thing is this wonderful Trust of yours. You might at least point out the place where the supposed omission occurs. See, here is our general scheme of Private Law. Are we to place this precious *Rechtsinstitut* under the title *Sachenrecht* [law of property] or should it stand under *Recht der Schuldverhältnisse* [law of debt], or, to use a term which may be more familiar, *Obligationenrecht* [law of obligations]?'

To this elementary question I know of no reply which would be given at once and as a matter of course by every English lawyer. We are told in one of our old books that in the year 1348 a certain English lawyer found himself face to face with the words *contra inhibitionem novi operis*,[v] and therefore said, 'there is no sense to be made of these words.' I am not at all sure that some men very learned in our law would not be inclined to give a similar answer if they were required to bring our Trust under any one of those rubrics which divide the German Code.

'English law' says Dr Redlich, 'knows no distinction between public and private law.' In the sense in which he wrote that sentence it is, I think, very true. Now-a-days young men who are beginning to study our law are expected to read books in which there is talk about this distinction: the distinction between Private Law and Public Law. Perhaps I might say that we regard those terms as potential rubrics. We think, or many of us think, that if all our law were put into a code that pair of terms might conveniently appear in very large letters. But they are not technical terms. If I saw in an English newspaper that Mr A. B. had written a book on 'Public Law', my first guess would be that he had been writing about International Law. If an English newspaper called Mr C. D. a 'publicist', I should think that he wrote articles in newspapers and magazines about political questions.

In the same sense it might be said that English Law knows no distinction between *Sachenrecht* [law of property] and *Obligationenrecht* [law of obligations]. It is needless to say that in England as elsewhere there is a great difference between owning a hundred gold coins and being owed a hundred pounds, and of course one of the first lessons that any beginner must learn is the apprehension of this difference. And then he will read in more or less speculative books – books of 'General Jurisprudence' – about *iura in rem* and *iura in personam*, and perhaps will be taught that if English law were put into a Code, this distinction would appear very prominently. But here again we have much rather potential rubrics than technical terms. The technical concepts with which the English lawyer will have to operate, the tools of his trade (if I may so speak), are of a different kind.

I have said this because, so it seems to me, the Trust could hardly have been evolved among a people who had clearly formulated the distinction between a right *in personam* and a right *in rem*, and had made that distinction one of the main outlines of their legal system. I am aware that the question how far this distinction was grasped in medieval Germany has been debated by distinguished Germanists, and I would not even appear to be intervening between Dr Laband and Dr Heusler.[vi] Still I cannot doubt who it is that has said the words that will satisfy the student of English legal history. In the thirteenth century Englishmen find a distinction between the *actio in rem* and the *actio in personam* in those Roman books which they regard as the representatives of enlightened jurisprudence. They try to put their own actions – and they have a large number of separate actions, each with its own name, each with his own procedure – under these cosmopolitan rubrics. And what is the result? Very soon the result is that which Dr Laband has admirably stated:

The action is characterised by what it is that the plaintiff claims, which the judge should help him to obtain, not by his reason for claiming it . . . By contrast, one searches the medieval sources in vain for a classification of the actions according to an underlying legal relationship and especially according to the distinction between real and personal actions. The expression *clage up gut* [in England *real action*], apparently corresponding to the Roman term *actio in rem*, bears absolutely no relation to the juridical nature of the plaintiff's right, but refers only to the fact that the property so described is claimed by the plaintiff.[2]

To this very day we are incumbered with those terms 'real property' and 'personal property' which serve us as approximate equivalents for *Liegenschaft* [immovable property] and *Fahrnis* [movable property]. The reason is that in the Middle Age, and indeed until 1854, the claimant of a movable could only obtain a judgment which gave his adversary a choice between giving up that thing and paying its value. And so, said we, there is no *actio realis* for a horse or a book. Such things are not 'realty'; they are not 'real property'. Whether this use of words is creditable to English lawyers who are living in the twentieth century is not here the question; but it seems to me exceedingly instructive.

For my own part if a foreign friend asked me to tell him in one word whether the right of the English *Destinatär* (the person for whom property is held in trust) is *dinglich* [real, *in rem*] or *obligatorisch* [contractual, *in personam*] I should be inclined to say: 'No, I cannot do that. If I said *dinglich*, that would be untrue. If I said *obligatorisch*, I should suggest what is false. In ultimate analysis the right may be *obligatorisch*; but for many practical purposes of great importance it has been treated as though it were *dinglich*, and indeed people habitually speak and think of it as a kind of *Eigentum* [property].'

This, then, is the first point to which I would ask attention; and I do so because, so far as my knowledge goes, this point is hardly to be seen upon the surface of those books about English law that a foreign student is most likely to read.[3]

---

[2] Laband, *Die Vermögensrechtlichen Klagen*, S. 5–7.

[3] Heymann in the sketch of English law that is included in the new edition of Holtzen-dorff's *Encyklopädie* has declined to place our Trust under 'Das Sachenrecht' or under 'Forderungsrecht'. It seems to me that in this as in many other instances he has shown a true insight into the structure of our system.

I

Before going further I should like to transcribe some sentences from an essay in legal history which has interested me deeply: I mean '*Die langobardische Treuhand und ihre Umbildung zur Testamentsvollstreckung*' by Dr Alfred Schultze.[4] I think that we may see what is at the root the same *Rechtsinstitut* taking two different shapes in different ages and different lands, and perhaps a German observer will find our Trust the easier after a short excursion into Lombardy.

To be brief, the Lombard cannot make a genuine testament. He therefore transfers the whole or some part of his property to a *Treuhänder* [trustee], who is to carry out his instructions. Such instructions may leave greater or less liberty of action to the *Treuhänder*. He may only have to transfer the things to some named person or some particular church, or, at the other extreme, he may have an unlimited choice among the various means by which the soul of a dead man can be benefited. And now we will listen to Dr Schultze.

The relationship of *Treuhand* [trust] is usually created by a contract between the testator and the person chosen by him as *Treuhänder* [trustee]. Where a direct power over corporeal things is assigned to the *Treuhänder*, this contract frequently takes the form and even the physical characteristics of a contract transferring title. The objects are conveyed to him *per cartam* [by charter] for the desired purpose, and there is explicit talk of *tradere res* [handing over the things] . . . Certain documents in the eleventh-century Register of Farfa refer to an investiture bestowed upon the *Treuhänder* by the donor. The donor conveys to the *Treuhänder* not merely the relevant piece of land, but also, in accordance with the Lombard legal custom governing the transfer of property rights, his own title deeds and those of his predecessors in title if he has them. If he is a Frank, he uses the Frankish symbols of investiture, twig, knife, clod of earth, branch and glove.

That is what I should have expected, an English reader would say. The land is conveyed to the trustee. Of course he has *ein dingliches Recht* [a real right]. He has *Eigentum* [proprietary right]. In the Middle Age he will be 'enfeoffed, vested and seised' (*feoffatus, vestitus et seisitus* or *feffé, vestu et seisi*). And naturally *die Erwerbsurkunden*, 'the title deeds', are handed over to him. But we must return to Dr Schultze's exposition.

---

[4] Gierke's *Untersuchungen*, 1895.

The trustee has, as we have just shown, his own real right as legal successor to the corporeal objects assigned to him. What is the nature of this right? In first place, we must draw attention to a number of documents which leave no doubt that the trustee here has full proprietary right, and is not limited either by proprietary or contractual rights of others in his enjoyment and his power to dispose of the things. These are all cases in which the donor wishes the things to be used for the good of his soul according to the free disposition of the trustee, who thus emerges as a *dispensator* in the true sense.

This, however, was not the common case. Generally what the *Treuhänder* has is not:

The full, free power to dispose of the things, but rather, a right of alienation subject to certain limitations. Here, in comparison with the legal position of the *dispensator* in the fullest sense outlined above, he occupies an inferior position. But wherein consists this limitation? We may pass over here the question of whether the trustee is limited by the law of obligations, of whether he has an obligation grounded in private law towards the donor or his heirs or anyone else. The question is rather whether his right is subject to any limitation arising from the law of property, to which the answer is yes.

Dr Schultze then proceeds to expound the *Treuhänder's* right as:

Property right, but property right subject to a condition; it is a conditional property right (*resolutiv bedingtes Eigentum*). The condition took effect when the object of the donation was used otherwise than for the stipulated purpose, or when for some reason or another that purpose became impossible to fulfil. The result was that the proprietary right of the trustee expired and without any new conveyance fell to the donor or his heirs, who could thus regain possession of the thing by the real action (property claim).

Now that is not true of the English trustee. His right is not *resolutiv bedingtes Eigentum* [conditional proprietary right]. I cite it, however, because of what follows. And what follows is highly instructive to those who would study English 'equity': indeed some of Dr Schultze's sentences might have been written about the England of the fourteenth or the England of the twentieth century.

The limitation of the ownership of the *Treuhänder* inherent in this hovering condition could also take effect against third parties who acquired the property under that same condition ... This presupposed the notoriety (publicity) of that limitation of proprietary right, in such measure that every third party who acquired the property could be subjected to the condition without suffering hardship, whether or not he actually knew about it in the specific case. Now it is possible that where land was concerned, the Lombards, too, had previously known a form of conveyance in their tribal law which made the act sufficiently public to the other members of the tribe at the very moment it took place (performance of the transaction on the piece of land itself, or *in mallo*). But in the period of interest here, conveyance of title deeds was by far and away the predominant form, and in any case the only one where formal donations in contemplation of death were concerned, including those in trust. Any transaction of property rights which had taken place by conveyance of title deeds was for that reason alone sufficiently public ... Whoever wanted to obtain a piece of land by derivative title could inform himself sufficiently about the title of the transferor by examining the title deed which had been issued to the transferor by his own predecessor in title. It was even customary from an early stage to have the deed transferred to oneself along with the actual land as a lasting guarantee of legitimacy, and – which followed but logically – not merely the transferor's title deed, but all the deeds in his possession of his predecessors in title. In this way, whoever wanted to buy a piece of land from a *Treuhänder* could immediately ascertain the *Treuhänder* status of his opposite number, the conditional nature of his title, upon inspection of all the title deeds finishing with his. But if, against legal usage, he did not concern himself with the title deeds, then there was no hardship if the condition unexpectedly took effect against him; the damage he thereby sustained was not undeserved.

But what have we here? – an Englishman might say – why, it is our 'doctrine of constructive notice', the key-stone which holds together the lofty edifice of trusts that we have raised. These Lombards, he would add, seem to have gone a little too far, and with a *resolutiv bedingtes Eigentum* [conditional proprietary right] we have not to do. But of course the *Eigentum* of a piece of land is conveyed by the conveyance of title deed. And of course every prudent buyer of land will expect to see the title deeds which are in the seller's hand and to have them handed over to himself when the sale is completed. 'But if, against legal usage, he did not concern himself with the title deeds', then there is no hardship if he is treated as knowing all that he would have discovered had he behaved as reasonable men behave. He has 'constructive notice' of it all. 'The damage he thereby sustains is not undeserved.'

We must make one other excerpt before we leave Lombardy.

Nevertheless this was only true of immovable property. Mechanisms for publicising to third parties a condition imposing limits on a transfer of chattels were entirely lacking, just as in the other Germanic laws. Certainly, the testamentary *Treuhänder* was objectively bound by the stipulation of the purpose of the trust in respect of movables, and only had a conditional property right, just as he did in land. But if he had already conveyed the movables to the wrong persons, the heirs of the donor had no redress against the third-party possessors, even if the latter had known how things stood at the time they acquired them. The reason all third parties were subject to the condition in the case of immovables did not apply here. If the movables assigned to the *Treuhänder* were no longer in his possession thanks to a breach of trust, and thus not subject to the proprietary action for recovery known as *Malo ordine possides* ['You are in unlawful possession'], then the way was open instead for a personal action for compensation.

That does not go quite far enough, the English critic might say. If it could be proved that *der dritte Besitzer* [the third holder] actually knew of the 'trust', it does not seem to me equitable that he should be able to disregard it. Also it does not seem to me clear that if the movables can no longer be pursued, the claim of the *Destinatär* [beneficiary] must of necessity be a mere *persönliche Schadenersatzklage* [personal action for compensation] against the *Treuhänder*. But it is most remarkable to see our cousins the Lombards in these very ancient days seizing a distinction that is very familiar to us. The doctrine of 'constructive notice' is not to be extended from land to movables.[5]

II

We may now turn to the England of the fourteenth century, and in the first place I may be suffered to recall a few general traits of the English

---

[5] I am aware that Schultze's construction of the right of the Lombard *Treuhänder* as 'resolutiv bedingtes Eigentum' is open to dispute. See, for example, Caillemer, *Exécution Testamentaire*, Lyon (1901), 351. A great deal of what M. Caillemer says about England in this excellent book seems to be both new and true.

law of that time, which, though they may be well enough known, should be had in memory.

A deep and wide gulf lies between *Liegenschaft* [immovables] and *Fahrnis* [movables]. It is deeper and wider in England than elsewhere. This is due in part to our rigorous primogeniture, and in part to the successful efforts of the Church to claim as her own an exclusive jurisdiction over the movables of a dead man, whether he has made a last will or whether he has died intestate. One offshoot of the ancient Germanic *Treuhandschaft* is already a well established and flourishing institute. The English last will is a will with executors. If there is no will or no executor, an 'administrator' appointed by the bishop fills the vacant place. This will is no longer *donatio post obitum* of the old kind, but under canonical influence has assumed a truly testamentary character. The process which makes the executor into the 'personal representative' of the dead man, his representative as regards all but his *Liegenschaft* [immovables], is already far advanced. It is a process which in course of time makes the English executor not unlike a Roman *haeres* [heir]. In later days when the Trust, strictly so called, had been developed, these two institutes, which indeed had a common root, began to influence each other. We began to think of the executor as being for many purposes very like a trustee. However, the Trust, properly so called, makes its appearance on the legal stage at a time when the Englishman can already make a true testament of his movables, and at a time when the relationship between the executor and the legatees is a matter with which the secular courts have no concern.

As to dealings with movables *inter vivos*, we cannot say that there is any great need for a new *Rechtsinstitut* [legal institution]. It is true that in the fourteenth century this part of our law is not highly developed. Still it meets the main wants of a community that knows little of commerce. We will notice in passing that the current language is often using a term which, when used in another context, will indicate the germ of the true Trust: namely the term that in Latin is *ad opus* [to the use], and in French *al oes*. Often it is said that one man holds goods or receives money *ad opus alterius* [to another's use]. But the Common Law is gradually acquiring such categories as deposit, mandate and so forth, which will adequately meet these cases. This part of our law is young and it can grow.

On the other hand, the land law is highly developed, and at every point it is stiffened by a complicated system of actions and writs (*brevia*). A wonderful scheme of 'estates' – I know not whether that word can be translated – has been elaborated: 'estates in fee simple, estates in fee tail, estates for life, estates in remainder, estates in reversion, etc'; and each 'estate' is protected by its corresponding writ (*breve*). The judges, even if they were less conservative than they are, would find it difficult to introduce a new figure into this crowded scene. In particular we may notice that a 'resolutiv bedingtes Eigentum', which Dr Schultze finds in Lombardy, is very well known and is doing very hard work. All our *Pfandrecht* [law of lien] is governed by this concept. More work than it is doing it could hardly do.

Then in the second half of the fourteenth century we see a new Court struggling for existence. It is that Court of Chancery whose name is to be inseverably connected with the Trust. The old idea that when ordinary justice fails, there is a reserve of extraordinary justice which the king can exercise is bearing new fruit. In civil (*privatrechtliche*) causes men make their way to the king's Chancellor begging him in piteous terms to intervene 'for the love of God and in the way of charity'. It is not of any defect in the material law that they complain; but somehow or another they cannot get justice. They are poor and helpless; their adversaries are rich and powerful. Sheriffs are partial; jurors are corrupt. But, whatever may be the case with penal justice, it is by no means clear that in civil suits there can be any room for a formless, extraordinary jurisdiction. Complaints against interference with the ordinary course of law were becoming loud, when something was found for the Chancellor to do, and something that he could do with general approval. I think it might be said that if the Court of Chancery saved the Trust, the Trust saved the Court of Chancery.

And now we come to the origin of the Trust. The Englishman cannot leave his land by will. In the case of land every germ of testamentary power has been ruthlessly stamped out in the twelfth century. But the Englishman would like to leave his land by will. He would like to provide for the weal of his sinful soul, and he would like to provide for his daughters and younger sons. That is the root of the matter.[6] But further, it is to be observed that the law is hard upon him at the hour of death, more especially if he is one of the great. If he leaves an heir of full age, there is a *relevium* [relief] to be paid to the lord. If he leaves an heir under age, the lord may take the profits of the land, perhaps for twenty years, and may sell

---

[6] I do not wish to deny that there were other causes for trusts; but comparatively they were of little importance.

the marriage of the heir. And then if there is no heir, the land falls back ('escheats') to the lord for good and all.

Once more recourse is had to the *Treuhänder*. The landowner conveys his land to some friends. They are to hold it 'to his use (*a son oes*)'. They will let him enjoy it while he lives, and he can tell them what they are to do with it after his death.

I say that he conveys his land, not to a friend, but to some friends. This is a point of some importance. If there were a single owner, a single *feoffatus*, he might die, and then the lord would claim the ordinary rights of a lord; *relevium, custodia haeredis* [wardship of the heir], *maritagium haeredis* [the sale of the heir in marriage], *escaeta* [escheats], all would follow as a matter of course. But here the Germanic *Gesamthandschaft* [joint ownership] comes to our help. Enfeoff five or perhaps ten friends *zu gesamter Hand* ('as joint tenants'). When one of them dies there is no inheritance; there is merely accrescence. The lord can claim nothing. If the number of the feoffees is running low, then indeed it will be prudent to introduce some new ones, and this can be done by some transferring and retransferring. But, if a little care be taken about this matter, the lord's chance of getting anything is very small.

Here is a principle that has served us well in the past and is serving us well in the present. The *Gesamthandprinzip* [principle of joint ownership] enables us to erect (if I may so speak) a wall of trustees which will not be always in need of repair. Some of those 'charitable' trusts of which I am to speak hereafter will start with numerous trustees, and many years may pass away before any new documents are necessary. Two may die, three may die; but there is no inheritance; there is merely accrescence; what was owned by ten men, is now owned by eight or by seven; that is all.[7]

In a land in which Roman law has long been seriously studied it would be needless, I should imagine, for me to say that it is not in Roman books that Englishmen of the fourteenth century have discovered this device; but it may be well to remark that any talk of *fides, fiducia, fideicommissum* is singularly absent from the earliest documents in which our new legal institution appears. The same may be said of the English word 'trust'. All is being done under the cover of *ad opus*. In Old French this becomes *al oes*,

---

[7] Our 'joint ownership' is not a very strong form of *Gesamthandschaft*. One of several 'joint owners' has a share that he can alienate *inter vivos*; but he has nothing to give by testament.

al ues or the like. In the degraded French of Stratford-atte-Bow we see many varieties of spelling. It is not unusual for learned persons to restore the Latin *p* and to write *oeps* or *eops*. Finally in English mouths (which do not easily pronounce a French *u*) this word becomes entangled with the French *use*. The English for 'ad opus meum' is 'to my use'.

It is always interesting, if we can, to detect the point at which a new institute or new concept enters the field of law. Hitherto the early history of our 'feoffments to uses' has been but too little explored: I fear that the credit of thoroughly exploring it is reserved for some French or German scholar. However, there can be little doubt that the new practice first makes its appearance in the highest and noblest circles of society. I will mention one early example. The 'feoffor' in this case is John of Gaunt, son of a King of England and himself at one time titular King of Castile. Among the persons who are to profit by the trust is his son Henry who will be our King Henry IV.

On the 3rd of February, 1399, 'old John of Gaunt, time-honoured Lancaster' makes his testament.[8] Thereby he disposes of his movables and he appoints seventeen executors, among whom are two bishops and three earls. To this instrument he annexes a 'Codicillus' (as he calls it) which begins thus:

> Further, whereas I John, son of the King of England, Duke of Lancaster, have bought and have had bought to my use diverse lordships, manors, lands, tenements, rents, services, possessions, reversions and advowsons of the benefices of Holy Church with their appurtenances . . . so I have had made this schedule appended to this my testament, containing my last and whole will concerning the aforementioned lordships, manors, lands, tenements, rents, services possessions, reversions, advowsons with their appurtenances . . .

He then says what is to be done with these lands. Thus for example:

> Further, I will that my most dear bachelor(s) Robert Nevill, William Gascoigne, my most dear squires Thomas Radcliffe and William Ketering, and my most dear clerk Thomas Langley, who are en-feoffed at my orders in the manor of Barnoldswick in the county of York are to pay annually to my executors . . .

---

[8] *Testamenta Eboracensia* (Surtees Society), vol. 1. p. 223. In the same volume (p. 113) an earlier example will be found, the will of William, Lord Latimer (13 April, 1381). See also the will of the Earl of Pembroke (5 May, 1372), and the will of the Earl of Arundel (4 March, 1392–3) in J. Nichols, *Royal Wills* (1870), pp. 91, 120.

To be brief, certain sums of money are to be paid to the executors, who will apply them for pious purposes, and:

> To the purpose that an estate be made of the said manor to my most beloved eldest son Henry Duke of Hereford and to the heirs of his body, and in default of issue of the said Henry the remainder is[9] to go to my rightful heirs.

Then at the end stand these words:

> Further, I will that all other lordships, manors, lands . . . with their appurtenances purchased to my use and remaining in the hands of those enfeoffed by me to this purpose, shall be given (if I make no further ordinance concerning them in my life) to the aforsaid Thomas, my son, to be had by him and the heirs of his body; and in default of issue of his body, the remainder is to be given to the aforesaid John his brother and to the heirs of his body; and in default of issue of the said John, the remainder is to be given to the above-mentioned Joanne, their sister, and to the heirs of her body; and in default of issue from the said Joanne, the remainder is to be given to my rightful heirs who shall be the heirs to the inheritance of Lancaster: willing always that all these my wishes, ordinances and devises contained in this schedule shall be fulfilled by those who shall have the estate and power, and by the advice, ordinance and counsel of lawyers in the surest manner possible.

We see what the situation is. The Duke has transferred various lands to various parties of friends and dependants. When he feels that death is approaching, he declares what his wishes are, and they fall under two heads. He desires to increase the funds which his executors are to expend for the good of his soul, and he desires also to make some provision for his younger and (so it happens) illegitimate children.

Apparently the new fashion spread with great rapidity. We have not in print so many collections of wills as we ought to have; but in such as have been published the mention of land held to the testator's 'use' begins to appear somewhat suddenly in the last years of the fourteenth century and thence forward it is common. We are obliged to suppose that the practice had existed for some time before it found legal protection. But that time seems to have been short. Between 1396 and 1403 the Chancellor's intervention had been demanded.[10]

---

[9] This is an *Anwartschaft*.
[10] *Select Cases in Chancery* (Selden Society), p. 69.

It would have been very difficult for the old Courts, 'the Courts of Common Law', to give any aid. As already said, the system of our land law had become prematurely osseous. The introduction without Act of Parliament of a new *dingliches Recht*, some new modification of *Eigentum* would have been impossible. In our documents we see no attempt to meet the new case by an adaptation of the terms that are employed when there is to be a '*resolutiv bedingtes Eigentum*'.[11] And on the other hand we see a remarkable absence of those phrases which are currently used when an *obligatorischer Vertrag* [obligatory contract] is being made. No care is taken to exact from the *Treuhänder* a formal promise that the trust shall be observed. From the first men seem to feel that a contract binding the trustees to the author of the trust, binding the feoffees to the enfeoffed, is not what is wanted.

Moreover, it was probably felt, though perhaps but dimly felt, that if once the old Courts began to take notice of these arrangements a great question of policy would have to be faced. The minds of the magnates were in all probability much divided. They wanted to make wills. But they were 'lords', and it was not to their advantage that their 'tenants' should make wills. And then there was one person in England who had much to gain and little to lose by a total suppression of this novelty. That person was the King, for he was always 'lord' and never 'tenant'. An open debate about this matter would have made it evident that if landowners, and more especially the magnates, were to make wills, the King would have a fair claim for compensation. Even medieval Englishmen must have seen that if the King could not 'live of his own', he must live by taxes. The State must have a revenue. Perhaps we may say, therefore, that the kindest thing that the old Courts could do for the nascent Trust was to look the other way. Certain it is that from a very early time some of our great lawyers were deeply engaged in the new practice. We have seen a certain William Gascoigne as a *Treuhänder* for John of Gaunt. He was already a distinguished lawyer. He was going to be Chief Justice of England and will be known to all Shakespeare's readers. Thomas Littleton (ob. 1481) when he expounds the English land law in a very famous book will hardly a word to say about 'feoffments to uses'; but when he makes his own will he will say, 'Also I wulle that the feoffees to myn use [of certain

---

[11] This is not quite true. A few attempts were made to attain the end by means of 'conditions', and Edward III himself made, so it seems, some attempt of this kind. But the mechanism of a 'condition' would have been very awkward.

lands] make a sure estate unto Richard Lyttelton my sonne, and to the heirs of his bodie.'

When we consider where the king's interest lay, it is somewhat surprising that the important step should be taken by his first minister, the Chancellor. It seems very possible, however, that the step was taken without any calculation of loss and gain.[12] We may suppose a scandalous case. Certain persons have been guilty of a flagrant act of dishonesty, condemned by all decent people. Here is an opportunity for the intervention of a Court which has been taught that it is not to intervene where the old Courts of Common Law offer a remedy. And as with politics, so with jurisprudence. I doubt whether in the first instance our Chancellor troubled his head about the 'juristic nature' of the new *Rechtsinstitut* or asked himself whether the new chapter of English law that he was beginning to write would fall under the title *Sachenrecht* or under the title *Obligationenrecht*. In some scandalous case he compelled the trustees to do what honesty required. Men often act first and think afterwards.

For some time we see hesitation at important points. For example, we hear a doubt whether the trust could be enforced against the heir of a sole trustee. As already said, efforts were generally made to prevent this question arising: to prevent the land coming to the hands of one man. So long as the wall was properly repaired, there would be no inheriting. But on the whole our new *Rechtsinstitut* seems soon to find the line of least resistance and to move irresistibly forward towards an appointed goal.

III

We are to speak of the rights of the *Destinatär*, or in our jargon *cestui que trust*.[13] Postponing the question against whom those rights will be valid, we may ask how those rights are treated within the sphere of their validity. And we soon see that within that sphere they are treated as *Eigentum* or as some of those modalities of *Eigentum* in which our medieval land law is so

---

[12] It may have been of decisive importance that at some critical moment the King himself wanted to leave some land by will. Edward III had tried ineffectually to do this. In 1417 King Henry V had a great mass of land in the hands of feoffees (including four bishops, a duke and three earls) and made a will in favour of his brothers. See Nichols, *Royal Wills*, 236.

[13] At starting the phrase would be *cestui a qui oes le feffement fut fait* [he to whose use the enfeoffment was made]. This degenerates into *cestui que use*; and then *cestui que trust* is made.

rich. The *Destinatär* has an 'estate', not in the land, but in 'the use'. This may be 'an estate in fee simple, an estate for life, an estate in remainder', and so forth. We might say that 'the use' is turned into an incorporeal thing, an incorporeal piece of land; and in this incorporeal thing you may have all those rights, those 'estates', which you could have in a real, tangible piece of land. And then in course of time movable goods and mere *Forderungen* [claims] are held in trust, and we get, as it were, a second edition of our whole *Vermögensrecht* [law of property]: a second and in some respects an amended edition. About all such matters as inheritance and alienation, the Chancellor's Equity, so we say, is to follow the Common Law.

Another point was settled at an early date. The earliest trust is in the first instance a trust for the author of the trust; he is not only the author of the trust but he is the *Destinatär*. But it is as *Destinatär* and not as contracting party that he obtains the Chancellor's assistance. The notion of contract is not that with which the Chancellor works in these cases: perhaps because the old Courts profess to enforce contracts. It is the destinatory who has the action, and he may be a person who was unborn when the trust was created. This is of importance for, curiously enough, after some vacillation our Courts of Common Law have adopted the rule that in the case of a *pactum in favorem tertii* [a contract in favour of a third party] the third party has no action.

But a true ownership, a truly *dingliches Recht*, the destinatory cannot have. In the common case a full and free and unconditioned ownership has been given to the trustees. Were the Chancellor to attempt to give the destinatory a truly *dingliches Recht*, the new Court would not be supplementing the work of the old Courts, but undoing it.

This brings us to the vital question, 'Against whom can the destinatory's right be enforced?' We see it enforced against the original trustees. Then after a little while we see it enforced against the heir of a trustee who has inherited the land; and, to speak more generally, we see it enforced against all those who by succession on death fill the place of a trustee. But what of a person to whom in breach of trust the trustee conveys the land? Such a person, so far as the old Courts can see, acquires ownership: full and free ownership: nothing less. The question is whether, although he be owner, he can be compelled to hold the land in trust for the destinatory. We soon learn that all is to depend upon the state of his 'conscience' at the time when he acquired the ownership. It is to be a question of 'notice'. This we are told already in 1471. 'If my trustee conveys the land to a third person who well knows that the trustee holds for my use, I shall have a remedy in the Chancery against both of them: as well against the buyer as against the trustee: for in conscience he buys my land.'[14]

That is a basis upon which a lofty structure is reared. The concept with which the Chancellor commences his operations is that of a guilty conscience. If any one knowing that the land is held upon trust for me obtains the ownership of it, he does what is unconscientious and must be treated as a trustee for me. In conscience the land is 'ma terre'.

This being established, no lawyer will be surprised to hear that the words 'if he knew' are after a while followed by the words 'or ought to have known', or that a certain degree of negligence is coordinated with fraud. By the side of 'actual notice' is placed 'constructive notice'.

And now we may refer once more to what Dr Schultze has said of the Lombards:

> Now it is possible that where land was concerned, the Lombards too had previously known a form of conveyance in their tribal law which made the act sufficiently public to the other members of the tribe at the very moment it took place. But in the period of interest here, conveyance of title deeds was by far and away the predominant form, and in any case the only one where formal donations in contemplation of death were concerned, including those in trust.

With some modifications, which it would be long to explain and which for our purpose are not very important, these words are true of the England in which the Trust was born and are yet truer of modern England. The buyer before he pays the price and obtains the land will investigate the seller's title. He will ask for and examine the *Urkunden* [deeds] which prove that the seller is owner, and unless the contract is specially worded, the seller of land is under a very onerous duty of demonstrating his ownership. This *Rechtssitte* [legal usage], as Dr Schultze calls it, enabled the Chancery to set up an external and objective standard of diligence for purchasers of land: namely the conduct of a prudent purchaser. The man who took a conveyance of land might be supposed to know (and he had 'constructive notice') of all such rights of destinatories as would have come to his knowledge if he had acted as a prudent purchaser would in his own interest have acted. 'But if, against legal usage, he did not concern himself with the title deeds, then there was no hardship if the condition unexpectedly took

---

[14] Year Book, 11 Edward IV, folio 8: 'Si mon feoffee de trust etc. enfeoffe un autre, que conust bien que le feoffor rien ad forsque a mon use, subpoena girra vers ambideux: scil. auxibien vers le feoffee come vers le feoffor . . . pur ceo que en conscience il purchase ma terre.'

effect against him; he shouldered the blame for any damage he sustained thereby.' Quite so. Such a purchaser himself became a trustee. We might say that he became a trustee *ex delicto vel quasi* [by delict or quasi-delict]. If not guilty of *dolus* [fraud], he was guilty of that sort of negligence which is equivalent to fraud. He had shut his eyes in order that he might not see.

A truly *dingliches Recht* the Chancellor could not create. The trustee is owner. It had to be admitted that if the purchaser who acquired ownership from the trustee was, not only ignorant, but excusably ignorant of the rights of the destinatory, then he must be left to enjoy the ownership that he had obtained. If he had acted as a prudent purchaser, as the reasonable man, behaves, then 'his conscience was unaffected' and the Chancellor's Equity had no hold upon him. But the Court of Chancery screwed up the standard of diligence ever higher and higher. The judges who sat in that Court were experts in the creation of trusts. We might say that they could smell a trust a long way off, and they were apt to attribute to every reasonable man their own keen scent. They were apt to attribute to him a constructive notice of all those facts which he would have discovered if he had followed up every trail that was suggested by those title deeds that he had seen or ought to have seen.

Of late years there has been some reaction in favour of purchasers. The standard, we are told, is not to be raised yet higher and perhaps it is being slightly lowered. Still it is very hard for any man to acquire land in England without acquiring 'constructive notice' of every trust that affects that land. I might almost say that this never happens except when some trustee has committed the grave crime of forgery.

It remains to be observed that a strong line was drawn in this as in other respects between the *entgeltliche Handlung* [transaction for value] and the *unentgeltliche Handlung* [free transaction]. A man who acquired the land from the trustee without giving 'value' for it was bound by the trust, even if at the time of acquisition he had no notice of it. It would be 'against conscience' for him to retain the gift after he knew that it had been made in breach of trust. It was only the 'purchaser for value' who could disregard the claims of the destinatory.

Also we see it established that the creditors of the trustee cannot exact payment of their debts out of the property that he holds in trust. And on the other hand the creditors of the destinatory can regard that property as part of his wealth. If we suppose that there is bankruptcy on both sides, this property will be divided, not among the creditors of the trustee but among the creditors of the destinatory. This, it need hardly be said, is an important point.

To produce all these results took a long time. The *Billigkeitsrecht* [law of equity] of the new Court moved slowly forward from precedent to precedent, but always towards one goal: namely, the strengthening at every point of the right of the destinatory. In our present context it may, for example, be interesting to notice that at one time it was currently said that the right of the destinatory could not be enforced against a corporation which had acquired the land, for a corporation has no conscience, and conscience is the basis of the equitable jurisdiction. But this precious deduction from the foreign *Fiktionstheorie* was long ago ignored, and it is the commonest thing to see a corporation as *Treuhänder*.

But perhaps the evolution of this *Rechtsinstitut* may be best seen in another quarter. To a modern Englishman it would seem plainly unjust and indeed intolerable that, if a sole trustee died intestate and without an heir, the rights of the destinatory should perish. And on the other hand it might seem to him unnatural that if the destinatory, 'the owner in equity', of this land died intestate and without an heir, the trustee should thenceforward hold the land for his own benefit. But the Court, working merely with the idea of good conscience, could not attain what we now regard as the right result. In the first case (trustee's death) the land fell back (escheat) to the King or to some other feudal lord. He did not claim any right through the trustee or through the creator of the trust, and equity had no hold upon him, for his conscience was clean.[15] In the second case (destinatory's death), the trust was at an end. The trustee was owner, and there was no more to be said. The King or the feudal lord was not a destinatory. In both respects, however, modern legislation has reversed these old rules.

Thus we come by the idea of an 'equitable ownership' or 'ownership in equity'. Supposing that a man is in equity the owner ('tenant in fee simple') of a piece of land, it makes very little difference to him that he is not also 'owner at law' and that, as we say, 'the legal ownership is outstanding in trustees'. The only serious danger that he is incurring is that this 'legal ownership' may come to a person who acquires it *bona fide*, for value, and without actual or constructive notice of his rights. And that is an uncommon event. It is an event of which practical lawyers must often be thinking when they give advice or compose documents;

---

[15] The law about this matter had become somewhat doubtful before Parliament intervened.

but still it is an uncommon event. I believe that for the ordinary thought of Englishmen 'equitable ownership' is just ownership pure and simple, though it is subject to a peculiar, technical and not very intelligible rule in favour of *bona fide* purchasers. A professor of law will tell his pupils that they must not think, or at any rate must not begin by thinking, in this manner. He may tell them that the destinatory's rights are in history and in ultimate analysis not *dinglich* but *obligatorisch*: that they are valid only against those who for some special reason are bound to respect them. But let the Herr Professor say what he likes, so many persons are bound to respect these rights that practically they are almost as valuable as if they were *dominium* [ownership].[16]

This is not all. Let us suppose that the thing that is held upon trust passes into the hands of one against whom the trust cannot be enforced. This may happen with land; it may more easily happen in the case of movables, because (for the reason that Dr Schultze has given) the Court could not extend its doctrine of constructive notice to traffic in movables. Now can we do no more for our destinatory than give him a mere *Schaden-ersatzklage* [action for compensation] against the dishonest trustee? That will not always be a very effectual remedy. Dishonest people are often impecunious, insolvent people.

The Court of Chancery managed to do something more for its darling. What it did I cannot well describe in abstract terms, but perhaps I may say that it converted the 'trust fund' into an incorporeal thing, capable of being 'invested' in different ways. Observe that metaphor of 'investment'. We conceive that the 'trust fund' can change its dress, but maintain its identity. To-day it appears as a piece of land; tomorrow it may be some gold coins in a purse; then it will be a sum of Consols; then it will be shares in a Railway Company, and then Peruvian Bonds. When all is going well, changes of investment may often be made; the trustees have been given power to make them. All along the 'trust fund' retains its identity. 'The price takes the place of the object' we might say, 'and the object takes the place of the price'. But the same idea is applied even when all is not going well. Suppose that a trustee sells land meaning to misappropriate

---

[16] Some writers even in theoretical discussion have allowed themselves to speak of the destinatory as 'the real owner', and of the trustee's ownership as 'nominal' and 'fictitious'. See Salmond, *Jurisprudence*, p. 278. But I think it is better and safer to say with a great American teacher that 'Equity could not create rights *in rem* if it would, and would not if it could.' See Langdell, *Harvard Law Review*, vol. 1, p. 60.

the price. The price is paid to him in the shape of a bank-note which is now in his pocket. That bank-note belongs 'in equity' to the destinatories. He pays it away as the price of shares in a company; those shares belong 'in equity' to the destinatories. He becomes bankrupt; those shares will not be part of the property that is divisible among his creditors; they will belong to the destinatories. And then, again, if the trustee mixes 'trust money' with his own money, we are taught to say that, so long as this is possible, we must suppose him to be an honest man and to be spending, not other people's money, but his own. This idea of a 'trust fund' that can be traced from investment to investment does not always work very easily, and for my own part I think it does scanty justice to the claims of the trustee's creditors. But it is an important part of our system. The Court of Chancery struggled hard to prevent its darling, the destinatory, from falling to the level of a mere creditor. And it should be understood that he may often have more than one remedy. He may be able both to pursue a piece of land and to attack the trustee who alienated it. It is not for others to say in what order he shall use his rights, so long as he has not got what he lost or an equivalent for it.

To complete the picture we must add that a very high degree not only of honesty but of diligence has been required of trustees. In common opinion it has been too high, and of late our legislature, without definitely lowering it, has given the courts a discretionary power of dealing mercifully with honest men who have made mistakes or acted unwisely. The honest man brought to ruin by the commission of 'a technical breach of trust', brought to ruin at the suit of his friend's children, has in the past been only too common a figure in English life. On the other hand, it was not until lately that the dishonest trustee who misappropriated money or other movables could be treated as a criminal. Naturally there was a difficulty here, for 'at law' the trustee was owner, and a man cannot be guilty of stealing what he both owns and possesses. But for half a century we have known the criminal breach of trust, and, though we do not call it theft, it can be severely punished.

Altogether it is certainly not of inadequate protection that a foreign jurist would speak if he examined the position of our destinatory. Rather I should suppose that he would say that this lucky being, the spoilt child of English jurisprudence, has been favoured at the expense of principles and distinctions that ought to have been held sacred. At any rate, those who would understand how our 'unincorporate bodies' have lived and flourished behind a hedge of trustees should understand that the right of the destinatory, though we must not call it a true *dominium rei*, is something far better than the mere benefit of a promise.

IV

To describe even in outline the various uses to which our Trust has been put would require many pages. As we all know, when once a *Rechtsinstitut* has been established, it does not perish or become atrophied merely because its original function becomes unnecessary. Trusts may be instituted because landowners want to make testaments but cannot make testaments. A statute gives them the power to make testaments; but by this time the trust has found other work to do and does not die. There is a long and very difficult story to be told about the action of Henry VIII. He was losing his feudal revenue and struck a blow which did a good deal of harm, and harm which we feel at the present day. But in such a survey as the present what he did looks like an ineffectual attempt to dam a mighty current. The stream sweeps onward, carrying some rubbish with it.

Soon the Trust became very busy. For a while its chief employment was 'the family settlement'. Of 'the family settlement' I must say no word, except this, that the trust thus entered the service of a wealthy and powerful class: the class of great landowners who could command the best legal advice and the highest technical skill. Whether we like the result or not, we must confess that skill of a very high order was applied to the construction of these 'settlements' of great landed estates. Everything that foresight could do was done to define the duties of the trustees. Sometimes they would be, as in the early cases, the mere depositaries of a nude *dominium*, bound only to keep it until it was asked for. At other times they would have many and complex duties to perform and wide discretionary powers. And then, if I may so speak, the 'settlement' descended from above: descended from the landed aristocracy to the rising monied class, until at last it was quite uncommon for any man or woman of any considerable wealth to marry without a 'marriage settlement'. Trusts of money or of invested funds became as usual as trusts of land. It may be worthy of notice that this was, at least in part, the effect of an extreme degree of testamentary freedom. Our law had got rid of the *Pflichtteil* [legal portion] altogether, and trusts in favour of the children of the projected marriage were a sort of substitute for it. However, in this region, what we have here to notice is that the trust became one of the commonest institutes of English law.

Almost every well-to-do man was a trustee; and though the usual trusts might fall under a few great headings, still all the details (which had to be punctually observed) were to be found in lengthy documents; and a large liberty of constructing unusual trusts was both conceded in law and exercised in fact. To classify trusts is like classifying contracts.

I am well aware that all this has its dark side, and I do not claim admiration for it. But it should not escape us that a very wide field was secured for what I may call social experimentation. Let me give one example. In 1882 a revolutionary change was made in our *eheliches Güterrecht* [law of marital property]. But this was no leap in the dark. It had been preceded by a prolonged course of experimentation. Our law about this matter had become osseous at an early time, and, especially as regards movable goods, was extremely unfavourable to the wife. There was no *Gemeinschaft* [community of ownership]. The bride's movables became the husband's; if the wife acquired, she acquired for her husband. Now *eheliches Güterrecht*, when once it has taken a definite shape, will not easily be altered. Legislators are not easily persuaded to touch so vital a point, and we cannot readily conceive that large changes can be gradually made by the practice of the courts. You cannot transfer ownership from the husband to the wife by slow degrees.

But here the Trust comes to our help. We are not now talking of ownership strictly so called. Some trustees are to be owners. We are only going to speak of their duties. What is to prevent us, if we use words enough, from binding them to pay the income of a fund into the very hands of the wife and to take her written receipt for it? But the wedge was in, and it could be driven home. It was a long process; but one successful experiment followed another. At length the time came when four well-tested words ('for her separate use') would give a married woman a *Vermögen* [property] of which she was the complete mistress 'in equity'; and if there was no other trustee appointed, her husband had to be trustee. Then, rightly or wrongly we came to the conclusion that all this experimentation had led to satisfactory results. Our law of husband and wife was revolutionised. But great as was the change, it was in fact little more than the extension to all marriages of rules which had long been applied to the marriages of the well-to-do.

But the liberty of action and experimentation that has been secured to us by the Trust is best seen in the freedom with which from a remote time until the present day *Anstalten* [institutions] and *Stiftungen* [foundations] of all sorts and kinds had been created by Englishmen.

Whether our law knows or ever has known what foreign lawyers would call a *selbstständige Anstalt* [autonomous institution] might be a vexed question among us, if we had – but we have not – any turn for juristic speculation. For some centuries we have kept among our technical notions that of a 'corporation sole'. Applied in the first instance to the parson of a parish church (*rector ecclesiae parochialis*) we have since the Reformation applied it also to bishops and to certain other ecclesiastical dignitaries. We have endeavoured to apply it also – much to our own disadvantage, so I think, – to our King or to the Crown; and in modern times we have been told by statute that we ought to apply it to a few officers of the central government, *e.g.* the Post Master General. It seems to me a most unhappy notion: an attempt at personification that has not succeeded. Upon examination, our 'corporation sole' turns out to be either a natural man or a juristic abortion: a sort of hybrid between *Anstalt* and *Mensch*. Our medieval lawyers were staunch realists. They would attribute the ownership of land to a man or to a body of men, but they would not attribute it to anything so unsubstantial as a personified *ecclesia* or a personified *dignitas*. Rather they would say that when the rector of a parish church died there was an interval during which the land attached to the church (*gleba ecclesiae*) was *herrenlos* [without an owner]. The *Eigentum*, they said, was *in nubibus* [in the clouds], or *in gremio legis* [in the lap of the law]; it existed only *en abéance* [in abeyance]; that is, *in spe* [in expectation only]. And I do not think that an English lawyer is entitled to say that this is not our orthodox theory at the present day. Practically the question is of no importance. For a long time past this part of our law has ceased to grow, and I hope that we are not destined to see any new 'corporations sole'.[17]

We have had no need to cultivate the idea of an 'autonomous institution' (*selbstständige Anstalt*), because with us the *unselbstständige Anstalt* [non-autonomous institution][vii] has long been a highly developed and flourishing *Rechtsinstitut*. I believe that the English term which most closely corresponds to the *Anstalt* or the *Stiftung* of German legal literature is 'a charity'. It is very possible that our concept of 'a charity' would not cover every *Anstalt* or *Stiftung* that is known to German lawyers: but it is and from a remote time has been enormously wide. For example, one of our courts had lately to decide that the mere encouragement of sport is not 'charity'. The annual giving of a prize to be competed for in a yacht-race is not a 'charitable' purpose. On the other hand, 'the total suppression of

[17] See above, pp. 32–51.

vivisection' is a charitable purpose, though it implies the repeal of an Act of Parliament, and though the judge who decides this question may be fully persuaded that this so-called 'charity' will do much more harm than good. English judges have carefully refrained from any exact definition of a 'charity'; but perhaps we may say that any *Zweck* [purpose] which any reasonable person could regard as directly beneficial to the public or to some large and indefinite class of men is a 'charitable' purpose. Some exception should be made of trusts which would fly in the face of morality or religion; but judges who were themselves stout adherents of the State Church have had to uphold as 'charitable', trusts which involved the maintenance of Catholicism, Presbyterianism, Judaism.

To the enforcement of charitable trusts we came in a very natural way and at an early date. A trust for persons shades off, we might say, into a trust for a *Zweck*. We are not, it will be remembered, speaking of true ownership. Ownership supposes an owner. We cannot put ownership into an indefinite mass of men; and, according to our English ideas, we cannot put ownership into a *Zweck*. I should say that there are vast masses of *Zweckvermögen* [special purpose funds] in England, but the owner is always man or corporation. As regards the trust, however, transitions are easy. You may start with a trust for the education of my son and for his education in a particular manner. It is easy to pass from this by slow degrees to the education of the boys of the neighbourhood, though in the process of transition the definite destinatary may disappear and leave only a *Zweck* behind him.[18]

At any rate, in 1601 there was already a vast mass of *Zweckvermögen* in the country; a very large number of *unselbstständige Stiftungen* had come into existence. A famous statute of that year became the basis of our law of Charitable Trusts,[viii] and their creation was directly encouraged. There being no problem about personality to be solved, the courts for a long while showed every favour to the authors of 'charitable' trusts. In particular, it was settled that where there was a 'charitable' *Zweck* there was to be no trouble about 'perpetuity'. The exact import of this remark could not be explained in two or three words. But, as might be supposed, even the Englishman, when he is making a trust of the ordinary private kind, finds that the law sets some limits to his power of bestowing benefits upon a long series of unborn destinatories; and these limits are formulated

---

[18] In the oldest cases the Court of Chancery seems to enforce the 'charitable' trust upon the complaint of anyone who is interested, without requiring the presence of any representative of the State.

in what we know as 'the rule against perpetuities'. Well, it was settled that where there is 'charity', there can be no trouble about 'perpetuity'.[19]

It will occur to my readers that it must have been necessary for English lawyers to make or to find some juristic person in whom the benefit of the 'charitable' trust would inhere and who would be the destinatory. But that is not true. It will be understood that in external litigation – *e.g.* if there were an adverse claim to a piece of land held by the trustees – the interests of the trust would be fully represented by the trustees. Then if it were necessary to take proceedings against the trustees to compel them to observe the trust, the *Reichsanwalt* (Attorney-General) would appear. We find it said long ago that it is for the King *ut parens patriae* [as the father of the country] to intervene for this purpose. But we have stopped far short of any theory which would make the State into the true destinatory (*cestui que trust*) of all charitable trusts. Catholics, Wesleyans, Jews would certainly be surprised if they were told that their cathedrals, chapels, synagogues were in any sense *Staatsvermögen* [public property]. We are not good at making juristic theories, but of the various concepts that seem to be offered to us by German books, it seems to me that *Zweckvermögen* is that which most nearly corresponds to our way of thinking about our 'charities'.

That great abuses took place in this matter of charitable trusts is undeniable. Slowly we were convinced by sad experience that in the way of supervision something more was necessary than the mere administration of the law (technically of 'equity') at the instance of a public *Staatsanwalt* [public prosecutor] who was casually set in motion by some person who happened to see that the trustees were not doing their duty. Since 1853 such supervision has been supplied by a central authority (the Charity Commissioners); but it is much rather supervision than control, and, so far from any check being placed on the creation of new *Stiftungen*, we in 1891 repealed a law which since 1736 had prevented men from giving land to 'charity' by testament.[20]

I understand that in the case of an *unselbstständige Stiftung* German legal doctrine knows a *Treuhänder* or *Fiduziar* [fiduciary], who in many respects would resemble our trustee, and I think that I might bring to light an important point by quoting some words that I read in Dr Regelsberger's *Pandekten*:

[19] An Englishman might say that § 2109 of the *B.G.B.* contains the German 'rule against perpetuities' and that it is considerably more severe than is the English.

[20] In some cases the land will have to be sold, but the 'charity' will get the price.

There are, moreover, good reasons for maintaining that a *Zweck-vermögen* is removed from the reach of the fiduciary's creditors, whose claims do not arise from the *Zweckvermögen* itself, and furthermore, that on bankruptcy of the fiduciary, or upon the confiscation of his property, a right of sequestration could be claimed for the *Zweck-vermögen*, since the recipient, although bearer of the proprietary right, is so only in another's interest.[21]

Now in England these would not be probable opinions: they would be obvious and elementary truths. The trustee's creditors have nothing whatever to do with the trust property. Our independent institution lives behind a wall that was erected in the interests of the richest and most powerful class of Englishmen: it is as safe as the duke and the millionaire.

But the wall will need repairs.

The subject of the right (says Dr Regelsberger) to whom the *Zweck-vermögen* is transferred at the creation of a non-autonomous public foundation is, as a rule, a juristic person, a corporation, for only a juristic person offers a lasting point of support.[22]

We have not found that to be true. Doubtless a corporation is, because of its permanence, a convenient trustee. But it is a matter of convenience. By means of the Germanic *Gesamthandschaft* [joint ownership] and of a power given to the surviving trustees – or perhaps to some destinatories, or perhaps to other people (*e.g.* the catholic bishop of the diocese for the time being) – of appointing new trustees, a great deal of permanence can be obtained at a cost that is not serious if the property is of any considerable value. Extreme cases, such as that of a sole trustee who is wandering about in Central Africa with the ownership of some English land in his nomadic person, can be met by an order of the Court ('a vesting order') taking the ownership out of him and putting it in some more accessible receptacle. We have spent a great deal of pains over this matter. I am far from saying that all our devices are elegant. On juristic elegance we do not pride ourselves, but we know how to keep the roof weather-tight.

And here it should be observed that many reformers of our 'charities' have deliberately preferred that 'charitable trusts' should be confided, not to corporations, but to 'natural persons'. It is said – and appeal is made to long experience – that men are more conscientious when they are doing

[21] *Pandekten*, 442.
[22] *Ibid.*, 341.

acts in their own names than when they are using the name of a corporation. In consequence of this prevailing opinion, all sorts of expedients have been devised by Parliament for simplifying and cheapening those transitions of *Eigentum* which are inevitable where mortal men are the basis of an *unselbstständige Stiftung*. Some of these would shock a theorist. In the case of certain places of worship, we may see the *dominium* taken out of one set of men and put into another set of men by the mere vote of an assembly – an unincorporated congregation of Nonconformists.[23] Of course no rules of merely private law can explain this; but that does not trouble us.

This brings us to a point at which the Trust performed a signal service. All that we English people mean by 'religious liberty' has been intimately connected with the making of trusts. When the time for a little toleration had come, there was the Trust ready to provide all that was needed by the barely tolerated sects. All that they had to ask from the State was that the open preaching of their doctrines should not be unlawful.

By way of contrast I may be allowed to cite a few words written by Dr Hinschius:

> When, as a result of new circumstances, the earlier State-Church or *Staatskirchentum* began to tolerate other individual religious societies, it could not regard these as purely private associations, since it saw religion as a state concern. Rather, it had accordingly to take the position that such associations should be treated to a certain extent as corporations of public law, but on the other hand subjected them to extensive controls and interventions by the state.[24]

But just what, according to Dr Hinschius, could not be done, was in England the easy and obvious thing to do. If in 1688 the choice had lain between conceding no toleration at all and forming corporations of Nonconformists, and even 'Korporationen mit öffentlichen Rechten' [corporations of public law], there can be little doubt that the dominant *Staatskirchentum* would have left them untolerated for a long time to come, for in England, as elsewhere, incorporation meant privilege and exceptional favour. And, on the other hand, there were among the Nonconformists many who would have thought that even toleration was dearly purchased if their religious affairs were subjected to State control. But if the State could be persuaded to do the very minimum, to repeal a few

---

[23] Trustees Appointment Acts, 1850–69–90.
[24] Marquardsen's *Handbuch des öffentlichen Rechts*, B. 1, S. 367.

persecuting laws, to say 'You shall not be punished for not going to the parish church, and you shall not be punished for going to your meeting-house', that was all that was requisite. Trust would do the rest, and the State and the *Staatskirchentum* could not be accused of any active participation in heresy and schism. Trust soon did the rest. I have been told that some of the earliest trust deeds of Nonconformist 'meeting-houses' say what is to be done with the buildings if the Toleration Act be repealed. After a little hesitation, the courts enforced these trusts, and even held that they were 'charitable'.

And now we have in England Jewish synagogues and Catholic cathedrals and the churches and chapels of countless sects. They are owned by natural persons. They are owned by trustees.

Now I know very well that our way of dealing with all the churches, except that which is 'by law established' (and in America and the great English colonies even that exception need not be made), looks grotesque to some of those who see it from the outside. They are surprised when they learn that such an 'historic organism' as the Church of Rome, 'is on a par with a private association, a sports club'.[25] But when they have done laughing at us, the upshot of their complaint or their warning is, not that we have not made this historic organism comfortable enough, but that we have made it too comfortable.

I have spoken of our 'charity' as an *Anstalt* or *Stiftung*; but, as might be expected in a land where men have been very free to create such 'charitable trusts' as they pleased, *anstaltliche* and *genossenschaftliche* [institutional and co-operative] threads have been interwoven in every conceivable fashion. And this has been so from the very first. In dealing with charitable trusts one by one, our Courts have not been compelled to make any severe classification. *Anstalt* or *Genossenschaft* was not a dilemma which every trust had to face, though I suppose that what would be called an *anstaltliches Element* [institutional element] is implicit in our notion of a charity. This seems particularly noticeable in the ecclesiastical region. There is a piece of ground with a building on it which is used as a place of worship. Who or what is it that in this instance stands behind the trustees? Shall we say *Anstalt* or shall we say *Verein* [society]?

No general answer could be given. We must look at the 'trust deed'. We may find that as a matter of fact the trustees are little better than automata whose springs are controlled by the catholic bishop, or by the

25 Hinschius, op. cit. S. 222–4.

central council ('Conference') of the Wesleyans; or we may find that the trustees themselves have wide discretionary powers. A certain amount of *Zweck* there must be, for otherwise the trust would not be 'charitable'. But this demand is satisfied by the fact that the building is to be used for public worship. If, however, we raise the question who shall preach here, what shall he preach, who shall appoint, who shall dismiss him, then we are face to face with almost every conceivable type of organisation from centralised and absolute monarchy to decentralised democracy and the autonomy of the independent congregation. To say nothing of the Catholics, it is well known that our Protestant Nonconformists have differed from each other much rather about Church government than about theological dogma: but all of them have found satisfaction for their various ideals of ecclesiastical polity under the shadow of our trusts.

V

This brings us to our 'unincorporated bodies', and by way of a first example I should like to mention the Wesleyans. They have a very elaborate and a highly centralised constitution, the primary outlines of which are to be found in a deed to which John Wesley set his seal in 1784. Thereby he declared the trusts upon which he was holding certain lands and buildings that had been conveyed to him in various parts of England. Now-a-days we see Wesleyan chapels in all our towns and in many of our villages. Generally every chapel has its separate set of trustees, but the trust deeds all follow one model, devised by a famous lawyer in 1832 – the printed copy that lies before me fills more than forty pages – and these deeds institute a form of government so centralised that Rome might be proud of it, though the central organ is no pope, but a council.

But we must not dwell any longer on cases in which there is a 'charitable trust', for, as already said, there is in these cases no pressing demand for a personal destinatary. We can, if we please, think of the charitable *Zweck* as filling the place that is filled by a person in the ordinary private trust. When, however, we leave behind us the province, the wide province, of 'charity', then – so we might argue *a priori* – a question about personality must arise. There will here be no *Zweck* that is protected as being 'beneficial to the public'. There will here be no intervention of a *Staatsanwalt* who represents the 'father of the country'. Must there not therefore be some destinatary who is either a natural or else a juristic person? Can we have a trust for a *Genossenschaft*, unless it is endowed with personality, or unless it is steadily regarded as being a mere collective name for certain natural persons? I believe that our answer should be that in theory we cannot, but that in practice we can.

If then we ask how there can be this divergence between theory and practice, we come upon what has to my mind been the chief merit of the Trust. It has served to protect the unincorporated *Genossenschaft* against the attacks of inadequate and individualistic theories.

We should all agree that, if an *Anstalt* or a *Genossenschaft* is to live and thrive, it must be efficiently defended by law against external enemies. On the other hand, experience seems to show that it can live and thrive, although the only theories that lawyers hold about its internal affairs are inadequate. Let me dwell for a moment on both of these truths.

Our *Anstalt*, or our *Genossenschaft*, or whatever it may be, has to live in a wicked world: a world full of thieves and rogues and other bad people. And apart from wickedness, there will be unfounded claims to be resisted: claims made by neighbours, claims made by the State. This sensitive being must have a hard, exterior shell. Now our Trust provides this hard, exterior shell for whatever lies within. If there is theft, the thief will be accused of stealing the goods of Mr A. B. and Mr C. D., and not one word will be said of the trust. If there is a dispute about a boundary, Mr A. B. and Mr C. D. will bring or defend the action. It is here to be remembered that during the age in which the Trust was taking shape all this external litigation went on before courts where nothing could be said about trusts. The judges in those courts, if I may so say, could only see the wall of trustees and could see nothing that lay beyond it. Thus in a conflict with an external foe no question about personality could arise. A great deal of ingenuity had been spent in bringing about this result.

But if there be this hard exterior shell, then there is no longer any pressing demand for juristic theory. Years may pass by, decades, even centuries, before jurisprudence is called upon to decide exactly what it is that lies within the shell. And if what lies within is some *Genossenschaft*, it may slowly and silently change its shape many times before it is compelled to explain its constitution to a public tribunal. Disputes there will be; but the disputants will be very unwilling to call in the policeman. This unwillingness may reach its highest point in the case of religious bodies. Englishmen are a litigious race, and religious people have always plenty to quarrel about. Still they are very reluctant to seek the judgment seat of Gallio.[ix] As is well known, our 'Law Reports', beginning in the day of Edward I, are a mountainous mass. Almost every side of English life is revealed in them. But if you search them through in the hope of discovering the organisation of our churches and sects (other than the established church) you will find only a few widely scattered hints. And what is true of religious bodies, is hardly less true of many other *Vereine*, such as our 'clubs'. Even the 'pugnacious Englishman' whom Ihering admired, would, as we say, think once, twice, thrice, before he appealed to a court of law against the decision of the committee or the general meeting. I say 'appealed', and believe that this is the word that he would use, for the thought of a 'jurisdiction' inherent in the *Genossenschaft* is strong in us, and I believe that it is at its strongest where there is no formal corporation. And so, the external wall being kept in good repair, our English legal *Dogmatik* [dogmatics] may have no theory or a wholly inadequate and antiquated theory of what goes on behind. And to some of us that seems a desirable state of affairs. Shameful though it may be to say this, we fear the petrifying action of juristic theory.

And now may I name a few typical instances of 'unincorporated bodies' that have lived behind the trustee wall?

I imagine a foreign tourist, with Bädeker in hand, visiting one of our 'Inns of Court': let us say Lincoln's Inn.[26] He sees the chapel and the library and the dining-hall; he sees the external gates that are shut at night. It is in many respects much like such colleges as he may see at Oxford and Cambridge. On inquiry he hears of an ancient constitution that had taken shape before 1422, and we know not how much earlier. He learns that something in the way of legal education is being done by these Inns of Court, and that for this purpose a federal organ, a Council of Legal Education, has been established. He learns that no man can practise as an advocate in any of the higher courts who is not a member of one of the four Inns and who has not there received the degree of 'barrister-at-law'. He would learn that these Inns have been very free to dictate the terms upon which this degree is given. He would learn that the Inn has in its hands a terrible, if rarely exercised, power of expelling ('disbarring') a member for dishonourable or unprofessional conduct, of excluding him from the courts in which he has been making his living, of ruining him and disgracing him. He would learn that in such a case there might be an appeal to the judges of our High Court: but not to them as a public tribunal: to them as 'visitors' and as constituting, we might say, a second instance of the domestic forum.

[26] In Latin documents the word corresponding to our *inn* is *hospitium*.

Well, he might say, apparently we have some curious hybrid – and we must expect such things in England – between an *Anstalt des öffentlichen Rechtes* [an institution of public law] and a *privilegierte Korporation* [privileged corporation]. Nothing of the sort, an English friend would reply; you have here a *Privatverein* [private society] which has not even juristic personality. It might – such at least our theory has been – dissolve itself tomorrow, and its members might divide the property that is held for them by trustees. And indeed there was until lately an Inn of a somewhat similar character, the ancient Inn of the 'Serjeants at Law', and, as there were to be no more serjeants, its members dissolved the *Verein* and divided their property. Many people thought that this dissolution of an ancient society was to be regretted; there was a little war in the newspapers about it; but as to the legal right we were told that there was no doubt.

It need hardly be said that the case of these Inns of Court is in a certain sense anomalous. Such powers as they wield could not be acquired at the present day by any *Privatverein*, and it would not be too much to say that we do not exactly know how or when those powers were acquired, for the beginning of these societies of lawyers was very humble and is very dark. But, before we leave them, let us remember that the English judges who received and repeated a great deal of the canonistic learning about corporations, *Fiktionstheorie*, *Konzessionstheorie* [fiction theory, concession theory] and so forth, were to a man members of these *Körperschaften* [corporate entities] and had never found that the want of juristic personality was a serious misfortune. Our lawyers were rich and influential people. They could easily have obtained incorporation had they desired it. They did not desire it.

But let us come to modern cases. To-day German ships and Austrian ships are carrying into all the seas the name of the keeper of a coffee-house, the name of Edward Lloyd. At the end of the seventeenth century he kept a coffee-house in the City of London, which was frequented by 'underwriters' or marine insurers. Now from 1720 onwards these men had to do their business in the most purely individualistic fashion. In order to protect two privileged corporations, which had lent money to the State, even a simple *Gesellschaft* [society] among underwriters was forbidden. Every insurer had to act for himself and for himself only. We might not expect to see such individualistic units coalescing so as to form a compactly organised body – and this too not in the middle age but in the eighteenth century. However, these men had common interests: an interest in obtaining information, an interest in exposing fraud and resisting fraudulent claims.

There was a subscription; there was a small 'trust fund'; the exclusive use of the 'coffee-house' was obtained. The *Verein* grew and grew. During the great wars of the Napoleonic age, 'the Committee for regulating the affairs of Lloyd's Coffee House' became a great power. But the organisation was still very loose until 1811, when a trust deed was executed and bore more than eleven hundred signatures. I must not attempt to tell all that 'Lloyd's' has done for England. The story should be the better known in Germany, because the hero of it, J. J. Angerstein, though he came to us from Russia, was of German parentage. But until 1871 Lloyd's was an unincorporated *Verein* without the least trace (at least so we said) of juristic personality about it. And when incorporation came in 1871, the chief reason for the change was to be found in no ordinary event, but in the recovery from the bottom of the Zuyder Zee of a large mass of treasure which had been lying there since 1799, and which belonged – well, owing to the destruction of records by an accidental fire, no one could exactly say to whom it belonged. In the life of such a *Verein* 'incorporation' appears as a mere event. We could not even compare it to the attainment of full age. Rather it is as if a 'natural person' bought a type-writing machine or took lessons in stenography.[27]

Even more instructive is the story of the London Stock Exchange.[28] Here also we see small beginnings. In the eighteenth century the men who deal in stocks frequent certain coffee-houses: in particular 'Jonathan's'. They begin to form a club. They pay the owner an annual sum to exclude those whom they have not elected into their society. In 1773 they moved to more commodious rooms. Those who used the rooms paid sixpence a day. In 1802 a costly site was bought, a costly building erected, and an elaborate constitution was formulated in a 'deed of settlement'. There was a capital of £20,000 divided into 400 shares. Behind the trustees stood a body of 'proprietors', who had found the money; and behind the 'proprietors' stood a much larger body of 'members', whose subscriptions formed the income that was divided among the 'proprietors'. And then there was building and always more building. In 1876 there was a new 'deed of settlement'; in 1882 large changes were made in it; there was a capital of £240,000 divided into 20,000 shares.

Into details we must not enter. Suffice it that the organisation is of a high type. It might, for example, strike one at first that the shares

[27] F. Martin, *History of Lloyd's*, 1876.
[28] C. Duguid, *Story of the Stock Exchange*, 1901.

of the 'proprietors' would, by the natural operation of private law, be often passing into the hands of people who were in no wise interested in the sort of business that is done on the Stock Exchange, and that thus the *genossenschaftliche* [co-operative] character of the constitution would be destroyed. But that danger could be obviated. There was nothing to prevent the original subscribers from agreeing that the shares could only be sold to members of the Stock Exchange, and that, if by inheritance a share came to other hands, it must be sold within a twelvemonth. Such regulations have not prevented the shares from being valuable.

In 1877 a Royal Commission was appointed to consider the Stock Exchange. It heard evidence; it issued a report; it made recommendations. A majority of its members recommended that the Stock Exchange should be incorporated by royal charter or Act of Parliament.

And so the Stock Exchange was incorporated? Certainly not. In England you cannot incorporate people who do not want incorporation, and the members of the Stock Exchange did not want it. Something had been said about the submission of the 'bye-laws' of the corporation to the approval of a central *Behörde* [authority] the Board of Trade. That was the cloven hoof. *Ex pede diabolum.*[29,x]

Now, unless we have regard to what an Englishman would call 'mere technicalities', it would not, I think, be easy to find anything that a corporation could do and that is not being done by this *nicht rechtsfähiger Verein* [society without legal capacity]. It legislates profusely. Its representative among the Royal Commissioners did not scruple to speak of 'legislation'. And then he told how it did justice and enforced a higher standard of morality than the law can reach. And a terrible justice it is. Expulsion brings with it disgrace and ruin, and minor punishments are inflicted. In current language the committee is said to 'pronounce a sentence' of suspension for a year, or two years or five years.

The 'quasi-judicial' power of the body over its members – *quasi* is one of the few Latin words that English lawyers really love – is made to look all the more judicial by the manner in which it is treated by our courts of law. A man who is expelled from one of our clubs – or (to use a delicate phrase) whose name is removed from the list of members – will sometimes complain to a public court. That court will insist on a strict observance of any procedure that is formulated in the written or printed 'rules' of the club; but also there may be talk of 'natural justice'. Thereby is meant an

---

[29] London Stock Exchange Commission, Parliamentary Papers, 1878, vol. XIX.

observance of those forms which should secure for every accused person a full and fair trail. In particular, a definite accusation should be definitely made, and the accused should have a sufficient opportunity of meeting it. Whatever the printed rules may say, it is not easy to be supposed that a man has placed his rights beyond that protection which should be afforded to all men by 'natural justice'. Theoretically the 'rules', written or unwritten, may only be the terms of a contract, still the thought that this man is complaining that justice has been denied to him by those who were bound to do it, often finds practical expression. The dread of *Vereinsherrschaft* [club-rule] is hardly represented among us.[xi]

I believe that in the eyes of a large number of my fellow-countrymen the most important and august tribunal in England is not the House of Lords but the Jockey Club; and in this case we might see 'jurisdiction' – they would use that word – exercised by the *Verein* over those who stand outside it. I must not aspire to tell this story. But the beginning of it seems to be that some gentlemen form a club, buy a race-course, the famous Newmarket Heath, which is conveyed to trustees for them, and then they can say who shall and who shall not be admitted to it. I fancy, however, that some men who have been excluded from this sacred heath ('warned off Newmarket Heath' is our phrase) would have much preferred the major excommunication of that 'historic organism' the Church of Rome.

It will have been observed that I have been choosing examples from the eighteenth century: a time when, if I am not mistaken, corporation theory sat heavy upon mankind in other countries. And we had a theory in England too, and it was of a very orthodox pattern; but it did not crush the spirit of association. So much could be done behind a trust, and the beginnings might be so very humble. All this tended to make our English jurisprudence disorderly, but also gave to it something of the character of an experimental science, and that I hope it will never lose.

But surely, it will be said, you must have some juristic theory about the constitution of the *Privatverein*: some theory, for example, about your clubs and those luxurious club-houses which we see in Pall Mall.

Yes, we have, and it is a purely individualistic theory. This it must necessarily be. As there is no 'charity' in the case, the trust must be a trust for persons, and any attempt to make it a trust for unascertained persons (future members) would soon come into collision with that 'rule against perpetuities' which keeps the *Familienfideicommiss* [family *fideicommissum*; entailed estate] within moderate bounds. So really we have no tools to work with except such as are well known to all lawyers. Behind the wall of trustees we have *Miteigentum* and *Vertrag* [co-ownership and contract]. We say that 'in equity' the original members were the only destinatories: they were *Miteigentümer* with *Gesamthandschaft* [co-owners with joint ownership]; but at the same time they contracted to observe certain rules.

I do not think that the result is satisfactory. The 'ownership in equity' that the member of the club has in land, buildings, furniture, books etc. is of a very strange kind. (1) Practically it is inalienable. (2) Practically his creditors cannot touch it by execution. (3) Practically, if he is bankrupt, there is nothing for them.[30] (4) It ceases if he does not pay his annual subscription. (5) It ceases if in accordance with the rules he is expelled. (6) His share – if of a share we may speak – is diminished whenever a new member is elected. (7) He cannot demand a partition. And (8) in order to explain all this, we have to suppose numerous tacit contracts which no one knows that he is making, for after every election there must be a fresh contract between the new member and all the old members. But every judge on the bench is a member of at least one club, and we know that, if a thousand tacit contracts have to be discovered, a tolerable result will be attained. We may remember that the State did not fall to pieces when philosophers and jurists declared that it was the outcome of contract.

There are some signs that in course of time we may be driven out of this theory. The State has begun to tax clubs as it taxes corporations.[31] When we have laid down as a very general principle that, when a man gains any property upon the death of another, he must pay something to the State, it becomes plain to us that the property of a club will escape this sort of taxation. It would be ridiculous, and indeed impossible, to hold that, whenever a member of a club dies, some taxable increment of wealth accrues to every one of his fellows. So the property of the 'unincorporated body' is to be taxed as if it belonged to a corporation. This is a step forward.

Strange operations with *Miteigentum* and *Vertrag* must, I should suppose, have been very familiar to German jurists in days when corporateness was not to be had upon easy terms. But what I am concerned to remark is that, owing to the hard exterior shell provided by a trust, the inadequacy of our theories was seldom brought to the light of day. Every now and again a court of law may have a word to say about a club; but you

---

[30] In a conceivable case the prospective right to an aliquot part of the property of a club that was going to be dissolved might be valuable to a member's creditors; but this would be a rare case, and I can find nothing written about it. Some clubs endeavour by their rules to extinguish the right of a bankrupt member.

[31] Customs and Inland Revenue Act, 1885, sec. 11.

will find nothing about club-property in our institutional treatises. And yet the value of those houses in London, their sites and their contents, is very great, and almost every English lawyer is interested, personally interested, in one of them.

A comparison between our unincorporated *Verein* and the *nicht rechtsfähiger Verein* [society without legal capacity] of the new German code might be very instructive; but perhaps the first difference that would strike anyone who undertook the task would be this, that, whereas in the German case almost every conceivable question has been forestalled by scientific and controversial discussion, there is in the English case very little to be read. We have a few decisions, dotted about here and there; but they have to be read with caution, for each decision deals only with some one type of *Verein*, and the types are endless. I might perhaps say that no attempt has been made to provide answers for half the questions that have been raised, for example, by Dr Gierke. And yet let me repeat that our *Vereine ohne Rechtsfähigkeit* [societies without legal capacity] are very numerous, that some of them are already old, and that some of them are wealthy.[32]

One of the points that is clear (and here we differ from the German code) is that our unincorporated *Verein* is not to be likened to a *Gesellschaft* (partnership): at all events this is not to be done when the *Verein* is a 'club' of the common type.[33] Parenthetically I may observe that for the present purpose the English for *Gesellschaft* is 'Partnership' and the English for *Verein* is 'Society'. Now in the early days of clubs an attempt was made to treat the club as a *Gesellschaft*. The *Gesellschaft* was an old well-established institute, and an effort was made to bring the new creature under the old rubric. That effort has, however, been definitely abandoned and we are now taught, not only that the club is not a *Gesellschaft*, but that you cannot as a general rule argue from the one to the other. Since 1890 we have a statutory definition of a *Gesellschaft*: 'Partnership is the relation which subsists between persons carrying on a business in common with a view of profit.'[34] A club would not fall within this definition.

---

[32] I believe that all the decisions given by our Courts in any way affecting our clubs will be found in a small book: J. Wertheimer, *Law relating to Clubs*, ed. 3, by A. W. Chaster, 1903.

[33] It was otherwise with the unincorporated *Aktiengesellschaft*; but that is almost a thing of the past. A few formed long ago may still be living in an unincorporated condition, e.g. the London Stock Exchange.

[34] Partnership Act, 1890, sec. 1. For the meaning of these words, see F. Pollock, *Digest of the Law of Partnership*, ed. 6.

The chief practical interest of this doctrine, that a club is not to be assimilated to a *Gesellschaft*, lies in the fact that the committee of an English club has no general power of contracting on behalf of the members within a sphere marked out by the affairs of the club. A true corporate liability could not be manufactured, and, as I shall remark below, our courts were setting their faces against any attempt to establish a limited liability. The supposition as regards the club is that the members pay their subscriptions in advance, and that the committee has ready money to meet all current expenses. On paper that is not satisfactory. I believe that cases must pretty frequently occur in which a tradesman who has supplied wine or books or other goods for the use of the club would have great difficulty in discovering the other contractor. We have no such rule (and here again we differ from the German code) as that the person who professes to act on behalf of an unincorporated *Verein* is always personally liable;[35] and I think the tradesman could often be forced to admit that he had not given credit to any man, the truth being that he thought of the club as a person. I can only say that scandals, though not absolutely unknown,[36] have been very rare; that the members of the club would in all probability treat the case as if it were one of corporate liability; and that London tradesmen are willing enough to supply goods to clubs on a large scale. If there is to be extraordinary expenditure, if, for example, a new wing is to be added to the building, money to a large amount can often be borrowed at a very moderate rate of interest. We know a 'mortgage without personal liability'; and that has been useful. Strictly speaking there is no debtor; but the creditor has various ways by which he can obtain payment: in particular he can sell the land.

Deliktsfähigkeit [capacity to commit an offence] is an interesting and at the present time it is perhaps a burning point. A little while ago English lawyers would probably have denied that anything resembling corporate liability could be established in this quarter. Any liability beyond that of the man who does the unlawful act must be that of a principal for the acts of an agent, or of a master for the acts of a servant, and if there is any liability at all, it must be unlimited. But this is now very doubtful. Our highest court (the House of Lords) has lately held that a trade union is *deliktsfähig*: in other words, that the damage done by the organised action of this unincorporated *Verein* must be paid for out of the property

---

[35] *B.G.B.* § 54.
[36] See Wertheimer, op. cit. p. 73.

held by its trustees. Now a trade union is an unincorporated *Verein* of a somewhat exceptional sort. It is the subject of special Statutes which have conferred upon it some, but not all, of those legal qualities which we associate with incorporation. Whether this decision, which made a great noise, is attributable to this exceptional element, or whether it is to be based upon a broader ground, is not absolutely plain. The trade unionists are dissatisfied about this and some other matters, and what the results of their agitation will be I cannot say. The one thing that it is safe to predict is that in England *sozialpolitische* [socio-political] will take precedence of *rechtswissenschaftliche* [jurisprudential] considerations. As to the broader question, now that a beginning has once been made, I believe that the situation could be well described in some words that I will borrow from Dr Gierke:

> Perhaps a custom is taking root subjecting clubs without legal capacity to corporation law as far as liability for unlawfully inflicted damage is concerned.[37]

The natural inclination of the members of an English club would, so I think, be to treat the case exactly as if it were a case of corporate liability. It has often struck me that morally there is most personality where legally there is none. A man thinks of his club as a living being, honourable as well as honest, while the joint-stock company is only a sort of machine into which he puts money and out of which he draws dividends.

As to the *Deliktsfähigkeit* of corporations it may not be out of place to observe that by this time English corporations have had to pay for almost every kind of wrong that one man can do to another. Thus recently an incorporated company had to pay for having instituted criminal proceedings against a man 'maliciously and without reasonable or probable cause'. In our theoretical moments we reconcile this with the *Fiktionstheorie* by saying that it is a case in which a master (*persona ficta*) pays for the act of his servant or a principal for the act of an agent, and, as our rule about the master's liability is very wide, the explanation is not obviously insufficient. I am not sure that this may not help us to attain the desirable result in the case of the unincorporated *Verein*.

Our practical doctrine about the *Vermögen* [property] of our clubs seems to me to be very much that which is stated by Dr Gierke in the following

---

[37] Gierke, *Vereine ohne Rechtsfähigkeit*, zweite Auflage, S. 20.

sentence, though (for the reason already given) we should have to omit a few words in which he refers to a *Gesellschaft* [partnership].[38]

> The club's property . . . belongs . . . to the members for the time being; but as partnership-property [club-property] it is a separate body of assets set aside from the remaining property of the members as property serving the purpose of the partnership [club], to be held in common by the partners [club-members] in undivided shares, which comes close to a corporation's property.

And then in England the *Sonderung* [separation] of this *Vermögen* from all the other *Vermögen* of the *Teilhaber* [members] can be all the plainer, because in legal analysis the owners of this *Vermögen* are not the *Vereinsmitglieder* [club members], but the trustees. It is true that for practical purposes this property of the trustees of a club may be hardly better than a *Scheineigentum* [sham property], and the trustees themselves may be hardly better than puppets whose wires are pulled by the committee and the general meeting. And it is to be observed that in the case of this class of trusts the destinatories are peculiarly well protected, for, even if deeds were forged, no man could say that he had bought one of our club-houses or a catholic cathedral without suspecting the existence of a trust: *res ipsa loquitur* [the matter speaks for itself]. Still the *nudum dominium* [bare proprietary right] of the trustees serves as a sort of external mark which keeps all this *Vermögen* together as a *Sondervermögen* [separate body of assets]. And when we remember that some great jurists have found it possible to speak of the juristic person as puppet, a not unimportant analogy is established.

> The club can acquire property not merely from living persons but also by succession to dead persons. For there is no obstacle to nominating the members at any given time in their partnership (club) solidarity as heirs, nor to making them a bequest.[39]

This is substantially true of our English law, though the words 'nominating as heirs' do not fit into our system. A little care on the part of the testator is requisite in such cases in order that he may not be accused of having endeavoured to create a trust in favour of a long series of unascertained persons (future members) and of having come into collision with our 'rule against perpetuities'. The less he says the better. Substantially

---

[38] *Vereine ohne Rechtsfähigkeit*, S. 14.
[39] Gierke, op. cit., S. 21.

the *Verein* is *vermächtnissfähig* [able to receive bequests]. Dr Gierke's next sentence also is true, though of course the first word is inappropriate.[xii] '[Laws of the federal states introducing (*landesgesetzlich*)] restrictions on the abilities of juristic persons to acquire rights cannot be extended to clubs having no legal capacity'.

Since our lawyers explained away a certain statute of Henry VIII, which will be mentioned below, our *nicht rechtsfähiger Verein* [society without legal capacity] has stood outside the scope of those statutes which forbad corporations to acquire land (Statutes of Mortmain). And this was at one time a great advantage that our *nicht rechtsfähiger Verein* had over the *rechtsfähiger Verein*. The Jockey Club, for example, could acquire Newmarket Heath without asking the King's or the State's permission. Even at the present day certain of our *nicht rechtsfähige Vereine* would lose their power of holding an unlimited quantity of land if they registered themselves under the Companies Acts and so became corporations.[40]

As regards *Prozessfähigkeit*, our doctrine regarded the capacity 'to sue and be sued' as one of the essential attributes of the corporation. Indeed at times this capacity seems to have appeared as the specific *differentia* of the corporation, though the common seal also was an important mark. And with this doctrine we have not openly broken. It will be understood, however, that in a very large class of disputes the concerns of the *nicht rechtsfähiger Verein* would be completely represented by the trustees. Especially would this be the case in all litigation concerning *Liegenschaft* [immovables]. Suppose a dispute with a neighbour about a servitude ('easement') or about a boundary, this can be brought into court and decided as if there were no trust in existence and no *Verein*. And so if the dispute is with some *Pächter* [leaseholder] or *Mieter* [tenant] of land or houses that belong 'in equity' to the *Verein*. There is a legal relationship between him and the trustees, but none between him and the *Verein*; and in general it will be impossible for him to give trouble by any talk about the constitution of the *Verein*. And then as regards internal controversies, the Court of Chancery developed a highly elastic doctrine about 'representative suits'. The beginning of this lies far away from the point that we are considering. It must suffice that in dealing with those complicated trusts that Englishmen are allowed to create, the court was driven to hold that a class of persons may be sufficiently represented in litigation by a member of that class. We became familiar with the plaintiff who was suing

---

[40] Companies Act, 1862, sec. 21.

'on behalf of himself and all other legatees' or 'all other cousins of the deceased' or 'all other creditors'. This practice came to the aid of the *Verein*. Our English tendency would be to argue that if in many cases a mere class (*e.g.* the testator's nephews) could be represented by a specimen, then *a fortiori* a *Verein* could be represented by its 'officers'. And we should do this without seeing that we were infringing the corporation's exclusive possession of *Prozessfähigkeit*.[41]

But with all its imperfections the position of the unincorporate *Verein* must be fairly comfortable. There is a simple test that we can apply. For the last forty years and more almost every *Verein* could have obtained the corporate quality had it wished to do this, and upon easy terms. When we opened the door we opened it wide. Any seven or more persons associated together for any lawful purpose can make a corporation.[42] No approval by any organ of the State is necessary, and there is no exceptional rule touching *politische, sozialpolitische oder religiöse Vereine* [political, sociopolitical or religious societies]. Many societies of the most various kinds have taken advantage of this offer; but many have not. I will not speak of humble societies which are going to have no property or very little: only some chess-men perhaps. Nor will I speak of those political societies which spring up in England whenever there is agitation: a 'Tariff Reform Association' or a 'Free Food League' or the like. It was hardly to be expected that bodies which have a temporary aim, and which perhaps are not quite certain what that aim is going to be, would care to appear as corporations. But many other bodies which are not poor, which hope to exist for a long time, and which have a definite purpose have not accepted the offer. It is so, for example, with clubs of what I may call the London type: clubs which have houses in which their members can pass the day. And it is so with many learned societies. In a case which came under my own observation a society had been formed for printing and distributing among its members books illustrating the history of English law.[xiii] The question was raised what to do with the copyright of these books, and it was proposed that the society should make itself into a corporation; but the council of the society – all of them lawyers, and some of them very distinguished lawyers – preferred the old plan: preferred trustees. As an instance of the big affairs which are carried on in the old way I may

---

[41] Our law about this matter is now represented by Rules of the Supreme Court of Judicature, XVI, 9.

[42] Companies Act, 1862, sec. 66.

mention the London Library, with a large house in the middle of London and more than 200,000 books which its members can borrow.

Why all this should be so it would not be easy to say. It is not, I believe, a matter of expense, for expense is involved in the maintenance of the hedge of trustees, and the account of merely pecuniary profit and loss would often, so I fancy, show a balance in favour of incorporation. But apparently there is a widespread, though not very definite belief, that by placing itself under an incorporating *Gesetz* [statute], however liberal and elastic that *Gesetz* may be, a *Verein* would forfeit some of its liberty, some of its autonomy, and would not be so completely the mistress of its own destiny as it is when it has asked nothing and obtained nothing from the State. This belief may wear out in course of time; but I feel sure that any attempt to drive our *Vereine* into corporateness, any *Registerzwang* [registration requirement] would excite opposition. And on the other hand a proposal to allow the courts of law openly to give the name of corporations to *Vereine* which have neither been chartered nor registered would not only arouse the complaint that an intolerable uncertainty was being introduced into the law (we know little of Austria) but also would awake the suspicion that the proposers had some secret aim in view: perhaps nothing worse than what we call 'red-tape', but perhaps taxation and 'spoliation'.

Hitherto (except when the Stock Exchange was mentioned) I have been speaking of societies that do not divide gain among their members. I must not attempt to tell the story of the English *Aktiengesellschaft* [joint stock company]. It has often been told in Germany and elsewhere. But there is just one point to which I would ask attention.

In 1862 Parliament placed corporate form and juristic personality within easy reach of 'any seven or more persons associated together for any lawful purpose'. I think we have cause to rejoice over the width of these words, for we in England are too much accustomed to half-measures, and this was no half-measure. But still we may represent it as an act of capitulation. The enemy was within the citadel.

In England before the end of the seventeenth century men were trying to make joint-stock companies with transferable shares or 'actions' (for that was the word then employed), and this process had gone so far that in 1694 a certain John Houghton could issue in his newspaper a price list which included the 'actions' of these unincorporated companies side by side with the stock of such chartered corporations as the Bank of England. We know something of the structure of these companies, but little of the manner in which their affairs were regarded by lawyers and courts of law. Then in 1720, as all know, the South Sea Bubble swelled and burst. A panic-stricken Parliament issued a law, which, even when we now read it, seems to scream at us from the statute book.[xiv] Unquestionably for a time this hindered the formation of joint-stock companies. But to this day there are living among us some insurance companies, in particular 'the Sun', which were living before 1720 and went on living in an unincorporate condition.[43] And then, later on when the great catastrophe was forgotten, lawyers began coldly to dissect the words of this terrible Act and to discover that after all it was not so terrible. For one thing, it threatened with punishment men who without lawful authority 'presumed to act as a corporation'. But how could this crime be committed?

From saying that organisation is corporateness English lawyers were precluded by a long history. They themselves were members of the Inns of Court. Really it did not seem clear that men could 'presume to act as a corporation' unless they said in so many words that they were incorporated, or unless they usurped that sacred symbol, the common seal. English law had been compelled to find the essence of real or spurious corporateness among comparatively superficial phenomena.

Even the more definite prohibitions in the Statute of 1720, such as that against 'raising or pretending to raise a transferable stock', were not, so the courts said, so stringent as they might seem to be at first sight. In its panic Parliament had spoken much of mischief to the public, and judges, whose conception of the mischievous was liable to change, were able to declare that where there was no mischievous tendency there was no offence. Before 'the Bubble Act' was repealed in 1825 most of its teeth had been drawn.

But the *unbeschränkte Haftbarkeit* [unlimited liability] of partners was still maintained. That was a thoroughly practical matter which Englishmen could thoroughly understand. Indeed from the first half of the nineteenth century we have Acts of Parliament which strongly suggest that this is the very kernel of the whole matter. All else Parliament was by this time very willing to grant: for instance, active and passive *Prozessfähigkeit*, the capacity of suing and being sued as unit in the name of some secretary or treasurer. And this, I may remark in passing, tended still further to enlarge our notion of what can be done by 'unincorporated companies'. It was the day of half-measures. In an interesting case an American court

[43] F. R. Relton, *Fire Insurance Companies*, 1893.

once decided that a certain English company was a corporation, though an Act of our Parliament had expressly said that it was not.

And if our legislature would not by any general measure grant full corporateness, our courts were equally earnest in maintaining the unlimited liability of the *Gesellschaftsmitglieder* [company members].

But the wedge was introduced. If a man sells goods and says in so many words that he will hold no one personally liable for the price, but will look only to a certain subscribed fund, must we not hold him to his bargain? Our courts were very unwilling to believe that men had done anything so foolish; but they had to admit that personal liability could be excluded by sufficiently explicit words. The wedge was in. If the State had not given way, we should have had in England joint-stock companies, unincorporated, but contracting with limited liability. We know now-a-days that men are not deterred from making contracts by the word 'limited'. We have no reason to suppose that they would have been deterred if that word were expanded into four or five lines printed at the head of the company's letter paper. It is needless to say that the directors of a company would have strong reasons for seeing that due notice of limited liability was given to every one who had contractual dealings with the company, for, if such notice were not given, they themselves would probably be the first sufferers.[44]

In England the State capitulated gracefully in 1862. And at the same time it prohibited the formation of large unincorporated *Gesellschaften*. No *Verein* or *Gesellschaft* [club or society] consisting of more than twenty persons was to be formed for the acquisition of gain unless it was registered and so became incorporate. We may say, however, that this prohibitory rule has become well-nigh a dead letter, and I doubt whether its existence is generally known, for no one desires to infringe it. If the making of gain be the society's object, the corporate form has proved itself to be so much more convenient than the unincorporate that a great deal of ingenuity has

[44] In England development along this line stopped at this point, because *wirtschaftliche Vereine* [clubs whose purpose is profit] became corporations under the *Gesetz* of 1862. English law had gone as far as the first, but not, I believe, as far as the second of the two following sentences. 'There is no obstacle to making the members subject to the obligations arising from legal transactions in such a way that each of them is only liable with a part of his property, specifically with his share of the club's assets (*Vereinsvermögen*). If such an agreement is in effect, then the committee's powers of representation can be limited by statute to the point at which it can only commit the members to an obligation with a liability limited to their share.' (Gierke, op. cit. 39.) Then as regards our clubs, there is, as already said, no presumption that the committee or the trustees can incur debts for which the members will be liable even to a limited degree.

been spent in the formation of very small corporations in which the will of a single man is predominant ('one-man companies'ˣᵛ). Indeed the simple *Gesellschaft* of English law, though we cannot call it a dying institution, has been rapidly losing ground.[45]

In America it has been otherwise. As I understand, the unincorporate *Aktiengesellschaft* [joint stock company] with its property reposing in trustees lived on beside the new trading corporations. I am told that any laws prohibiting men from forming large unincorporated partnerships would have been regarded as an unjustifiable interference with freedom of contract, and even that the validity of such a law might not always be beyond question. A large measure of limited liability was secured by carefully-worded clauses. I take the following as an example from an American 'trust deed'.

> The trustees shall have no power to bind the shareholders personally. In every written contract they may make, reference shall be made to this declaration of trust. The person or corporation contracting with the trustees shall look to the funds and property of the trust for the payment under such contract . . . and neither the trustees nor the shareholders, present or future, shall be personally liable therefor.

The larger the affairs in which the *Verein* or *Gesellschaft* is engaged, the more securely will such clauses work, for (to say nothing of legal requirements) big affairs will naturally take the shape of written documents.

Then those events occurred which have inseparably connected the two words 'trust' and 'corporation'. I am not qualified to state with any precision the reasons which induced American capitalists to avoid the corporate form when they were engaged in constructing the greatest aggregations of capital that the world had yet seen;ˣᵛⁱ but I believe that the American corporation has lived in greater fear of the State than the English corporation has felt for a long time past. A judgment dissolving a corporation at the suit of the *Staatsanwalt* [Attorney General] as a penalty for offences that it has committed has been well known in America. We have hardly heard of anything of the kind in England since the Revolution

---

[45] A distinction which, roughly speaking, is similar to that drawn by *B.G.B.* §§ 21, 22 was drawn by our Act of 1862, sec. 4: 'No company, association or partnership consisting of more than twenty persons [ten persons, if the business is banking] shall be formed for the purpose of carrying on any business that has for its object the acquisition of gain by the company, association or partnership, or by the individual members thereof unless it is registered.' I believe that in the space of forty years very few cases have arisen in which it was doubtful whether or not a *Verein* fell within these words.

of 1688. The dissolution of the civic corporation of London for its offences in the days of Charles II served as a *reductio ad absurdum*. At any rate 'trust' not 'corporation' was the form that the financial and industrial magnates of America chose when they were fashioning their immense designs.

Since then there has been a change. Certain of the States (especially New Jersey) began to relax their corporation laws in order to attract the great combinations. A very modest percentage is worth collecting when the capital of the company is reckoned in millions. So now-a-days the American 'trust' (in the sense in which economists and journalists use that term) is almost always if not quite always a corporation.

And so this old word, the 'trustis' of the Salica, has acquired a new sense. Any sort of capitalistic combination is popularly called a 'trust' if only it is powerful enough, and Englishmen believe that Germany is full of 'trusts'.

VI

And now let me once more repeat that the connection between Trust and Corporation is very ancient. It is at least four centuries old. Henry VIII saw it. An Act of Parliament in which we may hear his majestic voice has these words in its preamble.[46]

> Where by reason of feoffments . . . made of trust of . . . lands to the use of . . . guilds, fraternities, comminalties, companies or brotherheads erected . . . by common assent of the people without any corporation . . . there groweth to the King . . . and other lords and subjects of the realm the same like losses and inconveniences . . . as in case where lands be aliened into mortmain.

We see what the mischief is. The hedge of trustees will be kept in such good repair that there will be no escheat, no relief, no wardship, for behind will live a *Genossenschaft* [co-operative] keenly interested in the maintenance of the hedge, and a *Genossenschaft* which has made itself without asking the King's permission. Now no one, I think, can read this Act without seeing that it intends utterly to suppress this mischief.[47] Happily, however, the Act also set certain limits to trusts for obituary masses, and not long after Henry's death Protestant lawyers were able to say that the whole Act was directed against 'superstition'. Perhaps the

---

[46] Stat. 23 Hen. VIII, c.10.
[47] The trust is to be void unless it be one that must come to an end within twenty years.

members of the Inns of Court were not quite impartial expositors of the King's intentions. But in a classical case it was argued that the Act could not mean what it apparently said, since almost every town in England – and by 'town' was meant not *Stadt* but *Dorf* – had land held for it by trustees. Such a statement, it need hardly be said, is not to be taken literally. But the trust for a *Kommunalverband* [municipal association] or for certain purposes of a municipal association is very ancient and has been very common: it is a 'charity'. There was a manor (*Rittergut*) near Cambridge which was devoted to paying the wages of the knights who represented the county of Cambridge in Parliament.[48]

It is true that in this quarter the creation of trusts, though it was occasionally useful, could not directly repair the harm that was being done by that very sharp attack of the concession theory from which we suffered. All our municipal associations except the privileged boroughs, remained at a low stage of legal development. They even lost ground, for they underwent, as it were, a *capitis diminutio* when a privileged order of communities, namely the boroughs, was raised above them. The county of the thirteenth century (when in solemn records we find so bold a phrase as 'the county comes and says') was nearer to clear and unquestionable personality than was the county of the eighteenth century. But if the English county never descended to the level of a governmental district, and if there was always a certain element of 'self-government' in the strange system that Gneist[xvii] described under that name, that was due in a large measure (so it seems to me) to the work of the Trust. That work taught us to think of the corporate quality which the King kept for sale as a technical advantage. A very useful advantage it might be, enabling men to do in a straightforward fashion what otherwise they could only do by clumsy methods; but still an advantage of a highly technical kind. Much had been done behind the hedge of trustees in the way of constructing *Körper* ('bodies') which to the eye of the plain man looked extremely like *Korporationen* [corporations] and no one was prepared to set definite limits to this process.

---

[48] Porter's Case, 1 Coke's *Reports*, 60: 'For almost all the lands belonging to the towns or boroughs not incorporate are conveyed to several inhabitants of the parish and their heirs upon trust and confidence to employ the profits to such good uses as defraying the tax of the town, repairing the highways . . . and no such uses (although they are common almost in every town) were ever made void by the statute of 23 H. 8.' Some of the earliest instances of 'representative suits' that are known to me are cases of Elizabeth's day in which a few members of a village or parish 'on behalf of themselves and the others' complain against trustees.

All this reacted upon our system of local government. Action and reaction between our *Vereine* [societies] and our *Kommunalverbände* [municipal associations] was the easier, because we knew no formal severance of Public from Private Law. One of the marks of our *Korporation*, so soon as we have any doctrine about the matter, is its power of making 'bye-laws' (or better 'by-laws'); but, whatever meaning Englishmen may attach to that word now-a-days, its original meaning, so etymologists tell us, was not *Nebengesetz* [by-law] but *Dorfgesetz* [village law].[49] And then there comes the age when the very name 'corporation' has fallen into deep discredit, and stinks in the nostrils of all reformers. Gierke's account of the decadence of the German towns is in the main true of the English boroughs, though in the English case there is something to be added about parliamentary elections and the strife between Whig and Tory. And there is this also to be added that the Revolution of 1688 had sanctified the 'privileges' of the boroughs. Had not an attack upon their 'privileges', which were regarded as *wohlerworbene Rechte*, 'vested rights', cost a King his crown? The municipal corporations were both corrupt and sacrosanct. And so all sorts of devices were adopted in order that local government might be carried on without the creation of any new corporations. Bodies of 'commissioners' or of 'trustees' were instituted by *Gesetz*, now in this place, and now in that, now for this purpose, and now for that; but good care was taken not to incorporate them. Such by this time had been the development of private trusts and charitable trusts, that English law had many principles ready to meet these 'trusts of a public nature'. But no great step forward could be taken until the borough corporations had been radically reformed and the connection between corporateness and privilege had been decisively severed.

A natural result of all this long history is a certain carelessness in the use of terms and phrases which may puzzle a foreign observer. I can well understand that he might be struck by the fact that whereas our borough is (or, to speak with great strictness, the mayor, aldermen, and burgesses are) a corporation, our county, after all our reforms, is still not a corporation, though the County Council is. But though our modern statutes establish some important distinctions between counties and boroughs, I very much

---

[49] Murray, *New English Dictionary*. It will be known to my readers that in English books 'Statute' almost always means *Gesetz* (Statute of the Realm) and rarely *Statut*. Only in the case of universities, colleges, cathedral chapters and the like can we render *Statut* by 'Statute'. In other cases we must say 'by-laws', 'memorandum and articles of association' and so forth, varying the phrase according to the nature of the body of which we are speaking.

doubt whether any practical consequences could be deduced from the difference that has just been mentioned, and I am sure that it does not correspond to any vital principle.

I must bring to an end this long and disorderly paper, and yet I have said very little of those *Kommunalverbände* which gave Dr Redlich occasion to refer to what I had written. I thought, however, that the one small service that I could do to those who for many purposes are better able to see us than we are to see ourselves was to point out that an unincorporated *Kommunalverband* is no isolated phenomenon which can be studied by itself, but is a member of a great genus, with which we have been familiar ever since the days when we began to borrow a theory of corporations from the canonists. The technical machinery which has made the existence of 'unincorporated bodies' of many kinds possible and even comfortable deserves the attention of all who desire to study English life or any part of it. What the foreign observer should specially remember (if I may be bold enough to give advice) is that English law does not naturally fall into a number of independent pieces, one of which can be mastered while the others are ignored. It may be a clumsy whole; but it is a whole, and every part is closely connected with every other part. For example, it does not seem to me that a jurist is entitled to argue that the English county, being unincorporate, and having no juristic personality, can only be a 'passive' *Verband*, until he has considered whether he would apply the same argument to, let us say, the Church of Rome (as seen by English law), the Wesleyan 'Connexion', Lincoln's Inn, the London Stock Exchange, the London Library, the Jockey Club, and a Trade Union. Also it is to be remembered that the making of grand theories is not and never has been our strong point. The theory that lies upon the surface is sometimes a borrowed theory which has never penetrated far, while the really vital principles must be sought for in out-of-the-way places.

It would be easy therefore to attach too much importance to the fact that since 1889 we have had upon our statute-book the following words: – 'In this Act and in every Act passed after the commencement of this Act the expression "person" shall, unless the contrary intention appears, include any body of persons corporate or unincorporate.'[50] I can imagine a country in which a proposal to enact such a clause would give rise to vigorous controversy; but I feel safe in saying that there was nothing of the sort in England. For some years past a similar statutory interpretation had

[50] Interpretation Act, 1889, sec. 19.

been set upon the word 'person' in various Acts of Parliament relating to local government.[51] Some of our organs of local government, for example, the 'boards of health' had not been definitely incorporated, and it was, I suppose, to meet their case that the word 'person' was thus explained. It is not inconceivable that the above cited section of the Act of 1889 may do some work hereafter; but I have not heard of its having done any work as yet; and I fear that it cannot be treated as evidence that we are dissatisfied with such theories of personality as have descended to us in our classical books.

One more word may be allowed me. I think that a foreign jurist might find a very curious and instructive story to tell in what he would perhaps call the publicistic extension of our Trust *Begriff* [concept]. No one, I suppose, would deny that, at all events in the past, ideas whose native home was the system of Private Law have done hard work outside that sphere, though some would perhaps say that the time for this sort of thing has gone by. Now we in England have lived for a long while in an atmosphere of 'trust', and the effects that it has had upon us have become so much part of ourselves that we ourselves are not likely to detect them. The trustee, *der zwar Rechtsträger aber nur in fremdem Interesse ist* ['who, although bearer of the proprietary right, is so only in another's interest'], is well known to all of us, and he becomes a centre from which analogies radiate. He is not, it will be remembered, a mandatory. It is not contract that binds him to the *Destinatär* [beneficiary]. He is not, it will be remembered, a guardian. The *Destinatär* may well be a fully competent person. Again, there may be no *Destinatär* at all, his place being filled by some 'charitable' *Zweck* [purpose]. We have here a very elastic form of thought into which all manner of materials can be brought. So when new organs of local government are being developed, at first sporadically and afterwards by general laws, it is natural not only that any property they acquire, lands or money, should be thought of as 'trust property', but that their governmental powers should be regarded as being held in trust. Those powers are, we say, 'intrusted to them', or they are 'intrusted with' those powers. The fiduciary character of the *Rechtsträger* [bearer of the right] can in such a case be made apparent in legal proceedings, more or less analogous to those which are directed against other trustees. And, since practical questions will find an answer in the elaborate statutes which regulate the doings of these *Körper* [bodies], we have no great need to say

[51] Public Health Act, 1872, sec. 60.

whether the trust is for the State, or for the *Gemeinde* [local community], or for a *Zweck*. Some theorists who would like to put our institutions into their categories, may regret that this is so; but so it is.

Not content, however, with permeating this region, the Trust presses forward until it is imposing itself upon all wielders of political power, upon all the organs of the body politic. Open an English newspaper, and you will be unlucky if you do not see the word 'trustee' applied to 'the Crown' or to some high and mighty body. I have just made the experiment, and my lesson for to-day is, that as the Transvaal has not yet received a representative constitution, the Imperial parliament is 'a trustee for the colony'. There is metaphor here. Those who speak thus would admit that the trust was not one which any court could enforce, and might say that it was only a 'moral' trust. But I fancy that to a student of *Staatswissenschaft* legal metaphors should be of great interest, especially when they have become the commonplaces of political debate. Nor is it always easy to say where metaphor begins. When a Statute declared that the *Herrschaft* [rule] which the East India Company had acquired in India was held 'in trust' for the Crown of Great Britain, that was no idle proposition but the settlement of a great dispute. It is only the other day that American judges were saying that the United States acquired the sovereignty of Cuba upon trust for the Cubans.

But I have said enough and too much.[52]

Notes

i The text of 'Trust and Corporation' was originally written by Maitland in English and then translated into German by Josef Redlich. The question of this translation and other matters related to the text are discussed in some detail by Maitland in his letters to Redlich which are included in volume II of *The letters of F. W. Maitland* ed. P. N. Zutshi (London: Selden Society, 1995). See especially nos. 270, 271, 273, 276, 280, 285, 294, 302, 303.

[52] It did not seem expedient to burden this slight sketch with many references to books; but the following are among the best treatises which deal with those matters of which I have spoken: Lewin, *Law of Trusts*, ed. 10 (1898); Tudor, *Law of Charities and Mortmain*, ed. 3 (1889); Lindley, *Law of Partnership*, ed. 6 (1893); Lindley, *Law of Companies*, ed. 6 (1902); Pollock, *Digest of the Law of Partnership*, ed. 6 (1895); Buckley, *Law and Practice under the Companies Act*, 8 (1902); Palmer, *Company Law*, ed. 2 (1898); Wertheimer, *Law relating to Clubs*, ed. 3 (1903); Underhill, *Encyclopaedia of Forms*, vol. 3 (1903), pp. 728–814 (Clubs). As regards the early history of 'uses' or trusts, an epoch was made by O. W. Holmes, 'Early English Equity', *Law Quarterly Review*, vol. 1. p. 162.

ii J. Redlich, *Englische Lokalverwaltung* (Leipzig, 1901). The book was translated two years later by F. W. Hirst, and published in London with Hirst's
additions.

iii For some examples of these, see note xvi below.

iv That is, the *Bürgerliches Gesetzbuch*. See above, 'The Unincorporate
Body', note iii.

v This translates as 'against the inhibition of a new construction', a phrase
that Maitland implies would mean nothing to an English lawyer of the
fourteenth century.

vi By the time Maitland wrote, Paul Laband (1838–1918) was Germany's
dominant theorist of state-law or *Staatsrecht*, thanks to his three-volume
Das Staatsrecht des Deutschen Reiches (Strasburg 1876–82), which went
through five editions by 1911, and was heavily criticised by Gierke. He
had begun as a specialist in medieval German law, however, and it was
against his study of the proprietorial actions, *Die Vermögensrechtlichen
Klagen* (Königsberg 1869), that Andreas Heusler (1834–1921), Professor
of German law in Basel, directed a substantial section of his monumental *Die Institutionen des deutschen Privatrechts* (1885–6, pp. 376–96). The
debate turned on whether the all-important Roman law distinction between real and personal actions and rights had played a comparable role
in medieval Germanic law. As Maitland's quotations here show, Laband
thought all Germanic litigation had been determined by the kind of object,
action or omission sought by the plaintiff, rather than by the operation of
a ubiquitous, higher-order distinction between real and personal rights.
Germanic law was accordingly a less systematic legal culture for Laband,
because in it the object of litigation was of definitive importance, and
the right of the plaintiff a secondary concern. Heusler contradicted him
(*Institutionen* I, pp. 376–96), asserting the full operation of a systematic
distinction between real and personal right throughout the Germanic
sources. The evaluation of medieval German law was a major theme in
the controversy over whether the new German Empire needed a new,
codified law, with all the Romanist characteristics implied by the notion
of codification. By the time of 'Trust and Corporation', this aspect of the
debate had been settled by the appearance of the *Bürgerliches Gesetzbuch*.
Maitland wisely kept out of the debate about medieval Germanic law in
general; as far as medieval English law was concerned, he clearly sided with
Laband, for reasons which become abundantly clear in the course of this
essay.

vii The force of this distinction in German law relates to the ownership of
the property of an endowed institution. A non-autonomous institution
does not own the property with which it is endowed; rather, the property
passes to the fiduciary, who is bound only to the founder. An autonomous

institution remains owner by dint of having legal capacity (a capacity which under German law can only be bestowed by the state).

viii This is 43 Elizabeth I c. 4.

 ix See *Acts* 18, vv. 12–17. Gallio was the Roman governor before whom the Jews of Corinth accused Paul of heterodox teaching. He declined to give judgment, on the grounds that it was a matter for the Jews to decide.

  x 'We recognise the devil from his foot' (a play on the expression: '*Ex pede Herculem*').

 xi Maitland is making a play on the German terms for different forms of rule: '*Königsherrschaft*' [kingly rule], '*Adelsherrschaft*' [aristocratic rule], etc.

xii Maitland's point is that the term '*landesgesetzlich*' has no real English equivalent.

xiii This was the Selden Society, founded in 1887 'to encourage the study and advance the knowledge of English law'. The society was, in the words of H. A. L. Fisher, 'the creature of Maitland's enthusiasm, and of all his achievements stood nearest to his heart' (Fisher, *F. W. Maitland*, p. 52). Of the twenty-one volumes issued by the society during Maitland's lifetime, eight were by Maitland himself.

xiv 6 George I (1720), repealed by 4 George IV c. 94 (1825). In the words of Holdsworth, *A History of English Law* (7th edn, 14 vols., London, 1956), vol. VIII, pp. 220–1, the Bubble Act 'deliberately made it difficult for joint stock societies to assume a corporate form . . .'

 xv See Preface, note viii.

xvi Trusts were formed by corporations that wished to combine their interests without falling foul of the various laws that existed in the United States forbidding cartels and other restrictive practices. The first of these trusts was created in 1882 by Standard Oil, and was quickly followed by trust combinations in other industries, including steel, copper, tobacco, leather, rubber, mail and the telegraph business, in which the American Telephone and Telegraph Company (AT&T) was a trust already capitalised at the time Maitland was writing (1900) at $250,000,000. These trusts were formed by the legal device of allowing various corporations to contract to transfer their securities to trustees who ran the new corporate entity as one company, usually with the intention of coming to dominate or even monopolise a particular area of business. Soon, though, the term 'trust' came in America to denote any large-scale business or industrial enterprise that sought to corner the market. The formation of trusts was soon followed by pressure for anti-trust legislation, which resulted in the Sherman Anti-Trust Act of 1890. This act, however, was ambiguously framed and very haphazardly upheld by the courts, with the result that it did little to stop the spread of trusts and monopolistic practices into the early years of the twentieth century. The act was most effective not against big business but against trade unions and other labour movements, which, as in Britain, had sought to use the trust device to preserve their identity and bypass the legal constraints which acted on single corporations.

xvii R. von Gneist, *Selfgovernment, Communalverfassung und Verwaltungsgerichte in England* (Berlin, 1871).

Index

abbot, 16, 22, 27
actio in personam, xlvi, 77
actio in rem, xlvi, 77
ad opus, 53, 83, 85
advowson, xlvi, 17, 57
aid, xlvi, 22, 27
al oes, 53, 83, 85
Alexander III, Pope, xl, 16–17
Amalgamated Society of Railway Servants
    (ASRS), xxiii
America, 2. *See* United States of America
Anson, Sir William, xl, 40
Anstalt, 57, 59, 97, 98, 103,
    107
archdeacon, 27
associations, 67–8
Attorney-General, 58
Austin, John, xxvi, xl, 4, 5, 72
Australia, 44, 46
autonomous institution, 98

bailment, xlvii, 53
Balfour, Arthur, Lord, xli, 63, 70
Barker, Sir Ernest, xxvi, xxxviii–xxxix
benefice, xlvii, 17
beneficial owner. *See* destinatory
beneficium, xlvii, 17
Bermudas, 43
bishop, xv, 15–16, 27, 98
Blackstone, Sir William, xli
    on corporation sole, 10
    on fiction of law, 63
    on glebe, 16
    on the state, 38

patron the owner of parish church in
    twelfth century, 14
uses 'King' not 'Crown', 40
Board of Trade, 47, 109
body politic, xviii, 11, 16, 27, 34, 35–6, 46
boroughs, 123, 124–5
Bosanquet, Bernard, xxvi, 5
British North America Act (1867), xlvii, 44
Broke, Sir Robert, xli, 10–12, 14, 21, 26
Bürgerliches Gesetzbuch (B.G.B.), xx–xxi,
    12–13, 53, 58, 61, 76, 100, 113, 121

Canada, 44–5
canon law, xlvii, 10, 17–18, 33, 39, 44, 83,
    107, 125
cestui que trust, xlviii, 55, 56, 58–9, 89,
    100
cestui que use, xlviii, 89
Chamberlain of the City of London, 14, 46
Chancellor, 54, 87, 89, 90, 92
Chancery, Court of, 55, 84, 90, 91, 92, 94,
    95, 99, 116
chantry priests, 12–13, 100
charities, charitable trusts, xix
    and boroughs, 124
    and incorporation, 58
    and law of trusts, 57
    and personification, 59
    and religious organisations, 104
    as *Anstalt* or *Stiftung*, 57–8
    as non-autonomous institution
        (*unselbstständige Anstalt*), 98, 99–101
    destinatory not a juristic person, 100
    enforcement by Court of Chancery, 99

131

Index

Index

Index

Cambridge Texts in the History of Political Thought

Titles published in the series thus far

Aquinas *Political Writings* (edited by R. W. Dyson)
0 521 37595 9 paperback

Aristotle *The Politics* and *The Constitution of Athens* (edited by Stephen Everson)
0 521 48400 6 paperback

Arnold *Culture and Anarchy and Other Writings* (edited by Stefan Collini)
0 521 37796 X paperback

Astell *Political Writings* (edited by Patricia Springborg)
0 521 42845 9 paperback

Augustine *The City of God against the Pagans* (edited by R. W. Dyson)
0 521 46843 4 paperback

Augustine *Political Writings* (edited by E. M. Atkins and R. J. Dodaro)
0 521 44697 X paperback

Austin *The Province of Jurisprudence Determined* (edited by Wilfrid E. Rumble)
0 521 44756 9 paperback

Bacon *The History of the Reign of King Henry VII* (edited by Brian Vickers)
0 521 58663 1 paperback

Bagehot *The English Constitution* (edited by Paul Smith)
0 521 46942 2 paperback

Bakunin *Statism and Anarchy* (edited by Marshall Shatz)
0 521 36973 8 paperback

Baxter *Holy Commonwealth* (edited by William Lamont)
0 521 40580 7 paperback

Bayle *Political Writings* (edited by Sally L. Jenkinson)
0 521 47677 1 paperback

Beccaria *On Crimes and Punishments and Other Writings* (edited by Richard Bellamy)
0 521 47982 7 paperback

Bentham *Fragment on Government* (introduction by Ross Harrison)
0 521 35929 5 paperback

Bernstein *The Preconditions of Socialism* (edited by Henry Tudor)
0 521 39808 8 paperback

Bodin *On Sovereignty* (edited by Julian H. Franklin)
0 521 34992 3 paperback

Bolingbroke *Political Writings* (edited by David Armitage)
0 521 58697 6 paperback

Bossuet *Politics Drawn from the Very Words of Holy Scripture* (edited by Patrick Riley)
0 521 36807 3 paperback

The British Idealists (edited by David Boucher)
0 521 45951 6 paperback

Burke *Pre-Revolutionary Writings* (edited by Ian Harris)
0 521 36800 6 paperback

Cavendish *Political Writings* (edited by Susan James)
0 521 63350 8 paperback

Christine De Pizan *The Book of the Body Politic* (edited by Kate Langdon Forhan)
0 521 42259 0 paperback

Cicero *On Duties* (edited by M. T. Griffin and E. M. Atkins)
0 521 34835 8 paperback

Cicero *On the Commonwealth* and *On the Laws* (edited by James E. G. Zetzel)
0 521 45959 1 paperback

Comte *Early Political Writings* (edited by H. S. Jones)
0 521 46923 6 paperback

Conciliarism and Papalism (edited by J. H. Burns and Thomas M. Izbicki)
0 521 47674 7 paperback

Constant *Political Writings* (edited by Biancamaria Fontana)
0 521 31632 4 paperback

Dante *Monarchy* (edited by Prue Shaw)
0 521 56781 5 paperback

Diderot *Political Writings* (edited by John Hope Mason and Robert Wokler)
0 521 36911 8 paperback

The Dutch Revolt (edited by Martin van Gelderen)
0 521 39809 6 paperback

Early Greek Political Thought from Homer to the Sophists (edited by Michael Gagarin and Paul Woodruff)
0 521 43768 7 paperback

The Early Political Writings of the German Romantics (edited by Frederick C. Beiser)
0 521 44951 0 paperback

The English Levellers (edited by Andrew Sharp)
0 521 62511 4 paperback

Erasmus *The Education of a Christian Prince* (edited by Lisa Jardine)
0 521 58811 1 paperback

Fenelon *Telemachus* (edited by Patrick Riley)
0 521 45662 2 paperback

Ferguson *An Essay on the History of Civil Society* (edited by Fania Oz-Salzberger)
0 521 44736 4 paperback

Filmer *Patriarcha and Other Writings* (edited by Johann P. Sommerville)
0 521 39903 3 paperback

Fletcher *Political Works* (edited by John Robertson)
0 521 43994 9 paperback

Sir John Fortescue *On the Laws and Governance of England* (edited by Shelley Lockwood)
0 521 58996 7 paperback

Fourier *The Theory of the Four Movements* (edited by Gareth Stedman Jones and Ian Patterson)
0 521 35693 8 paperback

Kant *Political Writings* (edited by H. S. Reiss and H. B. Nisbet)
0 521 39837 1 paperback

Knox *On Rebellion* (edited by Roger A. Mason)
0 521 39988 2 paperback

Kropotkin *The Conquest of Bread and other writings* (edited by Marshall Shatz)
0 521 45990 7 paperback

Lawson *Politica sacra et civilis* (edited by Conal Condren)
0 521 39248 9 paperback

Leibniz *Political Writings* (edited by Patrick Riley)
0 521 35899 X paperback

The Levellers (edited by Andrew Sharp)
0 521 62511 4 paperback

Locke *Political Essays* (edited by Mark Goldie)
0 521 47861 8 paperback

Locke *Two Treatises of Government* (edited by Peter Laslett)
0 521 35730 6 paperback

Loyseau *A Treatise of Orders and Plain Dignities* (edited by Howell A. Lloyd)
0 521 45624 X paperback

Luther and Calvin on Secular Authority (edited by Harro Höpfl)
0 521 34986 9 paperback

Machiavelli *The Prince* (edited by Quentin Skinner and Russell Price)
0 521 34993 1 paperback

de Maistre *Considerations on France* (edited by Isaiah Berlin and Richard Lebrun)
0 521 46628 8 paperback

Maitland *State, Trust and Corporation* (edited by David Runciman and Magnus Ryan)
0 521 526302 paperback

Malthus *An Essay on the Principle of Population* (edited by Donald Winch)
0 521 42972 2 paperback

Marsiglio of Padua *Defensor minor* and *De translatione Imperii* (edited by Cary Nederman)
0 521 40846 6 paperback

Marx *Early Political Writings* (edited by Joseph O'Malley)
0 521 34994 X paperback

Marx *Later Political Writings* (edited by Terrell Carver)
0 521 36739 5 paperback

James Mill *Political Writings* (edited by Terence Ball)
0 521 38748 5 paperback

J. S. Mill *On Liberty*, with *The Subjection of Women* and *Chapters on Socialism* (edited by Stefan Collini)
0 521 37917 2 paperback

Milton *Political Writings* (edited by Martin Dzelzainis)
0 521 34866 8 paperback

Montesquieu *The Spirit of the Laws* (edited by Anne M. Cohler, Basia Carolyn Miller and Harold Samuel Stone)
0 521 36974 6 paperback

More *Utopia* (edited by George M. Logan and Robert M. Adams)
0 521 52540 3 paperback

Morris *News from Nowhere* (edited by Krishan Kumar)
0 521 42233 7 paperback

Nicholas of Cusa *The Catholic Concordance* (edited by Paul E. Sigmund)
0 521 56773 4 paperback

Nietzsche *On the Genealogy of Morality* (edited by Keith Ansell-Pearson)
0 521 40610 2 paperback

Paine *Political Writings* (edited by Bruce Kuklick)
0 521 66799 2 paperback

Plato *The Republic* (edited by G. R. F. Ferrari and Tom Griffith)
0 521 48443 X

Plato *Statesman* (edited by Julia Annas and Robin Waterfield)
0 521 44778 X paperback

Price *Political Writings* (edited by D. O. Thomas)
0 521 40969 1 paperback

Priestley *Political Writings* (edited by Peter Miller)
0 521 42561 1 paperback

Proudhon *What is Property?* (edited by Donald R. Kelley and Bonnie
G. Smith)
0 521 40556 4 paperback

Pufendorf *On the Duty of Man and Citizen according to Natural Law* (edited
by James Tully)
0 521 35980 5 paperback

The Radical Reformation (edited by Michael G. Baylor)
0521 37948 2 paperback

Rousseau *The Discourses and Other Early Political Writings* (edited by
Victor Gourevitch)
0 521 42445 3 paperback

Rousseau *The Social Contract and Other Later Political Writings* (edited by
Victor Gourevitch)
0 521 42446 1 paperback

Seneca *Moral and Political Essays* (edited by John Cooper and John
Procope)
0 521 34818 8 paperback

Sidney *Court Maxims* (edited by Hans W. Blom, Eco Haitsma Mulier and
Ronald Janse)
0 521 46736 5 paperback

Sorel *Reflections on Violence* (edited by Jeremy Jennings)
0 521 55910 3 paperback

Spencer *The Man versus the State* and *The Proper Sphere of Government*
(edited by John Offer)
0 521 43740 7 paperback

Stirner *The Ego and its Own* (edited by David Leopold)
0 521 45647 9 paperback

Thoreau *Political Writings* (edited by Nancy Rosenblum)
0 521 47675 5 paperback

Tönnies *Community and Civil Society* (edited by José Harris and Margaret Hollis)
0 521 56119 1 paperback

Utopias of the British Enlightenment (edited by Gregory Claeys)
0 521 45590 1 paperback

Vico *The First New Science* (edited by Leon Pompa)
0 521 38726 4 paperback

Vitoria *Political Writings* (edited by Anthony Pagden and Jeremy Lawrance)
0 521 36714 X paperback

Voltaire *Political Writings* (edited by David Williams)
0 521 43727 X paperback

Weber *Political Writings* (edited by Peter Lassman and Ronald Speirs)
0 521 39719 7 paperback

William of Ockham *A Short Discourse on Tyrannical Government* (edited by A. S. McGrade and John Kilcullen)
0 521 35803 5 paperback

William of Ockham *A Letter to the Friars Minor and other writings* (edited by A. S. McGrade and John Kilcullen)
0 521 35804 3 paperback

Wollstonecraft *A Vindication of the Rights of Men* and *A Vindication of the Rights of Woman* (edited by Sylvana Tomaselli)
0 521 43633 8 paperback